Using IGDIs

Using IGDIs

Monitoring Progress and Improving Intervention for Infants and Young Children

by

Judith J. Carta, Ph.D.
Charles Greenwood, Ph.D.
Dale Walker, Ph.D.
Jay Buzhardt, Ph.D.

Juniper Gardens Children's Project
University of Kansas

with invited contributors

·P·A·U·L·H·
BROOKES
PUBLISHING CO ®

Baltimore • London • Sydney

Paul H. Brookes Publishing Co.
Post Office Box 10624
Baltimore, Maryland 21285–0624
USA

www.brookespublishing.com

Typeset by Integrated Publishing Solutions, Grand Rapids, Michigan.
Manufactured in the United States of America by
Sheridan Books, Inc., Chelsea, Michigan.

Photographs on pages 45, 65, 66, 80, 81, 98, and 114 were taken by and are used with permission
of Jay Buzhardt.

The individuals described in this book are composites or real people whose situations are masked
and are based on the authors' experiences. In all instances, names and identifying details have been
changed to protect confidentiality.

Library of Congress Cataloging-in-Publication Data

Using IGDIs : monitoring progress and improving intervention for infants and young children / by
    Judith J. Carta . . . [et al.].
        p.   cm.
    Includes bibliographical references and index.
    ISBN-1: 978-1-59857-065-6 (pbk.)
    ISBN-10: 1-59857-065-X
    1. Child development.   2. Infants—Development.   3. Toddlers—Development.   4. Child
    development—Testing.   I. Carta, Judith J.
    HQ76.9.I552   2010
    305.231–dc22   2010003643

British Library Cataloguing in Publication data are available from the British Library.

2014   2013   2012   2011   2010

10   9   8   7   6   5   4   3   2   1

Contents

About the Authors

Judith J. Carta, Ph.D., University of Kansas and Juniper Gardens Children's Project, 444 Minnesota Avenue, Suite 300, Kansas City, Kansas 66101

Dr. Carta is Senior Scientist in the Schiefelbusch Institute for Life Span Studies, Professor of Special Education, and Director of Early Childhood Research at Juniper Gardens Children's Project at the University of Kansas. Dr. Carta earned her master's degree in child development and family life from Purdue University in 1974 and her doctorate in early childhood special education in 1983. She was a postdoctoral fellow at Juniper Gardens in 1983–1984 in educational research focused on developing interventions for children from high-poverty environments. Throughout her career, Dr. Carta has held positions as a classroom teacher of preschoolers with developmental disabilities, developer of interventions, curricula, and observational assessments aimed at young children, research director, faculty member, and teacher trainer. She has authored peer-reviewed publications include research syntheses, intervention research studies in language, early literacy and challenging behavior of young children, measurement, and conceptual papers. Her major research interests are evidence-based practices for young children, risk factors affecting children's development, monitoring progress in young children, and parenting interventions and their effects on young children. Since 1983 she has held 36 federally supported research projects on early intervention, parenting interventions, and early childhood special education. She has been a principal investigator of many multisite longitudinal studies funded by the National Institutes of Health (NIH), Centers for Disease Control and Prevention (CDC), and the U.S. Department of Education. Among her present roles is being Principal Investigator of a CDC-funded randomized trial to test to the effectiveness of a cellular-phone parenting intervention and the Institute of Education Sciences (IES)-funded Center for Response to Intervention in Early Childhood. Dr. Carta is currently Chair of the Conference on Research Innovation in Early Intervention. She was the past editor of *Topics in Early Childhood Special Education* and currently serves as an associate editor of that journal. She also currently serves on the editorial boards of *Journal of Early Intervention* and the *Journal of Special Education.* She received the Mary McEvoy Service to the Field Award from the Division of Early Childhood of the Council for Exceptional Children in 2007.

Charles Greenwood, Ph.D., Director, Senior Scientist, and Professor, Juniper Gardens Children's Project, 444 Minnesota Avenue, Suite 300, Kansas City, Kansas 66101

Dr. Greenwood is the Director of the Juniper Gardens Children's Project and Professor of Applied Behavioral Science at the University of Kansas. He is a founding author of progress monitoring measures for infants and toddlers and editor of *School-Wide Prevention Models: Lessons Learned in Elementary Schools* (Guilford Press, 2008). He is co-principal investigator of the Center for Response to Intervention in Early Childhood (CRTIEC). He has more than 100 publications in peer-reviewed journals to his credit. Under his leadership, the Juniper Gardens Children's Project was awarded the 1996 research award of the Council for Exceptional Children for its contributions to interventions for children with special needs. He was the recipient of the 2009 Higuchi Research Achievement Award in Applied Science at the University of Kansas.

Dale Walker Ph.D., Associate Research Professor, Juniper Gardens Children's Project, 444 Minnesota Avenue, Suite 300, Kansas City, Kansas 66101

Dr. Walker is an associate research professor in the Schiefelbusch Institute for Life Span Studies, Juniper Gardens Children's Project, at the University of Kansas, and holds courtesy positions in the departments of Special Education and Applied Behavioral Science at the University of Kansas. Her research is in the areas of early childhood intervention; language development; child care quality; and assessment and accountability practices with infants and toddlers at risk for, and with, disabilities. She was one of the original developers of the Infant-Toddler Individual Growth and Development Indicators (IGDIs). She directs and co-directs research projects related to early communication development, progress monitoring assessment, and accountability funded by the U.S. Department of Education, Office of Special Education Programs (OSEP), the Institute for Educational Science, and the NIH and Department of Health and Human Services. She is currently Research Chairperson for the Division of Early Childhood. Dr. Walker serves on the editorial boards for a number of journals including *Journal of Early Intervention, Early Childhood Research Quarterly, Young Exceptional Children,* and *Topics in Early Childhood Special Education.*

Jay Buzhardt, Ph.D., Assistant Research Professor, Juniper Gardens Children's Project, 444 Minnesota Avenue, Suite 300, Kansas City, Kansas 66101

Dr. Buzhardt is currently an assistant research professor at the University of Kansas, Juniper Gardens Children's Project. His interests focus on identifying factors that affect the implementation and effectiveness of technology-based intervention, assessment, and training. Since obtaining his doctoral degree in child development in 2002, Dr. Buzhardt has directed and co-directed several federally funded research projects from NIH, IES, OSEP, National Institute on Disability and Rehabilitation Research, and local foundations. Some examples of his work include the development and experimental evaluation of web-based progress monitoring and decision-making tools for early childhood service providers (described in this volume), the Online and Applied System for Intervention Skills (OASIS) distance training program to teach applied behavior analysis therapy to parents of young children with autism, a web-based foster parent training program, and technology-enhanced in-service professional development and coaching for K–8 teachers. Leveraging technology to streamline early intervention and data-based decision making for early childhood service providers is at the heart of his work with Infant-Toddler IGDIs. In addition to his research and development efforts at Juniper Gardens, his work with Integrated Behavioral Technologies, a nonprofit organization that serves children with disabilities, focuses on developing and maintaining sustainable web-based training solutions for paraprofessionals who provide in-home therapy for children with autism.

About the Contributors

Kathleen Baggett, Ph.D., Assistant Research Professor, University of Kansas, 650 Minnesota Avenue, 2nd Floor, Kansas City, Kansas 66101

Dr. Baggett is an assistant research professor at the University of Kansas. She is a licensed psychologist and clinical professional counselor whose clinical and research interests focus on early childhood social-emotional health promotion.

Scott McConnell, Ph.D., Fesler-Lampert Chair of Urban and Regional Affairs, Professor, Educational Psychology, University of Minnesota, Center for Early Education and Development, 56 East River Road, 4101, Minneapolis, Minnesota 55455

Dr. McConnell is Professor of Educational Psychology and Child Psychology and Director of Community Engagement for the Center for Early Education and Development at the University of Minnesota. He also has been appointed the Fesler-Lampert Chair in Urban and Regional Affairs, reflecting his community-based research on factors affecting young children's development. Dr. McConnell received his doctorate in educational psychology at the University of Oregon and has been at the University of Minnesota since 1986. In that time, he has served as Director of both the Institute on Community Integration (a University Center of Excellence in Developmental Disabilities) and the Center for Early Education and Development. Dr. McConnell was Principal Investigator of the Early Childhood Research Institute on Measuring Growth and Development, where IGDIs were first developed. He also serves as Investigator for the Center for Response to Intervention in Early Childhood, an IES-funded research enterprise conducting research, development, and dissemination of response to intervention resources for preschool children and teachers.

Kristen Missall, Ph.D., Associate Professor, The University of Iowa, 361 Lindquist Center, Iowa City, Iowa 52242-1529

Dr. Missall is an Associate Professor of School Psychology at The University of Iowa. She graduated from the University of Minnesota and completed a 2-year post-doctoral experience at the Center for Early Education and Development at the University of Minnesota. Dr. Missall conducts research in the areas of early literacy and social skill development, school adjustment, and general outcomes measurement and has particular interest in the skills and experiences of children making the transition from preschool to kindergarten. Dr. Missall has published several papers on technical and practical aspects of the Preschool Early Literacy IGDIs (EL IGDIs).

Acknowledgments

The preparation of any edited book always depends on a host of collaborators, and this volume is no exception. Of course, this book began with the idea of telling the story about IGDIs for Infants and Toddlers and so we are indebted to the funders who have helped us move that idea into reality: within the U.S. Department of Education (the Office of Special Education Programs) and the Institute of Educational Sciences (National Center for Special Education Research); within the Administration for Children and Families (the Office of Planning Research and Evaluation); and within Kansas State Rehabilitation Services (the Kansas Early Head Start office). Each of these agencies was instrumental in providing the funding for our research and development activities.

We would also like to thank the original team of researchers in the Early Childhood Research Institute for Measuring Growth and Development that was headed by Scott McConnell, Mary McEvoy, and Jeff Priest at the University of Minnesota; Ruth Kaminski, Roland Good, and Mark Shinn at the University of Oregon; and colleagues at the University of Kansas—Jane Atwater, Gayle Luze, Barbara Terry, Kere Hughes, Carol Leitschuh, Deb Linebarger, and Eva Horn. A whole host of research assistants at the University of Kansas provided invaluable assistance and they include Susan Higgins, Gabriel Cline, Debra Montagna, Christine Muehe, Annessa Staab, Kenneth Parsley, Sara Gould, Sarah Brown, Tina Yang, Rashida Banerjee, Gwiok Kim, Yumiko Saito, Kari Manier, Paige Bross, Jodi Gager, and Tonya Purnell. Also of tremendous help was the statistical analysis provided by Todd Little, Elizabeth McConnell, Rawni Anderson, and Waylon Howard and the web design expertise provided by Matt Garrett. We are also very grateful for the enthusiastic support and encouragement of Heather Shrestha and Johanna Cantler of Paul H. Brookes Publishing Company and for the careful editing and production work carried out by Johanna Cantler and Janet Krejci and their staff at Brookes.

A huge "thank you" goes to the staff of the programs in Kansas, Missouri, and Iowa who were partners with us in our IGDI studies and were willing to try out a new approach to measuring the progress of children. Finally, we extend our most profound gratitude to the children and families who were involved in the research and development of IGDIs with the hope that this experience will prove to be beneficial to them and other children in years to come.

To Mary McEvoy, our dear friend and colleague, who still inspires us to find better ways to measure and improve children's growth toward meaningful outcomes

I

What Are
IGDIs and Why
Are They Needed?

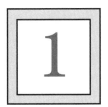

Background and Overview of IGDIs

Judith J. Carta and Charles Greenwood

Since the mid-1990s, the call for measurement systems to help teachers and parents understand how well young children are learning and developing has greatly increased. The need for more sensitive tools to gauge the rate of children's growth in learning is influenced by an array of sources, such as the expanding knowledge about early childhood years as a critical time for learning and the recognition that children should be identified as early as possible to minimize more serious delays and related problems. In addition, there is a growing recognition that the rate of children's growth in learning and development is to some extent a measure of program quality. Thus, in this era of accountability, we realize that one measure of program quality may be the extent to which children are making progress toward learning outcomes or specified learning standards (National Early Childhood Accountability Task Force, 2007). Although we understand that numerous forces influence children's development, it is certain that the strength of a program and the quality of instruction can affect the rate of children's progress toward socially valued outcomes. Therefore, just as the call for more accountability has affected educational programs for older children, programs serving young children must know whether they are on the right course as indicated by children's growth.

The Individual Growth and Development Indicators (IGDIs) offer a new approach that programs can use to improve child outcomes and reach measurable improvement goals. They can be used to ascertain how individual children, as well as groups of children in programs, are progressing. In this role, IGDIs serve a currently unmet need—determining quickly when changes need to be made in interventions being used to promote a child's development in the areas of communication, cognitive problem solving, movement, social, and parent–child interaction.

The value of the IGDI approach is best appreciated in terms of its differences from most current approaches to measurement. IGDIs are brief, frequently administered probes of an individual child's progress toward specific socially desired outcomes, such as learning to communicate or move in the environment. An IGDI is an indicator of progress and rate of growth. Unlike most measurement in early childhood, it is not intended to be a comprehensive measure of what a child knows and can do, but simply an *indicator*—a quick status check of where a child is with respect to a broader outcome.

We use many indicators in modern life, and reflecting on some examples is helpful in understanding IGDIs in early childhood. While traveling in a new city and trying to find our way to a restaurant or while in the middle of a large, unfamiliar state looking for the nearest gas station, for example, a Global Positioning System (GPS) can quickly indicate where we are, how far it is to the desired destination, and a specific course to follow. In addition, and perhaps most important, a GPS can quickly indicate if we are veering off track. The GPS reading is an indicator of our location.

When a child is sick and may have a fever, we use another indicator—a thermometer—to measure body temperature. If we see that the child's temperature is greater than 98.6 °F, our concern and vigilance grows. Our use of the thermometer repeatedly during a 24-hour period may indicate that the fever is continuing, which may prompt us to seek treatment. Under normal conditions, an effective treatment will result in the child's temperature returning to and maintaining the standard 98.6 °F benchmark.

The logic behind the thermometer and GPS technologies is the same as that behind IGDIs. IGDIs are simple, repeatable measurement tools that help both early childhood practitioners and parents or caregivers know whether individual children are on track and reaching learning outcomes, whether they are making progress in that direction, and, when the course is modified, whether or not they are getting closer to reaching the goal.

IGDIs, similar to a GPS, provide a picture of where one child or all children in a program stand compared with where they should be—the benchmark—and whether they are on the right track toward reaching the benchmark. Similar to the thermometer, monitoring progress using the IGDIs can provide feedback about whether an intervention is making a difference in terms of reaching the goal. IGDIs provide quick information that is easy to understand.

Another indicator that is similar to IGDIs and that we experience routinely is the height and weight chart used during well-child visits. By using quickly obtained measurements of height and weight, a medical professional can chart an individual child's growth relative to typically developing children of the same age in order to monitor a child's actual growth compared with expected growth. Similarly, IGDIs provide a picture of a child's rate of growth toward a specific outcome (e.g., ability to express oneself) compared with that of typically developing children. In addition, they clearly show a child's rate of growth before an intervention compared with growth during and after an intervention (e.g., language).

IGDIs as an Aid in Response to Intervention Approaches

As indicators of child progress, IGDIs are a sensitive way of looking at the effectiveness of interventions in changing a child's path toward an important outcome. This feature of IGDIs makes them valuable tools for improving child outcomes and the quality of programs using response to intervention (RTI) approaches (Fuchs, Fuchs, Hintze, & Lembke, 2006; Stecker & Fuchs, 2000). RTI is a decision-making framework within education and special education used to identify young children who show signs of learning difficulty and change instructional intervention in ways that help improve a child's rate of progress (Berkeley, Bender, Peaster, & Saunders, 2009; Council for Exceptional Children, 2007). IGDIs used in this RTI approach support universal screening of all children, identification of children below benchmark, frequent changes in the intensity of services provided these children and families, and monitoring of progress over time. IGDIs improve a program's ability to adjust the intensity of interventions being used with each child indexed to the child's own rate of growth. Use of IGDIs also improves the program's ability to strengthen key aspects of the curriculum.

Children's growth on measures such as IGDIs can be used to determine when a child's rate of progress is higher or lower than that of typically developing children or whether a child's trajectory of growth changes in response to a specific intervention. Thus, interventionists can *see* when they are making a difference in changing a child's developmental trajectory in a specific area and can quickly ascertain when a change in trajectory is necessary. Importantly for children with significant disabilities whose trajectories may be far different from that of typically developing children, a positive trendline deflection in response to an intervention can convey when changes are "closing the gap" or moving children closer toward average rates of growth.

As indicators, IGDIs are not as comprehensive in scope as more traditional measures for young children, such as curriculum-based tools. In the indicator model of measurement, indicators are used for universal screening and for progress monitoring. Comprehensive measures, however, given their greater expense and different purposes, are used to provide interventionists with information to help them diagnose or plan the appropriate intervention. Comprehensive, curriculum-based assessments are able to respond to questions such as "What skills does the child know and need to learn?" Comprehensive measures in the context of IGDIs play the role of helping to explore options and solutions to what needs to be done. However, because of their scope, cost, and infrequency of administration, these comprehensive measures are only used when the indicator suggests that a problem exists and a solution is needed.

Differences Between IGDIs and Currently Available Measures

Although many types of assessment are available for measuring young children, few have been designed specifically to help practitioners universally screen and monitor the progress of young children. Most have been developed to determine a child's status relative to norms or standards. Although curriculum-based assessments such as these may help determine whether children have developmental delays or are eligible for special education, most of these measures are too long and cumbersome to be implemented by practitioners. For example, it can easily take 30–45 minutes for a practitioner to carry out a curriculum-based assessment in a single developmental domain. As a consequence, this type of measure cannot be implemented often enough to provide frequent, ongoing information about how a child is changing in response to an intervention. IGDIs, on the other hand, typically take approximately 6–8 minutes and, as such, they can be repeated often to check on a child's growth. Another distinction between curriculum-based assessments and IGDIs is that curriculum-based assessments typically tap a comprehensive set of developmentally or instructionally sequenced skills that are used by classroom staff to determine what to teach. Although this sequenced set of skills can be used for progress monitoring, it is difficult to generate information about a child's rate of growth from this type of measure. Furthermore, with curriculum-based measures, a child's progress may only be measured with reference to a specific curriculum and not apply to some other curriculum. It is, therefore, difficult to use these types of measures to track children's changes in response to modifications in interventions in the same way as IGDIs. This creates a gap between measures available to assess young children's performance and tools needed to inform practitioners who are trying to influence children's progress. The IGDIs have characteristics that make them ideal for filling this gap. These characteristics are discussed in the following section.

Features Needed in Progress Monitoring Tools for Young Children

Besides having the psychometric properties of sound measurement, progress monitoring tools must have a set of features, listed here, that address their feasibility when used by practitioners and community-based programs.

1. They must be efficient (i.e., they must be as brief as possible and easy to administer and score).

2. They must be relatively inexpensive.

3. They must yield information about children that is readily understandable to the widest possible audience, including all stakeholders in early childhood settings (i.e., teachers, teaching assistants, administrators, parents).

4. They must be sensitive to intervention after relatively short periods of time if they are to be used for intervention decision making.

5. They should allow for the monitoring of growth of individual children and, when data are aggregated, allow for the evaluation of the progress of groups of children (e.g., all children or subsets of children in programs, regions, or states).

Features such as these are necessary for progress monitoring tools. If these measures will be applied to young children, however, the tools also need to embody the following features that are critical for any measures used with young children:

1. They must be authentic and collect information to the greatest extent possible in children's natural environments during situations that are familiar and comfortable.

2. They should be functional and generate information that is meaningful in under-standing children's skills and needs.

3. They should be culturally sensitive and applicable across a diverse array of chil-dren, as well as understandable to their families.

4. They must be technically adequate and produce information that is valid and re-liable for their intended use.

How IGDIs Fill the Gap in Assessment that Informs Practice

IGDIs can fill the gap in assessment by providing helpful information about chil-dren's growth toward socially valued outcomes. These new tools for young children are part of an approach to assessment called *general outcomes measurement (GOM)* (Deno, 1997). With this approach, key skill elements that have been specifi-cally linked to important outcomes and selected to represent the domain of interest are measured. An important distinction between this approach and other more tra-ditional assessment is that IGDIs use the same set of key skill elements that are measured repeatedly over time and allow for the depiction of growth toward iden-tified outcomes. Although growth on indicators does not provide a comprehensive measure of a child's development, it does provide helpful information because indi-cators are highly correlated to more general outcomes. Their relative simplicity al-lows them to be used repeatedly and often and to provide an important picture of the way a child is responding to the intervention(s) that may be currently in place.

Conclusion

This book is designed for individuals who serve infants and toddlers. Because IGDIs are appropriate for universal screening as well as for measuring progress of chil-dren in specialized interventions, children may be served in programs for typically developing children (e.g., infant and toddler programs, child care), at-risk children (e.g., Early Head Start), or children with developmental delays or disabilities (e.g., Part C programs). Early intervention practitioners will find a tool to determine whether individual children are "on target" and whether the practitioners can an-swer questions about specific interventions (e.g., Is Stacy making greater progress now that her parents are incorporating some of our intervention strategies in home routines on a regular basis?). Parents will be able to see how their children are responding to changes in early intervention programs (e.g., Is my child's communi-cation growing more quickly now that he's using an augmentative and alternative communication approach?). Program directors will be able to access reports for all children for use in making program-level decisions (e.g., Are children making faster progress this year now that we're implementing the XYZ curriculum?). State or local administrators can aggregate data across children in their respective areas and ex-amine trends resulting from policy shifts or reallocation of resources. Finally, re-searchers will also find that these tools can be useful in studies examining specific interventions or in large-scale program evaluations.

This book is for individuals who want to learn about the rationale for these measures and want to learn more about how they were developed, as well as for individuals who just want to learn how to administer and score one of the measures and to obtain progress reports. The next two chapters provide the conceptual background for IGDIs and the big ideas behind their development, as well as explanations of IGDI administration. Chapters in the second section of this book describe each of the five IGDIs for infants and toddlers (i.e., communication, cognitive problem solving, movement, social, and parent–child interaction), how they are administered, and how their data can be used. The third section of this book describes technical information related to training and certification, as well as psychometric properties of the measures. The final section explains the applications for these measures and IGDIs for older children.

Conceptual Background

Charles Greenwood and Judith J. Carta

Individual program planning to bring about change in child performance is the ultimate goal of early intervention services for infants, toddlers, and preschoolers, as well as their teachers, caregivers, and families (Bagnato, 2006; Bagnato & Neisworth, 1991; Neisworth & Bagnato, 2001). Yet, traditional forms of early childhood assessment have not always provided information useful in making individual programming decisions and monitoring intervention results. In traditional assessment approaches, assessment and intervention have often been treated as completely separate activities (Meisels, 1996).

In 1997, the Early Childhood Research Institute on Measuring Growth and Development was funded by the Office of Special Education Programs (OSEP) to develop and validate a growth and development measurement system capable of improving individual children's results, that could fill the gap between assessment and intervention in early childhood assessment. The goal was to develop

> A small set of common child and family growth and development indicators that would assist the early intervention and early childhood special education community to improve child outcomes, that would be consistent with calls for greater accountability, and that would respect and contribute to the unique perspectives of special education and related services for young children and their families. (Early Childhood Research Institute on Measuring Growth and Development, 1998a, p. 4)

To address the need for a better measurement system of children's learning and quality of instruction (see Chapter 1), a system was envisioned with various distinguishing features. This system would maintain a focus on individual children's skills and levels of developmental functioning as well as on factors that promote growth and development. It would place the growth and development of each child within a broader, more consistent psychometric context (or *common metric*) of important, more widely held values for child outcomes. It would also directly support the spirit and intent of individualized family service plans (IFSPs) and individualized education programs (IEPs). As a result, it would provide families and practitioners information and measurement strategies that would help operationalize many (but not all) of their long-term goals for children, as well as support creativity, individualization, and a focus on the effectiveness of short-term objectives to reach these goals. In addition, as a natural by-product of individual child assessment and program planning, this system would gather information that could be "rolled up" or aggregated across individual children and families to provide useful information about groups of children in classrooms, programs, districts, or even states.

To achieve this system, the following features of a design framework were used to guide development:

1. *A small number of common measurements for different age groups* of children and their families, with links in measurements across ages that reflect levels of development and developmental expectations, as well as the ways in which children of different ages and their families receive services

2. *Clear guidelines (or decision rules) for monitoring growth and development,* that help to decide when the rate of growth and development is less than desired and when to consider intervention-referenced information to plan changes for children and families

3. *Focus on in vivo behaviors and other "authentic" assessments* to ensure that measures of growth and development are meaningful and representative of functional skills in the child's life

4. *Active and wide-reaching dissemination of information* about the system to parents, early intervention service providers, and administrators, policy makers, researchers, and preservice trainers to initiate its wide-scale adoption, as well as ongoing technical assistance and training to support its implementation (Early Childhood Institute on Measuring Growth and Development, 1998a).

IGDIs Today

The product of this effort, that is the progress toward a small but comprehensive set of Individual Growth and Development Indicators (IGDIs) for infants, toddlers, and preschoolers, has led to the development of this volume. Five IGDIs for infants and toddlers were completed: communication, cognitive problem solving, movement, social, and parent–child interaction. Three more IGDIs were completed for preschoolers: vocabulary, alliteration, and rhyming. They are all discussed in this book. This work for children younger than kindergarten age was modeled on the development of the Dynamic Indicators of Basic Early Literacy Skills (DIBELS) for students in early elementary school (Kaminski, Cummings, Powell-Smith, & Good, 2008; Kaminski & Good, 1996). DIBELS are widely used measures of letter naming fluency, onset sound fluency, nonsense word fluency, and word segmentation fluency, among others (https://dibels.uoregon.edu/). Although substantial progress was achieved toward this goal, more work remains to develop new measures and improve existing measures for early childhood (see Chapter 13).

The development effort behind each IGDI included: 1) a national survey of parents of children with disabilities and professionals in early childhood education and early childhood special education (ECSE) to identify a set of the most socially valid desired outcomes for young children (Priest et al., 2001); 2) studies documenting the psychometric properties and feasibility of the indicators, including longitudinal studies illustrating sensitivity to growth over time; and 3) studies showing sensitivity to short-term growth and change in intervention (see Chapter 11). Today, all IGDIs are accessible on the following web sites: IGDIs for Infants and Toddlers (www.igdi.ku.edu) and Get It, Got It, Go! for preschoolers (http://ggg.umn.edu/).

The Conceptual Basis of IGDIs

How do we find out if a child's development is on track? How do we know if development problems are adversely affecting a child's growth? How do we know if a change in early intervention is working or not? Pediatricians answer some of these questions as part of well-child visits by measuring and charting brief, easy-to-collect indicators, such as height, weight, body temperature, and so forth (Centers for Disease Control and Prevention, 2000) (see Figure 2.1). By using growth charts to map normative growth patterns for girls and boys, it is possible to see if a child's height and weight measurements are normal and on track. Because height and weight measurements use simple measurement tools, they are quick and repeatable. Growth in height and weight are sensitive indicators of an infant's general health status; therefore, lack of expected growth rate or irregular patterns over time signal concern and set the occasion for reflection on causes and possible solutions (McConnell, 2000). Although height and weight certainly do not provide a comprehensive statement of a child's general health status, they are important *indicators* of it. Indicators such as these provide helpful information because they are correlates of (i.e., proxies for) the general outcome of good health and because their ease of use allows them to be used repeatedly to create rich data records of progress.

For example, consider a child demonstrating a typical pattern of growth until 18 months of age when he or she suddenly slows down compared with earlier measures and other children of the same age. Such a pattern may signal a health problem. The pediatrician is alerted that a problem may exist and that a more in-depth and detailed assessment is needed to confirm and rule out possible causes.

Causes that should be considered as possibly influencing a child's growth trend may be gender, genetics, hormones, nutrition, health issues, physical activity, age, and environmental factors, among others. Other growth charts pediatricians use for young boys and girls include head circumference, weight-for-length, or stature (for older children), and body mass index. Each provides an important contribution to understanding and making decisions about an individual child's physical growth and need for intervention.

Using this information, the pediatrician will consider all possible causal factors based on family history, parent interview, child's general well-being, prematurity, and additional assessment data, including other expert opinions. Based on synthesis of these results, treatment decisions are made, and the charts are later used to evaluate response to intervention (RTI) in subsequent visits (Centers for Disease Control and Prevention, 2000).

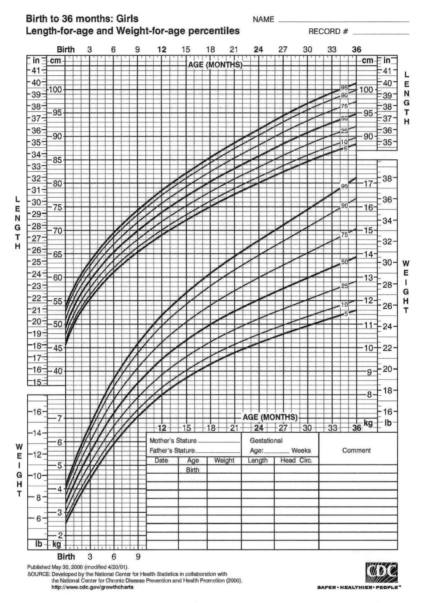

Figure 2.1. Centers for Disease Control and Prevention height and weight chart. (Copyright © 2000 by the National Center for Health Statistics in collaboration with the National Center for Chronic Disease Prevention and Health Promotion; http://www.cdc.gov/growthcharts)

Where possible, the pediatrician uses two synergetic strategies to maximize the effectiveness and reduce costs with individual children. They are 1) universal assessment of key indicators, and 2) a problem-solving, decision-making logic for determining and guiding intervention and service coordination over time. In this case, the key indicators used by pediatricians are analogous to the general outcomes measurement (GOM) approach in special education and IGDIs in early childhood (Deno, 2002; Greenwood, Carta, Baggett, et al., 2008; McConnell, Priest, Davis, & McEvoy, 2002). For example, curriculum-based measurement (CBM) based on a

GOM approach has been used in special education to support reading instruction for more than 20 years (e.g., Shinn, 1989). Both the pediatrician's growth charts and the special educator's CBM support the interventionist's problem solving and decision making regarding intervention effectiveness and the need for changing intervention to better meet an individual child's needs (Fuchs & Fuchs, 2007). Early childhood IGDIs provide practitioners with the foundational concepts for progress monitoring (i.e., GOMs), empirical support, and data collection protocols for an assessment of growth and development in young children.

General Outcome Measurement in Early Childhood

IGDIs are the product of the GOM approach to the design, development, and validation of progress-monitoring measures. Measures based on the GOM approach typically produce data that describe rate of growth across developmental or programmatically important chronological periods (e.g., birth to 3, or 4–5 years of age). For example, when children are able to produce 20 multiword utterances per minute by 36 months of age, we know that they have acquired the expressive communication skills needed by the time they are headed to preschool. Information such as this enables parents and professionals to judge not only proximal intervention effectiveness, but also the extent that intervention services are increasing the probability of desired long-term outcomes (Early Childhood Research Institute on Measuring Growth and Development, 1998b). Because GOMs are brief and relatively few in number, more professional time can be devoted to design, evaluation, and improvement of interventions and programs. GOM growth charts are intuitive and readily understood by parents, which contributes to more effective communication with parents as well as experts. GOMs yield data that are comparable within individual children across time, between children over time, and across children in programs on single occasions or over time.

GOMs are designed to be indicators of a child's performance on a few skill items that probe the child's acquisition of simple to more complex skills within the universe of skills in an age range. These skills may be precursors of more developmentally advanced performances (e.g., horizontal locomotion precedes vertical locomotion) or simple skills that should be taught first so that more difficult skills can be easily learned later in a curriculum (e.g., onset sounds before word segmentation). To be a robust measure of a general outcome, what is actually measured by a GOM must sample from a universe of simple to complex key skill elements in the outcome domain of interest. A score on a GOM at any single point in time represents a child's partial attainment on the path to full attainment of the universe of skills and, therefore, of the general outcome. Scores on a GOM over several time points result in the child's rate of growth (i.e., slope) in skill attainment over time.

For example, based on research, four key skill elements for children in the birth to 3 years age span were selected for direct measurement of the General Outcome of early communication proficiency. Those key skill elements were: Gestures, Vocalizations, Single Words, and Multiple Words (see Chapter 4). Increasing fluency

in these four skills is somewhat sequential across the age range, Gestures and Vocalizations in the youngest children after birth, followed by growth in Single and
Multiple Word fluency in children beginning around 12 months (Single), and 18
months (Multiple Words) for typically developing children. Similarly, with the
movement IGDI (e.g., change in position, horizontal locomotion, vertical locomotion), as well as the other IGDIs described in this volume, a few key skills in the age
range were identified and selected for direct measurement (see Chapter 11). These
key skills individually and as a total score were validated against traditional, frequently used measures of these outcomes (expressive language, movement). Thus,
each IGDI measures a few key skill elements across an age range representing
progress toward a general outcome, using tools that are brief, easy to administer,
valid, reliable, and repeatable in the short term.

General Outcomes Measurements versus Mastery Monitoring

GOMs differ in important ways from the traditional mastery monitoring approach
used in early childhood and K–12 special education. Whereas GOMs are designed
to be indicators, early childhood mastery monitoring measures are designed to provide a comprehensive profile of current status with respect to all of what a child
knows and is able to do within an outcome, domain, or skill category at a point in
time (Fuchs & Deno, 1991). Mastery monitoring traditions in early childhood measurement are most often represented by curriculum-based assessments in early
childhood and by curriculum-referenced assessments in K–12 education. Each is
designed to measure a child's proficiency in performing a specific set of defined
skills that are acquired through a typical developmental process or through a pre-
scribed intervention. Mastery monitoring measures are linked to all the skill sets
and the skills within each taught in a curriculum or intervention.

Some of the characteristics of mastery monitoring are that the skills are identified and well defined and that they are linked to a curriculum or intervention's
scope and sequence and the procedures teachers and/or parents use to teach them.
Skill mastery or proficiency is defined according to a high standard (typically 90%
correct). Performance on mastery monitoring measures informs the teacher in one
of two ways: 1) that the child has not yet mastered the skills and more teaching and
experience is needed; or 2) that the child's performance indicates that he or she has
achieved at least 90% mastery. Mastery indicates that he or she is ready to learn the
next skills and is ready for new measurements of those skills. Progress in mastery
monitoring is indicated by growth within a skill set and mastery across multiple skill
sets, each of which is measured by a different set of domain, or domain subscale
measures.

Screening, Problem Solving, and Decision Making

The pediatrician's approach to combining indicators of progress with a problem-
solving, decision-making logic has been translated for use with early childhood
IGDIs as shown in Figure 2.2. Using IGDIs in a pattern of quarterly monitoring es-

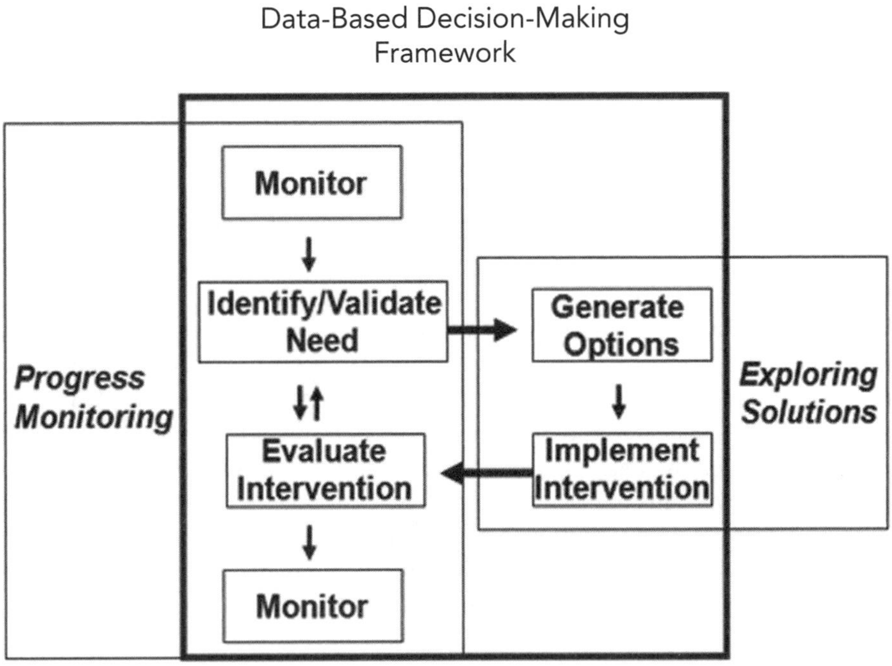

Data-Based Decision-Making Framework

Figure 2.2. Problem-solving, decision-making model using IGDIs. (Copyright © Juniper Gardens Children's Project; reprinted by permission.)

tablishes a universal screening system in which all children's performances can be observed and evaluated (Division for Early Childhood, 2007; Sandall, Hemmeter, Smith, & McLean, 2005). When a child's performance is low relative to normative levels, and when it exhibits a pattern of slow growth over time compared to peers, the early interventionist is alerted that a problem may exist. This identification is possible every 3 months in a quarterly system, which allows for change in intervention to occur as needed within this timeframe. This approach generally allows for a more timely call to action.

If a problem is validated in comparison to benchmarks (i.e., growth norms), a process of exploring solutions that includes additional assessments and hypotheses about likely causes leads to the development of an intervention that is implemented with family involvement (see Figure 2.2). The effects of the implementation are monitored using the appropriate IGDI, which is increased in frequency to monthly in order to monitor change in rate of growth in the presence of the intervention. Intervention effectiveness is evaluated in cycles of monitoring short-term results and continuous improvement made toward an outcome.

This approach in early childhood represents a paradigm shift compared with traditional practice because it overcomes a number of the "unresolved" challenges. These challenges include 1) the lack of short-term (monthly or quarterly) empirical data on early intervention results to guide intervention decisions in which typical practice is to collect data once or at most twice per year; 2) the relatively scant consideration given in the past to the utility of child-based results for making program decisions (Kagan, Rosenkoetter, & Cohen, 1997); and 3) the reliance on pathology as a cause for delay and the use of stigmatizing labels as compared with the search for intervention strategies most likely to lead to improvement (Reschly & Ysseldyke, 2002).

The problem-solving model avoids these and other issues because of its focus on the continuous progress of individual children and changing early intervention ingredients, particularly those under the influence of the early interventionist and parents. A specific example of this progress monitoring and problem solving is shown in the chart of an individual child's progress (see Figure 2.3). For this 20-month-old child, the first two measures reflected a level of performance and rate of growth well below expectation. However, using strategies in a language intervention tool kit, this child's rate of growth accelerated toward the mean with regular home visits, which the data suggest should be continued in the future to maintain this rate of growth. This approach is highly consistent with the Council for Exceptional Children's Division of Early Childhood's recommended practices (Sandall, Hemmeter, Smith, & McLean, 2005). Criteria recommended for evaluating assessment practices indicate that assessments should 1) point to behavioral objectives for change that are judged important and acceptable; 2) guide change in intervention activities; 3) incorporate several instruments, including observation and interviews; 4) incorporate input from parents; and 5) be implemented on multiple occasions (i.e., Neisworth, 2000).

Distinctive Features of IGDIs

The utility of IGDIs is due to a number of features that set them apart from traditional assessment in early childhood and make them particularly relevant and meaningful in terms of the intervention-related decisions that practitioners and parents need to make. We now highlight these features.

IGDIs Identify "Authentic" Child Behaviors in Natural Environments   Authentic behaviors are particularly important for young children because compared with older children and adults, young children are less able and willing to "perform" specific skills on demand. When asked to interact with unfamiliar people in unfamiliar situations, young children are less likely to engage in desired behaviors. However, given an opportunity to engage in real-life tasks in natural environments with familiar adults, a much more accurate representation of skills and abilities can be obtained.

IGDIs Assess Key Skill Elements that Are Representative of Important Child Outcomes   The skills measured by IGDIs should be linked to evidence of their social validity and predictive utility. With respect to social validity, the outcomes of early intervention should be those highly valued by professionals, parents, and policy makers. With respect to predictive validity, skills measured should be supported by evidence that they are predictive of both short- and longer-term outcomes (see Chapter 11).

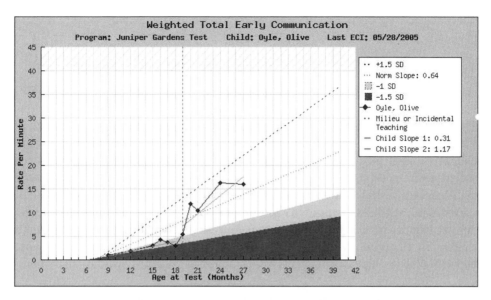

Figure 2.3. One child's early communication growth chart. (Copyright © Juniper Gardens Children's Project; reprinted by permission.)

IGDI Data from Separate Administrations Are Comparable within a Child and Between Children The results of IGDI administrations enable comparison of scores from one occasion to the next for an individual child, and comparisons of scores between an individual child and other children. Guidelines for administration of IGDIs are standardized so that each administrator conducts a measurement using a consistent protocol. Thus, assessors are taught to use the same procedures in each IGDI administration (see Chapter 3). Supporting this training is the IGDI web site (www.igdi.ku.edu) and specifically the section on IGDI Training and Certification (see Chapter 10). In addition, assessors are certified and trained by completing a standard training sequence, and IGDIs are calibrated to a standard coding test to establish comparability and continuity of procedures and results. This ensures that changes in children's performances are not caused by vast differences in how the IGDI was administered.

IGDI Data Meet Standards of Measurement Reliability The accuracy of IGDI results is further enhanced by reliability in the coding and recording of children's behaviors through interrater agreement, internal consistency, and/or alternate forms. Interrater agreement is a measure of how similarly two assessors score a child's performance either live or from video. Internal consistency indicates that an individual's key skill elements scores are correlated to one another. Alternate forms reliability is a measure of the extent that change in IGDI scores over time is due to growth in proficiency rather than simply memorizing the test.

IGDIs Are Efficient and Economical for Practitioners IGDIs are designed for use by early interventionists, whether they are teachers, home visitors, speech and language pathologists, occupational therapists, and so forth. IGDIs are designed to provide practitioners with information on a child's current level of proficiency, response to intervention, rate of growth over time, and likelihood of reaching benchmark goals in the future given current rates of progress.

IGDIs Are Sensitive to Children's Individual Differences   IGDIs have been shown to be highly sensitive to the individual differences of children. They allow for the wide variation in children who are not typically developing or who have sensory or physical challenges. A problem with traditional measures of children this age is that the measures are not universally designed. As a result, some children with special developmental needs may score zeros on the scales of interest. Measures with this problem are described as having "floor effects" because the measure has not been designed to capture the skill level of low-performing children. Zero scores are of little help in tracking progress or evaluating what a child needs to learn. IGDIs typically do not suffer from floor effects because they are able to capture some frequency of response from children at the lower levels of functioning.

IGDIs Are Sensitive to Individual Growth over Time and Intervention   To be useful in making decisions about an individual's response to intervention and determining whether a change in early intervention is needed, IGDIs must be supported by evidence that they are sensitive to short-term growth over time (Greenwood, Carta, Baggett, et al., 2008). IGDIs are repeatable, and for children receiving interventions, they should be administered with increased frequency to indicate whether or not the intervention is working and the child's performance is improving.

IGDIs were designed to capture change in performance due to 1) learning and development (e.g., adding horizontal locomotion to change in position skills); 2) use of augmentative or assistive technologies (e.g., positioning board, wheelchair, mobility training); or 3) accommodations in testing (e.g., assessors who speak the same language, including sign language). Consequently, IGDIs offer significant sensitivity and advantages in the education and intervention of children not making expected rates of progress. They are also appropriate for use in response to intervention approaches using multiple systems of support (three tier) models (Greenwood, Carta, Baggett, et al., 2008).

How IGDIs Address the Purposes of Assessment for Young Children

Monitor Progress and Growth over Time   The most important reason programs will want to use IGDIs is to monitor a child's short-term response to intervention and pattern of growth over time. IGDIs are unique among measures in their sensitivity to the short-term progress (slope or the rate of change) that individual children are making toward a socially desired outcome. This property enables one to forecast a child's future status given his or her current rate of growth, and it allows one to set goals for future progress to improve the child's outcome.

IGDIs are designed to be administered repeatedly—as frequently as weekly, monthly, and/or quarterly to reflect growth, which is a feature not common among other measurement tools. Frequent, repeatable assessments make IGDIs sensitive to short-term growth. This sensitivity to growth enables IGDIs to be used adaptively or as frequently as needed. Thus, IGDI information can be helpful to practitioners in deciding when to continue or change an intervention designed to promote the outcome of interest or to set goals for future progress. IGDIs also play important roles in screening. They identify risk and need for change in early intervention, identify a problem and prescribe a likely solution, and evaluate program effectiveness and set goals for improvement in program-level strategies and practices.

Screen to Identify a Need for Change in Early Intervention

Screening is a process of assessing all children in a program for the purpose of identifying the children who are at risk and in need of early intervention. Because of program costs to assess all children, many screening approaches use strategies and measures that reduce assessment time to increase efficiency. These strategies include brief assessments of a few key skills as compared with a comprehensive curriculum-based assessment or multigating strategy, such as teacher ranking of all children followed by a more detailed assessment of just those children flagged as at risk.

IGDIs may be used for screening because their brevity makes them suitable for universal administration. As a result, they are appropriate for administration to all children in a program in a pattern of 3–4 times per year as a means of monitoring progress and risk. When IGDI scores are compared with normative benchmarks, children at relatively higher risk and those who may not be responding to current interventions can be identified.

Identify Children Who Have Low Levels of Performance and Propose a Solution

Assessment for the purpose of identifying a need and then proposing a solution in the decision-making model is about exploring solutions that are matched to a child's progress data. Within the decision-making model, the focus is on identifying a problem in child performance, and learning how it can be addressed in the context of early intervention; therefore, the focus is not on diagnosis of a specific disability. IGDIs contribute to developing solutions by pointing to children whose lower performance indicates a need for more comprehensive information to determine what a child does and does not know and what a child needs to learn. This either leads to referral to experts or to additional comprehensive assessment to help identify the problem and the most likely solutions.

Evaluate Program Effectiveness and Improve the Effectiveness of Services Provided

The purpose of evaluating program effectiveness is to examine how well desired results are being obtained by a program and to help set goals and strategies for advancing further improvement. Two examples of the kind of program decisions to be made in response to evaluation data are 1) to move to evidence-based intervention strategies and provide staff with the professional development and supporting resources needed to implement them; and 2) to deploy staff differently to affect a particularly large group of children at particular ages or needs in the program. IGDIs may be used to support program-level evaluation through aggregation of all data to reflect the group or subgroups of interest (e.g., within an annual program of quarterly IGDI measurements). In this case, children have four data points that can be aggregated to provide a programwide indication of rate of growth toward desired outcomes. IGDIs may also contribute to eligibility and accountability purposes, as described next.

Determine Eligibility for Early Intervention or Early Childhood Special Education Services   The purpose of assessment for eligibility is to make qualifying decisions for the receipt of ECSE services (Individuals with Disabilities Education Improvement Act [IDEA] of 2004, PL 108-446 [Part C, Part B-619]). Federal and state policies define the process for determining a child's eligibility. One common feature is that more than one measure and source of information are required. IGDI data can be one piece of this information as they can contribute meaningful information regarding a child's degree of relative risk and lack of response to intervention for a specific outcome (e.g., early communication proficiency). This information may be cause for more comprehensive assessment, and, in combination with other data, including parent and expert judgment, it may contribute to eligibility decisions as required by IDEA 2004 and state policies. Furthermore, when a child is determined eligible for services, IGDI measurements can contribute to developing goals, intervention plans, and to measure progress in the context of the child's IFSP.

State and Federal Accountability for Child Results

The purpose of state and federal accountability is to provide policy makers and stakeholders evidence that the program is advancing child results and that dollars spent to finance the programs are effective, leading to improvement, and worth maintaining. IGDIs support accountability because they reflect progress toward socially valued general outcomes (Priest et al., 2001), and the data can be combined with other indicators used in federal and state accountability policies. Measures used in a state OSEP accountability report may include IGDIs (Greenwood, Carta, Baggett, et al., 2008).

Conclusion

IGDIs are beneficial in the care, education, and intervention of young children. They provide early childhood practitioners with a sensitive tool for monitoring children's progress toward attaining socially desired outcomes and confirming the success of early intervention based on child's response to it. Because this approach provides a strong basis for individualizing early intervention, it also offers a potential for larger and better intervention outcomes for children because needs are met more rapidly, ineffective interventions are changed in a more timely manner, successful interventions are quickly identified, and practitioners generally become more effective.

With pressure coming from accountability policies and requirements that programs set target goals for improvement in child results, IGDIs are a reasonable means of changing "business as usual" regarding prevention, early intervention, and use of evidence-based practice. IGDIs are especially important tools because 1) they contribute useful information to making individual programming decisions and monitoring child progress; 2) they alert staff of the need to consider change in intervention; 3) they contribute to the IFSP process; 4) they are efficient in terms of time to administer and cost; 5) they are designed for use by practitioners, which allows more time to be spent on intervention compared with assessment; 6) their growth charts are intuitive and lead to effective communication among practitioners, parents, and outside experts compared with typical assessment reports; and 7) they may be used to support the other important purposes of assessment, including program-level evaluation, accountability, and eligibility.

IGDI Administration

Coding, Scoring, and Graphing

Dale Walker and Jay Buzhardt

Each of the five Individual Growth and Development Indicators (IGDIs) described in this volume share common features related to their administration, coding, scoring protocol, and user training and certification. As described in Chapter 2, the IGDI general outcome measures adhere to several general defining features that characterize appropriate assessment practices with young children. These include the following:

- Authentic assessment

- Easy administration and scoring

- Standard protocol and a certification process, which promote reliable administration across assessors and consistency across children

This chapter describes the general administration format used across all of the IGDIs, as well as the common features related to their coding and scoring protocol. Elsewhere in this volume (Chapter 10), the general procedures for training and certification of the IGDIs are described.

Administration Protocol for the IGDIs

Given that the goal of each of the IGDIs is to capture a child's typical performance of the general outcome across repeated observations to monitor progress over time and any response to intervention (RTI), it is important to administer the IGDIs using the same protocol across assessments and to ensure that the assessments are representative of the child's performance. To accomplish this, standardized administration protocols have been developed and toys have been identified for each IGDI that encourage a child's behaviors relevant to each general outcome. These common protocols and the materials needed for administration are described in this chapter. Information specific to each of the IGDIs can be found in the individual IGDI chapters in this book (Chapters 4–8) and on the IGDI web site (http://www.igdi.ku.edu). A list of helpful links to administration and certification materials and information relevant to each IGDI are provided in Table 3.1.

Who Can Administer and Score IGDIs?

Accurate and reliable administration and scoring are critical to using IGDIs and to capturing a valid indication of children's growth and performance on general outcomes. Individuals who administer and score IGDIs should be trained and certified according to the guidelines described in Chapter 10. Links to certification steps are also available on the IGDI web site (http://www.igdi.ku.edu) (see also Table 3.1).

There are four primary roles in the administration and scoring of IGDIs.

1. Assessor

2. Familiar adult play partner

3. Coder

4. Data entry person

These roles may be assumed by one person or across several people depending on available staff resources and where assessments take place. The *assessor* is responsible for arranging the assessment, providing appropriate materials, and ensuring that the assessment is administered with a high level of fidelity. The *adult play partner* interacts with the child during the assessment and keeps the child engaged with the toys for the specified assessment period. The *coder* counts each occurrence of the identified key skills of the IGDI for the entire session duration. For the IGDIs described in this volume, the duration of assessment sessions ranges from 6 to 10 minutes (see individual IGDI chapters for the duration of each IGDI).

It is very important that the play partner who administers the IGDI is familiar to the child and supports the child's play by commenting on the child's interest and following his or her lead during the session. Persons taking the role of play partner who are not initially familiar with the child will need to spend some time playing with and getting to know the child. This can typically be accomplished by spending time playing with the child when the parent or another familiar caregiver is present so that the child feels safe and can explore toys along with the play partner.

Options for Administering and Scoring the IGDIs

There are three primary options available for administering and scoring IGDIs depending on staff availability and responsibilities, availability of video-recording equipment, and location of assessments. The first option is to have two people present during the session. An adult play partner and a coder or assessor who codes the child's behaviors on the IGDI scoring form while the play partner interacts with the child. (See Figure 3.1 for a sample form and Table 3.1 for links to online scoring forms.) The second option is to have an assessor who also acts as the play partner

Table 3.1. Links to IGDI administration and certification materials on the IGDI web site

Administration checklists: List of required protocol to follow before, during, and after administering an IGDI. Also used to certify assessors for administration.

- http://www.igdi.ku.edu/measures/admin_checklists.htm

Administration instructions and scoring forms: Detailed instructions for administering each IGDI and scoring forms for each.

- http://www.igdi.ku.edu/measures/observation_forms.htm

Scoring definitions: Comprehensive coding rules and definitions of key skill elements for each IGDI.

- http://www.igdi.ku.edu/measures/scoring.htm

IGDI toys: Information about toys to be used for each IGDI, including descriptions of the toys, how to use them, costs, and links to online stores that sell the toys.

- http://www.igdi.ku.edu/measures/toys.htm

Certification steps: Summary of requirements for certification, as well as links to training materials, certification videos, and other materials needed for certification.

- http://www.igdi.ku.edu/training/Assessor_Training/certification_steps.htm

Technical specifications: Description of the methods and results of studies undertaken to test each IGDI's technical soundness (e.g., reliability, validity, sensitivity to growth over time)

- http://www.igdi.ku.edu/measures/technical.html

© Juniper Gardens Children's Project; reprinted by permission.

while recording the session for later coding. (The protocol for video recording is described later in this chapter.)

The last option is to have a parent, teacher, interventionist, or other familiar caregiver act as the play partner while the assessor either codes the session as it occurs or records it for later coding. This option is particularly helpful if the infant or toddler is bashful or fearful of the assessor and will not engage in play with him or her. Although caregivers who act as play partners do not need to be certified, the certified assessor should review the administration instructions and checklist (see Table 3.1) with the play partner prior to the assessment session. Coaching or modeling from a certified assessor is also recommended as a way to learn how to be an effective play partner.

Setting Up the IGDI Administration Sessions

All IGDI assessments are administered as semistructured, play-based sessions using specific toy sets for 6–10 minutes depending on the IGDI (see individual IGDI chapters [Chapters 4–8] for specific information about administration duration). Sessions take place in a convenient, comfortable environment with minimal distractions to provide opportunities to observe the child's play with the toys and interactions with the play partner. Setting up an IGDI assessment session involves preparing the toys, ensuring that the child is positioned in a way that is developmentally and functionally appropriate, setting up the video equipment, if necessary, and starting the timer when appropriate.

Before beginning a session, it is recommended that the appropriate toys are available and ready for use. The IGDI web site regularly updates its lists of recommended toys (see Table 3.1). Although the specific toys recommended on the web

Early Movement Indicator (EMI)

Add EMI Data [▾] [Go!]

New primary EMI data for Smith, John T.

* = required

*Test Date:	March [▾] 11 [▾] , 2006 [▾]	*Test Duration	*Minutes:	6 [▾]
			Seconds:	- [▾]
*Form:	A [▾]	*Condition Change:	None [▾]	
*Primary Coder:	Buzhardt, Jay [▾]	*Assessor:	Buzhardt, Jay [▾]	
*Location:	Home [▾]	*Language of Administration:	English [▾]	
Note:	Sample Movement Data			

	transitional movements	grounded locomotion	vertical locomotion	throwing/rolling	catching/trapping
0:00	2	2	3	3	8
1:00	2	9	2	10	1
2:00	1	4	7	2	0
3:00	0	0	2	1	7
4:00	6	3	1	0	2
5:00	0	0	2	3	4

[Submit Data]   [Cancel]

Figure 3.1. Sample online IGDI recording form for the early movement indicator (EMI). (Copyright © Juniper Gardens Children's Project; reprinted by permission.)

site may occasionally change due to changes in the toy design, price, or availability, older toy models that are in good condition may be used. For toys with multiple pieces, recommendations for replacement toys are available, as well as recommendations for items to make the toys more appealing to children and families from a wide range of cultures and ethnicities. Prior to an assessment, the IGDI toys should be set up so that they are ready and inviting for the child to begin play immediately.

Each IGDI has at least two types of toys that may be used during sessions. Toys are alternated between assessments to keep the child's attention across repeated assessments. For example, the Early Communication Indicator (ECI) uses a barn and house as its two alternating toys. So, if the barn was used for the last administration of the ECI, the house would be used at the next quarterly or monthly ECI, and so forth. Therefore, it is important to note what toy or toy set was used for each assessment so that the next assessor will know which toy to use. This information is entered into the IGDI web site for efficient record keeping.

After finishing IGDI assessment sessions, it is important to ensure that all toys are clean and in good condition with no loose or damaged pieces. It is also important to note that although the toys identified for IGDI assessments are reported to be safe, children should be closely supervised at all times while engaged with any toys.

Conducting IGDI Assessment Sessions

Familiar Play Partners   When a potential play partner for the IGDI assessment is unfamiliar to the child, it is recommended that he or she spend time with the child in the home or child care classroom so that they have the opportunity to become familiar with one another. This will give the play partner time to join in the child's play along with someone already familiar to the child. The play partner should be positive and enthusiastic with the child to facilitate interaction during the assessment session.

After the child is comfortable, the next step is to let the child know that there are fun toys to play with together. To facilitate play, one strategy is for the adult to comment and label what they are doing while they are playing (e.g., "We are going to see the toys," or "Let's look in this house and see what's in there."). During the assessment session, the adult play partner should interact with the child in a way that encourages play and interaction with the toy and the adult. If the child becomes distressed, the assessment should be stopped until the child is interested in continuing, or it may be postponed for another time.

Positioning During Assessment Sessions   During the session, the play partner and child should sit in an area that is comfortable for them and suitable for free play with the toys (e.g., at a table or on the floor). There are several positioning options for children who are at various levels of development or who may require additional support. Suggested options can be found in the administration instructions available on the web site (see Table 3.1). For example, if a child is not independent in sitting, he or she could be placed in a chair with back and leg support; held or propped up by the play partner; or supported by a pillow, towels, or bolster seat. The play partner or assessor should make sure that the toys are in front of and within reach of the child, and that the child's neck, torso, and feet are properly supported during the play session. The play partner should be positioned so that he or she can maintain eye contact and reach the child as well as the toys.

Keeping Infants and Toddlers Engaged   The adult play partner needs to be engaging and interesting for the child during the IGDI sessions. If the child becomes bored, he or she may want to crawl or walk away from the area where the assessment is being conducted. If the child becomes interested in another toy or activity, the adult should try and bring the child back to the session by talking about the toys used for the assessment and by letting the child know that together they can play with the other toy after they finish playing with the current toys. The adult play partner can play with the toys or talk about new topics if the child does not become engaged with the toys or loses interest in playing. Although it is acceptable to ask some questions, asking questions should not be the primary manner of interacting with the child because interactions that are characterized primarily by questions may be too directive and may discourage a child from playing. Given the importance of having interactions that are positive and conducive to promoting the behaviors being assessed with each IGDI, the adult needs to remain positive and be an engaging play partner.

Timing and Ending IGDI Sessions

All IGDI assessments are timed, and they end after the specified amount of time has elapsed. Ideally, the assessment occurs for a continuous, uninterrupted period, but sometimes circumstances arise that may require pauses during the assessment. For example, an assessment may need to be paused due to unavoidable interruptions, such as a sibling who wants to join in the play during in-home assessments, a child who becomes distressed and needs to be comforted, or a child who is distracted by something and refuses to return to the play setting. If these or other circumstances occur, the play partner should stop the timer and restart it when the child returns to the play setting and reengages with the play partner and toys. If for some reason the child does not return to the play setting during that visit, start the session over on the next visit rather than continuing the timer where it left off during the previous session.

Completing Assessment Sessions

At the end of the timed IGDI assessment session, the assessor or play partner lets the child know that the play session has ended for the day, thanks the child for playing, and assists with transitioning the child to a new toy or activity (this may take a minute or two so that the child does not feel rushed). The toy(s) used for the session can then be put away. If the child becomes upset at having to leave the toys or the play session, the play partner can mention that he or she will be able to play with the toys another day, but that it is now time to play with other toys or friends or return to their routine activities. This transition is facilitated if the child has immediate access to another toy to play with at the end of the session. All toys should be sanitized after each session to prevent bacteria growth and the spread of germs. It is recommended that the play partner waits until the child is engaged in another activity or taken back to the classroom before cleaning the toys.

Modifying Administration Protocol

Modifications for Children with Disabilities

There are various ways to adapt the IGDI administration to accommodate children with physical disabilities, visual impairments, or hearing impairments. The suggestions described in this section should not be considered inclusive of all possible modifications. The important point is to arrange the assessment so that the child is afforded the best opportunity to demonstrate the IGDI key skills without providing excessive prompts that the child would not have in his or her natural environment.

For children with *physical disabilities*, ensure that the toy is arranged so that the child can easily reach it. This may mean moving the toy closer, propping the child up in a way that allows best access to the pieces, or having the play partner physically move the toys (e.g., if the child wants the farmer to drive the tractor but cannot get the farmer onto the tractor and move it, the play partner can move the farmer at the child's request and then make the farmer drive the tractor where the child directs).

For children with *visual impairments*, the assessor or play partner should orient the child to the toys during each session. The child might be introduced to each of the toy pieces and parts of the toy sets by allowing him or her to touch each part of, for example, the house, blocks, or balls. The play partner can tell the child where the toys have been placed so that the child might be able to pick them up or touch the toys. The play materials should be set up in a consistent arrangement from play session to play session to encourage familiarity as well as safe movement. Toys in each play set may be augmented to include animals that can be distinguished from one another by feel (e.g., pigs are smaller than cows and have tails, hooves, and so forth that may be distinguished by touch).

For children with *hearing impairments*, the play partner should be positioned with the toy between him- or herself and the child to allow them both to see each other easily for using sign language or lip reading to communicate. If the child uses a hearing aid or audio trainer, the play partner should be positioned so that the child can best hear what is being said or see what is being signed.

Modifications for Children Who Speak English as a Second Language   IGDIs may be given to children who speak English as a second language or who speak another language as long as the play partner and coder speak the same language as the child and are able to understand the child's initiations and responses. This is particularly important for the communication (ECI), social (ESI), and parent–child interaction (IPCI) IGDIs because coding these assessments requires that the coder understand what the child and play partner are saying. Other modifications are related to what should or should not be coded. For instance, in Spanish, as well as in some other languages, articles preceding words, such as "la" in "la vaca" (i.e., "the cow") should be counted as part of a multiple-word utterance. All IGDI scoring forms include a section to indicate the child's primary language (see Table 3.1 for the link to scoring forms on the web site) should there be an interest in looking at how children who speak English as a second language or a different language progress in their communication development.

Should modifications in the assessment protocol or format be made, the focus of the assessment should remain on encouraging the child to play with the toys and to interact with the adult play partner. Modifications that are made should be noted for each assessment on the paper and online scoring form (see Figure 3.1) so that future assessors will know to make similar modifications in subsequent assessments.

Video Recording of Assessments

Coders may either score the administration in person or from a video recording of the IGDI assessment. Prior to video recording of children, it may be the case that written permission from the child's parent or guardian should be obtained and kept on file. It is recommended that prior to video recording, the protocol related to video recording is reviewed. When setting up the video recording, special care should be taken to ensure that the entire play area is in the field of view and that both the child and play partner are clearly audible throughout the session. We recommend testing the audio levels by conducting a brief recording of the child and play partner interacting with the toys. In some cases, particularly for the ECI, ESI, and IPCI in which accurate coding depends on hearing the child's and play partner's communications, it may be necessary to attach a small microphone to the child, the play partner, or both. If microphones are used, it is recommended that they are light and wireless to avoid interfering with the play activity. When coding recorded sessions, it is recommended that coders wear earphones to cancel outside noise and to improve audio fidelity during playback.

If possible, a parent or another person should operate the video camera during the assessment. Home visitors have reported this to be an ideal opportunity to model effective parent–child interactions for parents if the parent is the person operating the video camera. The video operator should stay as still and quiet as possible to avoid distracting the child or play partner. The camera should be positioned so that the faces of the child and play partner are in full view as is the play situation. In most cases, particularly for the ESI and EMI in which the toys invite high levels of activity, it is important to hold the camera or set it up on a tripod that allows the camera to swivel in order to track children who move beyond the boundaries of the play area. When the session begins, the play partner or camera operator should indicate the start of the session for the coder by saying "start" to record a voice marker for the beginning of the timing and "stop" at the end of 6 minutes to mark the end of the session. Noting the beginning and end of the session will assist in later scoring of the assessments.

Coding the IGDIs

Key Skill Elements   Each of the IGDIs is comprised of key skills that are specifically defined behaviors coded by trained independent assessors during IGDI assessments. As described in Chapter 2, the key skill elements are indicators of the general outcome of interest and do not constitute all of the skills that make up an outcome. For each of the IGDIs, the key skill elements observed during the assessment are tallied or coded onto the recording form for the IGDI. For example, *gestures* observed during the ECI (communication IGDI) would be coded along with other key skill elements that would be summarized at the end of the assessment and would form the *total communication* score. Transition in *position* under the EMI (movement IGDI) would be similarly tallied and then summed across the key skills to derive a *total movement* score. The key skill elements are graphed separately in individual graphs (see Figure 3.3) that provide the opportunity to follow the growth pattern of each of the four key skill elements for the ECI in addition to the total score. The specific key skill elements for each of the IGDIs are described in Section II of this book.

Certification to Ensure Accuracy of Coding   As with most assessments, the accuracy of the information provided by IGDI assessments is highly dependent on the accuracy of the coding. It is imperative, therefore, that coders complete the required certification steps, including reliably scoring the online certification videos and continuing annual recertification to avoid inaccurate coding of child behavior that may happen if safeguards are not in place to ensure accuracy. (See Chapter 10 for more information about training and Table 3.1 for web links to certification steps and materials.)

Methods for Coding IGDIs

Each IGDI has a unique scoring form on which to enter information about the assessment that is important to identifying the child, general contextual information about the assessment, and codes for the key skill elements. Table 3.1 provides links to each of the IGDI's respective scoring forms on the IGDI web site. Before scoring an assessment, ensure that the fields for identifying information at the top of the form are complete. The fields provide valuable information about the context of the assessment, relevant interventions that are in place, and the people involved with the assessment.

Each key skill element that is observed during an IGDI assessment is tallied and recorded on the appropriate scoring form for each minute of the assessment. The assessor observes and tallies the key skill elements while the child and play partner are playing or later from a video recording of the assessment. An advantage of coding from video is that the session can be reviewed by multiple coders to establish that the coding was being accurately conducted. They are able to easily review parts of the recording if necessary. Listening to the session with earphones while coding will improve the audio quality and potentially improve reliability.

Entering Assessment Information into the Online System for Graphing and Reporting

After coding an assessment, the coder is ready to enter the minute-by-minute totals for each key skill element into the online data system using the online scoring form for the specific IGDI (see Figure 3.1 for an example of the EMI online scoring form). Scores can also be manually summed, but this may be more difficult, particularly for the ECI that requires some mathematics to weight key skill elements according to complexity. Entering data for all of the IGDIs into the online data system is recommended because the system automatically calculates total scores and individual slope scores, provides individual and group reports, allows for use of the Making Online Decisions (MOD) system for facilitating intervention decision making (described in Chapter 9), and provides a secure data management solution for all IGDIs. Technical information and screenshots of the IGDI web site and online data system are provided in the appendix of this book.

Immediately after an IGDI assessment is entered into the data system, graphs are generated in the online system that show the child's proficiency on the IGDI relative to normed benchmark performance (see Chapters 4–8 for information about how norms were derived for the individual IGDIs, as well as Chapter 11 for information on the technical adequacy of the IGDIs). The format of these graphs was designed to provide a quick visual picture of a child's performance and growth on an IGDI's general outcome and the key skill elements. All graphs plot data against the child's chronological age, and no corrections are made to adjust for premature birth

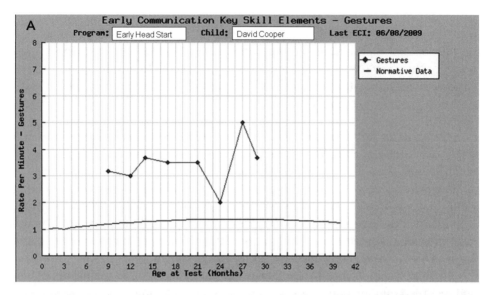

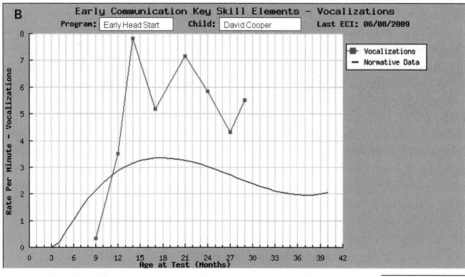

(continued)

Figure 3.2.   Key skill element graphs for the ECI: gestures (A), vocalizations (B), single words (C), and multiple words (D). (Copyright © Juniper Gardens Children's Project; reprinted by permission.)

or developmental age. Graphs are available for all of the IGDIs described in this volume.

Figure 3.3 shows a graph of a child's weighted total early communication scores, which is a sum of the child's rate per minute across all four ECI key skill elements. In addition to plotting the child's raw scores, which may have a considerable amount of variability, the orange line depicts the child's slope, which is essentially a trend line showing the average performance over time. If an intervention is used and the coder selects an intervention on the data entry form (see Figure 3.1), two slopes will be shown—one before the intervention and another after intervention. The graphed information allows interventionists to determine quickly whether or

Figure 3.2. *(continued)*

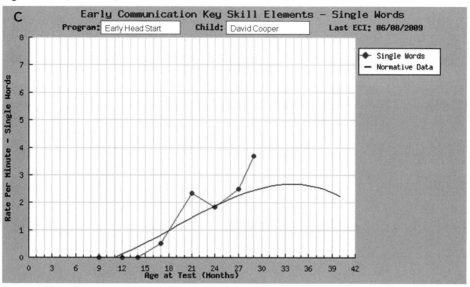

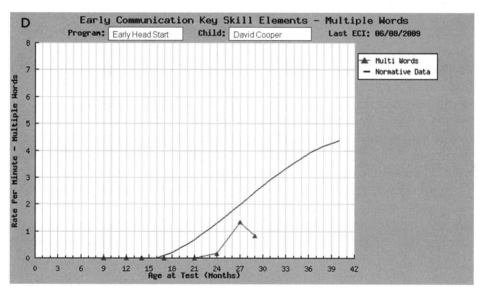

not the child's average growth over time has improved since beginning intervention. Imposed on the graph are shaded regions indicating 1.0 *SD* below norm performance (light grey) and 1.5 *SD* below benchmark (dark grey). Although IGDIs are not meant to be used as stand-alone diagnostic instruments, scores that fall in these regions may provide information for service providers and interventionists because they may suggest that the child is falling below expected performance. Chapters 2 and 9 discuss strategies for using these graphs for progress monitoring and to inform intervention decision making.

The ECI key skill elements that make up the total communication score are gestures, vocalizations, single words, and multiple words (see Chapter 4 for more

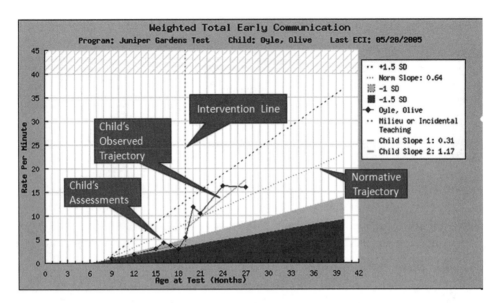

Figure 3.3. Weighted total early communication graph for ECI. (Copyright © Juniper Gardens Children's Project; reprinted by permission.)

information about these key skill elements). The graphs displayed in Figure 3.2 show the child's performance on each of these key skill elements and expected benchmark performance as depicted by curvilinear normative growth trajectories over time. For example, Figure 3.3 shows that the assessment conducted at the 18-month point just before intervention shows the child's total communication performance beginning to dip into the dark grey area or –1.5 *SD* below benchmark. A look at the key skill elements graphs gives a richer depiction of the child's communication and areas that need improvement. This information can provide valuable guidance for interventionists who are trying to identify appropriate language intervention strategies. At 18 months, this child is showing little growth in vocalizations and multiple words, and, although single words were previously at benchmark, the last assessment showed a marked decrease. Because the normed trajectories are showing that the child should be growing on single and multiple words at 18 months, and vocalizations should be decreasing because of increases in single and multiple words, the interventionist would likely identify strategies targeted at increasing single and multiple words.

The graphs shown in Figure 3.2 and ones similar to these for each of the IGDIs are available in the online data system either as stand-alone graphs or as part of a child's Individual Child Report. These graphs were designed to provide service providers and interventionists with a quick and easy way to interpret the child's current performance, his or her growth over time as indicated by the slope, and his or her response to intervention (if an intervention has been used) as indicated by the vertical line and separate slopes before and after intervention.

Group reports are also available that offer aggregate graphs of multiple children within a single program or across multiple programs, identification of children falling below benchmark, the context under which assessments are administered, and information about assessors and the assessments they have entered. See the Appendix of this book for details about the online data system, the support it provides, and additional samples of reports and data forms.

Conclusion

All of the IGDIs described in this volume share a number of features related to their administration, coding, data management, use of key skill elements related to a general outcome, and certification requirements to ensure high quality assessment. The key skill elements for each of the IGDIs are coded during brief, timed, play-based assessment sessions. Coded data are then entered into the online data system specifically developed for each IGDI. The focus of assessment, the toys used to facilitate child performance, and the coding definitions for each IGDI are different from one another as they each focus on a unique general outcome. The chapters in the next section describe the distinctive properties of each IGDI, including the corresponding key skill elements, and coding definitions (see the Appendix for links to the IGDI web site).

II

IGDIs
for Infants
and Toddlers

4

The Communication IGDI

Early Communication Indicator (ECI)

Dale Walker and Judith J. Carta

T he Early Communication Indicator (ECI) was designed for use by early educators, interventionists, home visitors, and researchers interested in measuring the expressive communication outcomes of infants and toddlers between 6 and 36 months of age. It was designed to meet the early educator's need for a quick, repeatable, reliable, and valid measure of children's progress in developing expressive communication and their response to intervention (Carta et al., 2002; Walker, Carta, Greenwood, & Buzhardt, 2008).

As previously discussed in Chapter 1 of this volume, a key to IGDIs is facilitating early educators' ability to monitor the progress of children and to quickly identify those children who are falling below benchmark so that a change in program or intervention may be initiated. Being informed about children's communication skills using the ECI provides early educators and parents with valuable information about children's developing communication as compared with other children their age. It also provides information on how well a general program or intervention is moving an individual child or group of children toward proficiency. Monitoring ECI growth for all children in a program can help to inform programmatic decisions regarding the general outcome of communication. When used on a statewide basis, monitoring children's growth on the ECI can be an important indicator of program, regional, or statewide outcomes.

Overview of the ECI and Its Importance to Development

The ECI is one of five IGDIs developed for infants and toddlers (Carta et al., 2002; Luze et al., 2001) that measure information toward socially valued outcomes and

ECI

guide intervention decision making. The ECI is the infant-toddler IGDI that has been used most often by practitioners in the field and for which there has been the most research related to its use for progress monitoring (e.g., Greenwood, Carta, Walker, Hughes, & Weathers, 2006). When parents and early childhood educators were canvassed in a national study about which general outcomes were considered most important for young children, expressive communication or "*Child uses gestures, sounds, words and word combinations to express meaning to others*" emerged as the most highly rated general outcome (Priest et al., 2001). This is not surprising given that proficiency in early communication has an impact on children's social interactions and forms the foundation for their later language development and emergent literacy skills (Cunningham & Stanovich, 1997; Fey, Catts, & Larrivee, 1995; Hart & Risley, 1995; Whitehurst & Lonigan, 2001). When there are gaps in the development of early communication skills and children do not develop along expected timelines, the impact on their later social and cognitive functioning can be extensive (Warren & Walker, 2005).

Delays in communication and language may significantly affect how young children access and participate in activities related to social development, as well as their early literacy skills and later school success (Burchinal et al., 2000; NICHD Early Child Care Research Network, 2000; Walker, Greenwood, Hart, & Carta, 1994). Children who have delays in communication may be less likely to use communication skills during social situations and more likely to use aggression or unwanted behaviors to communicate their wants and needs (Greenwood, Walker, & Utley, 2001; Kaiser, Hancock, Cai, Foster, & Hester, 2000; Long, Gurka, & Blackman, 2008). In addition to frustration at not being able to communicate, they may eventually experience social isolation.

Delays in the acquisition of language milestones may also be one of the first indicators that a young child may have developmental problems (Dale, Price, Bishop, & Plomin, 2003; Schwartz, Carta, & Grant, 1996). In the National Early Intervention Longitudinal Study (NEILS; Hebbeler et al., 2007), it was reported that more than 75% of children between 24 and 36 months of age who were eligible for early intervention services were identified because of a speech or communication delay (Hebbeler et al., 2007). Speech therapy was reported to be one of the most frequently provided services for children with identified disabilities. Furthermore, when children from the NEILS sample entered kindergarten, 84% of children with individualized education programs (IEPs) continued to receive speech services (Hebbeler et al., 2007).

Current State of Assessment of Infants' and Toddlers' Communication Skills

Given the prevalence of children receiving speech services and the importance of communication to later social, literacy, and educational outcomes, educators need to have a valid and reliable way to identify when there is a delay, and then to monitor children's growth in communication as a function of intervention or programmatic changes. Measures designed to meet the increased demand to document the effectiveness of intervention and children's growth in communication have not been widely available to practitioners and researchers who work with very young children (Missall, Carta, McConnell, Walker, & Greenwood, 2008). The ECI was developed as a means for giving practitioners and researchers the tools to regularly monitor children's growth toward the important outcome of being able to express themselves through gestures, vocalizations, words, and sentences (Greenwood, Carta et al., 2006; Greenwood, Carta, & Walker, 2004; Luze et al., 2001).

Developmental Course of Expressive Communication

The developmental path of expressive communication moves from prelinguistic (e.g., gaze, gesturing, and vocalizations) to linguistic forms of expression (single words and multiple word combinations). Although there is a generally consistent progression from prelinguistic to linguistic communication (e.g., Brady, Bredin-Oja, & Warren, 2008), considerable variability exists around the ages at which children actually begin using different forms of expressive communication (Fenson et al., 1994). In general, when infants are between 4 and 6 months of age, they may begin to make vocalizations, such as cooing and vocalizing pleasure or displeasure. Between 6 and 12 months of age, infants' communication becomes more intentional as they begin to reach toward an adult when they want to be picked up, show someone a toy by holding it up toward the person, or use a gesture to request something they want to hold or eat (e.g., Iverson & Thal, 1997; McLean, 1990). They will increasingly use more complex gestures and speech-like vocalizations (e.g., canonical babbling) with combinations of vowels and consonants to communicate their needs and wants and to interact socially (e.g., Stoel-Gammon, 1998). Later during this period, infants begin pointing to an item they want or when asked to identify something (Butterworth & Morisette, 1996). Around 12–18 months of age, infants gradually start to communicate using single words (e.g., Acredolo & Goodwyn, 1988; Hart, 1991). Between 18 and 24 months, children use single words to request desired objects and events (e.g., "more," "out") and move from single words to beginning to combine two or more words together into multiple-word phrases (e.g., "What's that?") (e.g., Fenson et al., 2007). Between 24 and 36 months of age and beyond, children's communication repertoires increase and become more complex as they begin to use multiple words in sentences to communicate socially (McCormick, 1990).

What Does the ECI Assess?

The four communicative behaviors or *key skill elements* that comprise the ECI and make up the total communication indicator include gestures, vocalizations, single words, and multiple words (see Figure 4.1). These skills were selected based on a review of the literature and existing measures of communication (e.g., Fenson et

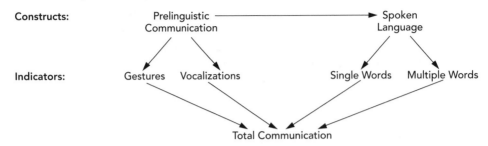

General Outcome: "The child uses gestures, sounds, words, or sentences to convey wants and needs or to express meaning to others."

Figure 4.1. Early Communication Indicator (ECI) conceptual framework. (© Juniper Gardens Children's Project; reprinted by permission.)

al., 1994; Hart & Risley, 1992; Huttenlocher, Haight, Bryk, Seltzer, & Lyons, 1991; Wetherby & Prizant, 1992) and confirmed through a validation process with other measures of expressive communication (Greenwood, Carta et al., 2006; Luze et al., 2001). The key skill elements of expressive communication for infants and toddlers 6-36 months of age include those skill areas representing prelinguistic communication (gestures and vocalizations) and linguistic forms of spoken or signed language (words and multiple words). Although there are many other indicators of communication, such as social attention, eye contact, and crying, these were not included as key skills for the ECI because, when evaluated, they did not show growth over time or were difficult for two independent observers to document reliably without specialized equipment. Therefore, the key skills that comprise the ECI include those most closely associated with proficiency in expressive communication and language that increased in rate per minute over time and could be reliably coded by two independent observers. Figure 4.1 shows each of the key skill elements and their relationship to the composite indicator of total communication. The definitions and how to code each of the key skill elements are provided later in this chapter.

Technical Adequacy of the ECI

To document the basic psychometric properties and feasibility of the ECI, a longitudinal study with 50 children; a cross-sectional study with 1,486 infants and toddlers in Early Head Start, child care, and early intervention programs (Greenwood, Carta et al., 2006; Luze et al., 2001); and a series of small-scale studies demonstrating sensitivity to intervention were conducted (Bigelow, 2006; Greenwood, Dunn, Ward, & Luze, 2003; Harjusola-Webb, 2006; Kirk, 2006; Murray, 2002; Small, 2004). These studies, among others, have demonstrated that observers are able to become reliable in administration and coding of the ECI (meeting the 85% criterion level). Early childhood educators were able to use the ECI reliably with high levels of agreement (90% overall) (Luze et al., 2001). The sensitivity of the ECI to communication growth over time was demonstrated when children's rates of total communication on the ECI continued to increase when they were followed longitudinally. It was also determined that the ECI was sensitive to differences in the performance of children with and without disabilities across different age groups and for children with English as a second language. In addition, the ECI was sensitive to differences following intervention.

When compared with two other measures of expressive communication—a standardized measure and a parent report measure—it was found that the ECI compared highly to both measures of communication, thus demonstrating criterion validity. Studies of the psychometric integrity of the ECI have indicated that it is an instrument that can be reliably administered, measure what it is intended to measure, and be sensitive to differences across children of different communicative abilities. (See also Chapter 11 or http://www.igdi.ku.edu/measures/index.htm for a more detailed discussion regarding the psychometric information for the ECI.)

Protocol for Administering the ECI

Given that the goal of the ECI is to capture a child's typical communication across repeated observations to monitor progress over time, as well as any response to changes in intervention, it is important to administer the ECI using the same protocol across assessments and to ensure that the assessment is representative of the child's communication. To accomplish this, it is recommended that assessors who administer the ECI are familiar to the child and support the child's communicative behavior through commenting on the child's interests and encouraging communication during ECI administration.

During ECI administration, play is centered on either the Fisher-Price barn or Fisher-Price house for a 6-minute session (see Figures 4.2 and 4.3). The administration session takes place in a convenient, comfortable setting with minimal distractions so that there are opportunities to observe and record the child's communication within a semistructured play-based format. There are several options available for administering and scoring the ECI. The following ECI administration protocol chart clarifies the process. (See also Chapter 3 for more information on administering IGDIs.) Figure 4.4. is an example of an ECI recording form, which is available on the IGDI web site. Figure 4.5 is an example of an ECI administration checklist, which is also available on the IGDI web site.

Coding the ECI

A child's frequency of communication using the key skill elements described earlier in the chapter of gesturing, vocalizing, and using words or multiple word utterances is recorded on a manual recording form (see Figure 4.4) and transferred to a form on the IGDI web site following the observation (see Figure 4.6).

The frequencies of each of the communicative behaviors that are tallied are then entered into the IGDI web site where they are summed, weighted by a computer program according to complexity of communication (e.g., single words multiplied by two, multiple words multiplied by three), and divided by the number of minutes of observation (i.e., typically 6 minutes) to form a weighted total communication rate that is automatically graphed for each child (see Figure 4.7). This weighted total communication rate is the indicator used to monitor children's communication progress. The weighted total communication graph displays the child's ECI total communication data at the age (in months) of the child at each ECI assessment occasion. The child's individual mean and his or her slope of growth are displayed on the graph in comparison with a normative sample or benchmark mean rate of communication and the norm slope. Shaded regions on the graph depict growth that is (1 *SD* below the mean [light grey area] or 1.5 *SD* below [dark grey area]). The ECI norms are currently based on a composite sample that includes more than 1,400 children (Greenwood, Carta et al., 2006).

In addition, each key skill element is graphed individually (see Figures 4.8, 4.9, 4.10, and 4.11 for examples of these graphs), which together comprise the total communication rate. Each key skill indicator graph displays the child's rate per minute for the key skill compared to normative data for that skill.

Definitions of Key Skill Elements of Communication   Assessors observe a child while he or she is engaged with a play partner (either in person or from a video-recorded ECI assessment) and tally the child's use of the following key skills: gestures, vocalizations, single words and multiple words.

Gestures   Gestures are coded when physical movements are made by the child in an attempt to communicate with the play partner. An episode during which a gesture is observed is counted from when the gesture begins to when there is a clear and distinct change in the child's movement. Gestures include:

- Giving or handing an object to a play partner

- Pushing away or rejecting an object

- Reaching toward a partner or object the partner is holding

- Pointing toward an object or person

- Nodding or shaking the head or shrugging shoulders to indicate "yes" or "no"

Gestures are not coded when the child

- Reaches for toys or objects that the play partner is not holding

- Moves toys in a way that does not involve interaction with the partner

- Makes a physical movement that shows excitement or pleasure that is not in direct communication with the partner (e.g., waving arms)

Vocalizations   Vocalizations are nonword or unintelligible verbal utterances voiced by the child to a partner. Utterances that are coded as vocalizations are those

Figure 4.2. Fisher-Price house used as one of the two alternate ECI assessment toys.

Figure 4.3. Fisher-Price barn used as one of the two alternate ECI assessment toys.

that cannot be understood as single or multiple words. When vocalizations co-occur in utterances in which single or multiple words are understood, the vocalization(s) should not be recorded. Vocalizations are only recorded when they occur in an utterance consisting only of vocalizations or gestures and vocalizations that occur together. An utterance ends when there has been a breath or a clear break of at least one second without vocalizations. The best way to determine this is to count to yourself "one thousand one." Vocalizations are coded when the child does the following:

- Laughs out loud during the play session

- Makes animal sounds (e.g., "moo") when looking at a toy, transportation/motor sounds (e.g., "vroom") when pushing a tractor, or other vowel-vowel or vowel-consonant combinations or babbling and cooing sounds or fillers, such as "mm" or "huh"

**Early Communication
Indicator (ECI)**

Child Name or #: Sheila Johnson_____   Assess Date 7/1/2009 (MM/DD/YYYY)

Assessment Duration: 6   00
                    Min   Sec

Form: (House) or Barn   Condition Change (see list below): None_____

Primary Coder: Samantha Dornan_____   Assessor: Samantha Dornan_____

Location (Circle One) (Home) Center   Other (explain in Notes)

Language of Administration: English_____

If Reliability, Reliability Coder's Name: Jose Hernandez_____

Notes: _____

Condition List

ABA/TEACH
Child Psychiatrist
Interpreter
Language Intervention Toolkit
Medical Intervention (e.g., Tubes)
Mental Health Consultant
Milieu or Incidental Teaching
MOD Recommendations
None
Other
Primary Care Provider
Registered Nurse
Responsive Interaction
Social Worker
Speech/Language Therapist

	Gestures	Vocalizations	Single Words	Multiple Words
Begin 0:00 Sec.	G ///	V /	W //	M ////
1:00 Sec.	G	V ///	W 卌 //	M ////
2:00 Sec.	G /	V	W ///	M 卌 //
3:00 Sec.	G	V //	W ///	M 卌 ///
4:00 Sec.	G //	V	W ///	M 卌
5:00 Sec.	G /	V //	W /	M ///
6 min. End Total	G 7	V 8	W 19	M 31

Figure 4.4. The ECI recording form available on the IGDI web site: http://www.igdi.ku.edu/measures/observation_forms.htm#ECI. (© Juniper Gardens Children's Project; reprinted by permission.)

The following are not coded as vocalizations:

- Crying

- Involuntary noises, such as hiccups

- An utterance that includes a recognizable word or word combination

A single-word utterance is a single word voiced by the child that is understood as a single word and not a vocalization or an approximation of a word (e.g., "baba" for *bottle* or "og" for *dog*). Single words are recorded when the child says a single

ECI Administration Checklist

ECI Assessor: _Alicia Hernandez_   Date: _June 13, 2009_   Tape: _N/A (live observation)_

This checklist may be used to score the administration tapes for the ECI. To be certified to administer the ECI, the adult play partner should complete the administration steps to at least an 81% (13 out of 16) criterion level.

	Item	Yes	No
Setting up the ECI Administration Situation: Materials & Positioning			
1. Adult play partner sets up the House or Barn prior to session.	1	X	
2. The toys inside have been arranged to attract child's attention.	2	X	
3. Barn or house is set up so it is facing the child and accessible.	3	X	
4. Adult and child are positioned so they can see and reach toys.	4	X	
5. Adult play partner and child can have eye contact.	5	X	
6. Child is positioned appropriately for his/her developmental level (head, neck and feet supported as needed).	6	X	
7. Session is timed	7	X	
ECI Assessment Administration: Play Situation			
8. Adult play partner follows child's lead in play situation.	8	X	
9. Adult play partner comments about what child is doing.	9	X	
10. Adult play partner describes what he/she is doing.	10	X	
11. Adult play partner interacts in non-directive, friendly manner.	11	X	
12. Adult play partner uses questions sparingly.	12		X
Ending ECI Session			
13. Session ends exactly after 6 minutes have elapsed.	13	X	
14. Adult play partner lets child know that it is time to stop.	14	X	
15. Adult play partner thanks child for playing.	15		X
16. Adult play partner cleans toys (may be reported).	16	X	
	Total	14 Yes	2 No

Administration Accuracy = [(Total Number of Steps Completed Correctly/16 Steps) × 100] = _87.5_ % (Need 81%)

Figure 4.5. The ECI administration checklist available on the IGDI web site: http://www.igdi.ku.edu/measures/observation_forms.htm#ECI. (© Juniper Gardens Children's Project; reprinted by permission.)

word in an utterance in which no other recognizable words are said. Single words are coded when the child

- Says the labels of objects (e.g., "cow," "horse," "potty")

- Repeats words in a continuous sequential repetition (e.g., "go, go, go")

- Says compound words (e.g., "mailbox," "necklace")

- Uses ritualized duplications, such as "bye-bye," "uh-oh," or "night-night," or two-part proper names, such as Big Bird or Mary Jane

- Sequentially describes or names objects, such as "block, red, blue, girl" (each is tallied as a single word)

- Uses standard sign language when one word is signed

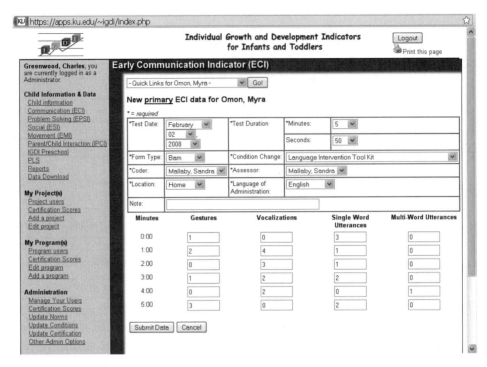

Figure 4.6. The ECI online individual child data entry form filled in at http://www.igdi.ku.edu/data_system/index .htm (© Juniper Gardens Children's Project; reprinted by permission.)

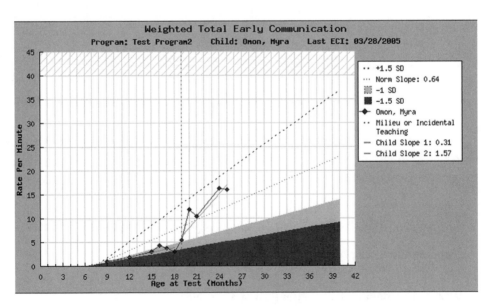

Figure 4.7. The ECI weighted total early communication graph for Myra displaying ECI total communication data, slope, and time at which the intervention was implemented. The light grey region indicates total communication that is –1 *SD* below the mean. The dark grey region indicates total communication that is –1.5 *SD* below the mean. The slope line indicates the slope of growth of Myra's communication. (© Juniper Gardens Children's Project; reprinted by permission.)

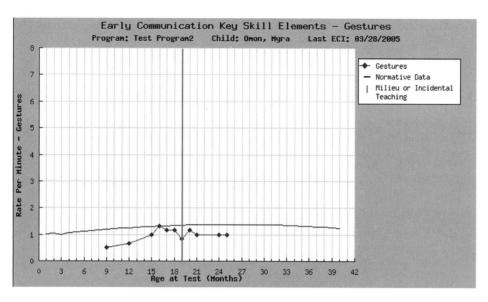

Figure 4.8. Myra's key skill element graph generated from the online IGDI child data system shows her rate per minute of gestures compared with normative data. (© Juniper Gardens Children's Project; reprinted by permission.)

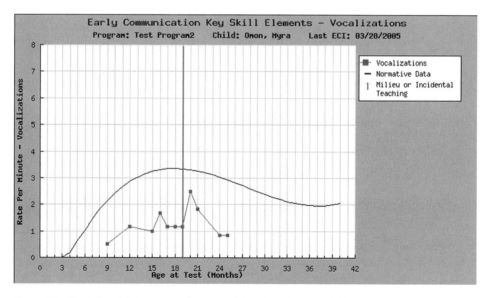

Figure 4.9. Myra's key skill element graph generated from the online IGDI child data system shows her rate per minute of vocalizations compared with normative data. (© Juniper Gardens Children's Project; reprinted by permission.)

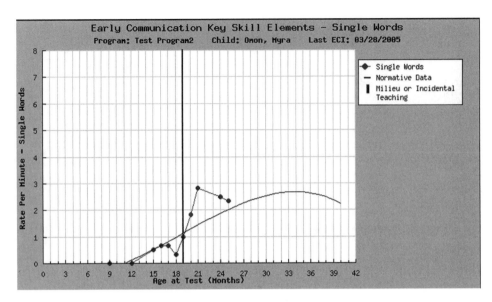

Figure 4.10. Myra's key skill element graph generated from the online IGDI child data system shows her rate per minute of single words compared with normative data. (© Juniper Gardens Children's Project; reprinted by permission.)

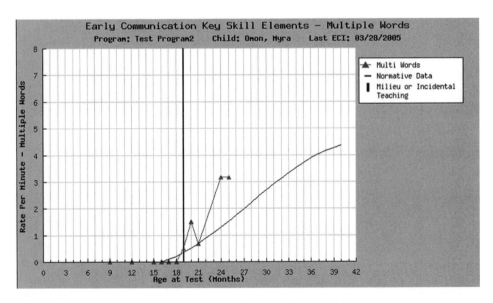

Figure 4.11. Myra's key skill element graph generated from the online IGDI child data system shows her rate per minute of multiple words compared with normative data. (© Juniper Gardens Children's Project; reprinted by permission.)

ECI

A multiple-word utterance is a combination of two or more different words voiced by the child that are understood by the person coding as being a word combination. In this case, an utterance consists of a sentence of two or more multiple words that fit together in a meaningful way that approximates a phrase or sentence. Multiple words are coded under the following circumstances:

- The word combination is grammatically correct or incorrect (e.g., "Me go to store").

- The meaning of a word combination is clear or not clear (e.g., "Cow rides tractor").

- Standard sign language for multiple-word utterances is used as long as the child signs two or more signs put together to convey meaning in a sentence format.

- False starts to sentences or stuttering into another utterance occurs. False starts are when a child starts to say something, but before finishing the sentence or thought he or she changes the wording to another sentence. For example, "I think this is . . . This looks like a dog." This would be considered to be one multiple-word utterance. In this case, the false start would not be counted.

- If only one word in an utterance is understandable, it should be considered a single word.

Web Site Support for Training and Certification in Scoring and Coding   An online certification process ensures that users attain a satisfactory level of reliability agreement in coding the key communication skills. (See Chapter 10 for training and certification information). In general, users may be certified in coding the ECI by 1) reviewing the coding definitions, 2) practicing coding on the two certification video examples provided on the web site, 3) coding the certification videos, and 4) totaling the tally marks on the recording sheet and entering the scores into the online system. An overall observer agreement score of 85% is required for each of the two certification videos.

When ready to code and enter scores into the online recording form for each individual child after an ECI assessment is completed, tally marks are counted up from the manual recording sheet, and the totals are entered into the web site. There, the scores are automatically weighted in the computer program and the total communication and key skill element graphs are made. These graphs may be printed off and shared in team meetings and with parents to monitor a child's progress in communication.

 ## Myra: An Example of Using the ECI in an RTI Framework for Intervention Decision Making

In this section, we present a case illustration of a child who was given the ECI by her home visitor as part of a statewide Early Head Start (EHS) initiative to conduct regular progress monitoring. Also illustrated is an example of using the decision-making model for intervention within an EHS program to document progress using the current curriculum and to provide information about individual and group progress in communication. As described previously in this volume (see Chapter 2), the decision-making approach gives early educators practical tools for continuous monitoring of child progress and a set of decision rules about when to begin or modify an intervention when a child shows insufficient growth on the progress monitoring indicator. The decision-making model used within an RTI framework gives early educators a practical basis for either altering their practices when needed as indicated by lack of growth on key skill indicators or confirming their practices when they are promoting sufficient growth toward the general outcome (Carta et al. 2002; VanDerHeyden, Snyder, Broussard, & Ramsdell, 2008; Walker, Carta et al., 2008).

Myra was 9 months old when she began receiving ongoing progress monitoring along with the other children in the Brown County EHS program. Myra had experienced several different home visitors, but her current home visitor was Alicia. When Alicia started her job as a home visitor in the Brown County EHS program, one of her initial tasks was to become certified using the web-based program to administer and code the ECI. (See Chapter 10 for IGDI training information.)

During recent home visits, Alicia had observed that Myra rarely communicated her wants and needs. This observation was confirmed by Myra's mother who reported that Myra seemed to be frustrated lately when she wanted something but could not tell her mother or siblings what it was. It was becoming a source of frustration not only for Myra, but for everyone in the family. Because Myra's scores on the ECI were in the "slightly below benchmark" (light grey area) of the ECI graph (see Figure 4.7), the EHS team and Myra's mother decided to begin more frequent monitoring of Myra's communication using the ECI. The team also did this for some other children in the program who were performing below benchmark.

After administering the ECI again at 15 months, Alicia entered Myra's ECI data into the ECI web site and printed an individual report (see appendix for example of a report) and graph of Myra's total communication (see Figure 4.7), as well as her key skill element graphs (see Figures 4.8, 4.9, 4.10, and 4.11) to share with the team and Myra's mother. Alicia noted that at the 9-, 12-, and 15-month assessments, Myra's ECI scores were −1 *SD* below the norm line for children her age. In addition, the key skill element graphs indicated that Myra's use of gestures or vocalizations were at rates that were lower than other children her age. A meeting with Myra's mother and the EHS team ruled out possible health concerns, such as hearing or vision problems, that might account for Myra's lower communication rate, and it was decided that they would begin more frequent monthly monitoring using the ECI. If Myra's scores continued to be low, they would explore possible intervention options to promote Myra's use of expressive communication.

After more frequent monitoring of Myra's communication progress, the ECI graph again showed that Myra was in the −1.5 *SD* range (see Figure 4.7 at 18 months). Alicia, the EHS team, and Myra's mother all agreed that Myra would benefit from planned communication intervention. They would continue using the ECI to monitor Myra's progress after they started the intervention to make sure that the intervention was helping to improve Myra's communication.

Following the initiation of the intervention that included evidence-based milieu and responsive teaching strategies for promoting communication (e.g., Kaiser, Hancock, &

Nietfeld, 2000; Walker, Bigelow, & Harjusola-Webb, 2008; Yoder & Warren, 2002), Alicia worked with Myra's mother to follow Myra's lead, use more commenting and labeling during daily routine activities, and other strategies known to promote communication. The intervention provided Myra with increased opportunities to be exposed to language and to practice communicating. After beginning the intervention, both Alicia and Myra's mother noticed an increase in Myra's use of communication. At the next ECI assessment, it was observed that Myra's communication had begun to increase. The slope on the total communication graph approached the mean level, and subsequent ECI assessments documented that Myra's total communication rate increased to levels above the mean for children her age. Those increases were maintained well above the normative level following the intervention; therefore, it was decided to return to quarterly progress monitoring. By 26 months of age, Myra was using multiple words at a level equivalent to the norm group (see Figure 4.7). Alicia continued to monitor Myra's overall communication to provide regular feedback on the fidelity of Myra's mother's use of the strategies, as well as consultation on how to use the strategies across a variety of activities at home and in the community.

Using progress monitoring within an RTI decision-making framework permitted the EHS home visitor and Myra's mother to be informed about the impact of the intervention on the toddler's communication levels. In addition, through progress monitoring, Myra's home visitor and parent continued to receive feedback about Myra's communication growth in the context of RTI.

Conclusion

Monitoring the growth of communication is important for giving practitioners and others working with young children a quick and reliable tool for determining whether an individual child or group of children is developing communication at a rate comparable to other children the same age. As shown in Myra's story, the ECI can be used for intervention decision making within an RTI framework. As discussed earlier in this volume (see Chapter 2), the IGDI decision-making model for making intervention decisions has implications for guiding changes in individual children's intervention, early identification and prevention, and the identification of children whose needs are not met by the curriculum or intervention being implemented. This model gives early educators a practical basis for either altering their practices when needed or confirming their practices when children are progressing along the expected trajectory (Carta et al., 2002). The decision-making model enables the connection between the evaluation of child progress in communication and the impact of intervention on progress toward the outcome. Some challenges still exist in facilitating how practitioners utilize the ECI information for purposes of informing intervention. As developed, the ECI is used as a monitoring tool to provide guidelines to users to determine when children may need additional support for their communication development. For some, the flexibility of the decision-making system to use interventions of their choosing is an important feature. However, we have found that some interventionists and programs can benefit from more

ECI

support for intervention decision making, especially in the role of home visitor. Therefore, a next step with the ECI, and with all of the IGDIs, is having a way to quickly provide parents or early educators with individualized intervention recommendations that are indexed to the general outcome measure. A process for making online intervention decisions within the ECI web site is described further in Chapter 11 of this volume.

Administration Protocol for the Early Communication Indicator

 Materials

Digital timer

Required toys
- Fisher-Price house (with furnishings; batteries removed) (see Figure 4.2)
- Fisher-Price barn (with animals) (see Figure 4.3)
- Something that shakes (e.g., a rattle)

Suggested toy substitutions
- Multiethnic dolls
- Rattles

 Administration options

1. Two people
   - Play partner (certified ECI administrator)
   - Certified assessor
2. One person as each of the following:
   - Play partner
   - Certified assessor**
3. Two people
   - Parent as play partner
   - Certified assessor

**This option would be video recorded for later coding.

 Forms

ECI recording form (see Figure 4.4)

 Setup

Comfortable area
- At a table
- Sitting on the floor

Arrangement of toys
- Farm or house with sides open
- Set up toys in an inviting manner (e.g., set up table and chairs, put animals in their stalls)
- Allow sufficient room for play

 Time

One timed 6-minute session

 Conducting the session**

If the child becomes interested in another toy, try to bring his or her attention back to the ECI assessment by talking about the ECI toys.

Follow the child's communicative lead (i.e., play with and talk about things that interest the child or that the child is doing).

Do not rely on asking questions as the primary manner of interacting with the child.

(continued)

ECI

Let the child know when the session has ended, assist him or her in ending play, and thank the child for playing.

Offer immediate access to another toy to play with at the end of the session.

**See Chapter 3 for more detailed information.

The Cognitive
Problem-Solving IGDI

Early Problem-Solving Indicator (EPSI)

Dale Walker and Charles Greenwood

The Individual Growth and Development Indicator (IGDI) for problem solving, the Early Problem-Solving Indicator (EPSI), was designed for use by early educators, interventionists, home visitors, and researchers interested in measuring early cognitive outcomes for infants and toddlers between 12 and 48 months of age. Similar in structure to the other IGDIs, the EPSI was designed to meet early educators' needs for a quick, repeatable, reliable, and valid measure of children's progress in developing early problem-solving skills and children's response to early cognitive interventions (Greenwood, Walker, Carta, & Higgins, 2006).

As discussed in Chapter 1, a key to IGDIs is to facilitate early educators' ability to monitor the progress of children and to quickly identify those children who are falling below benchmark in an area of development so that a change in program or intervention may be initiated. Being informed about children's early cognitive outcomes related to problem solving provides educators and parents with valuable information as to whether infants and toddlers are developing problem-solving skills at levels comparable with other children their age, and, if not, how well the general program or intervention is moving an individual child or group of children toward proficiency. Monitoring proficiency in problem solving for all children in a program can provide helpful information about the program's effectiveness and can help to inform programmatic decisions regarding the early cognitive abilities of the children being served.

Overview of the EPSI

Proficiency in problem solving is an important outcome in early childhood related to cognitive and social-emotional development. Children's early problem-solving

EPSI

skills and their perseverance toward achieving goals set the stage for their later intellectual competence. Moreover, children's early cognitive problem-solving skills affect the way they navigate and explore their environment, their reasoning ability, and their ability to adapt to challenging circumstances (Siegler & Alibali, 2004). Consequently, a major focus of early education and early care is the development of young children's cognitive development, including problem solving (National Research Council, 2001).

Developmental Course of Problem Solving and Early Cognition

Problem solving is a cognitive ability that requires the integration of a number of fundamental cognitive skills. Among the skills that must be harnessed for success in this realm are various components of attention (i.e., engagement, shifting, persistence, and resistance to distraction); memory (i.e., short- and long-term); and the ability to use these skills to direct some motor action (e.g., reaching for a toy, pushing a button to make a toy pop up) (Colombo & Cheatham, 2006; Garon, Bryson, & Smith, 2008).

Similar to other early developmental skills, there is variability in the age range at which certain early cognitive and problem-solving behaviors emerge. However, there is also some continuity seen in the pattern of development for infants and toddlers (Kannass & Oakes, 2008). For instance, infants between 4 and 6 months of age may shift their attention, visually explore a toy, and try to obtain a toy they see (Colombo, 2004). Between 6 and 12 months, infants will explore objects and may play with toys to produce effects (Willatts, 1999). Solving simple problems through sustained attention and persistence, even using adults to assist with solving a problem by asking for help, is a skill that toddlers may develop when they are between 12 and 18 months of age (Hupp & Abbeduto, 1991; Jennings, Yarrow, & Martin, 1984). Between 20 and 24 months, toddlers may begin to play independently with toys that require goal-directed problem solving, such as operating switches or buttons to produce effects (e.g., Bauer, Schwade, Wewerka, & Delaney, 1999). Proficiency with creating solutions becomes increasingly complex so that by 3 years of age, children can show persistence under distracting conditions and may use verbal cues to maintain persistence (Kannass & Colombo, 2007). At this age, children sometimes show other people how toys work and are increasingly able to focus their attention (e.g., Ruff & Capozzoli, 2003).

Considerable individual variation exists, however, in the problem-solving abilities of young children. Although some differences may be related to personality or inherited characteristics, most children's skills in this area appear to grow as a result of early experience (National Research Council and Institute of Medicine, 2000). For some children, development of these skills may be slower than for others because of experiential deficits due to low stimulation, restricted opportunities to play with toys, and limited verbal and play interaction by adults and caregivers. Early identification of a delay in problem-solving skills and the receipt of effective early intervention may help to move children toward age-expected out-comes (Colombo, 2004; Lyon, 1996; National Research Council and Institute of Medicine, 2000).

Parents and professionals identify problem-solving skills as an important general outcome for young children (Priest et al., 2001). The EPSI general outcome statement—*"Child solves problems that require reasoning about objects, concepts, situations and people"*—was one of 15 general child outcome statements investigated by a national sample of parents ($n = 351$) and professionals ($n = 672$) (Priest et al., 2001). Of the 15 general outcomes examined in the study, problem solving was highly rated. Other highly valued general outcomes included expressive communication, movement, and social skills, among others (Carta et al., 2002; Priest et al., 2001).

Importance of Problem-Solving Skills for Later Development

Among the most critical skills for school success involve the ability to engage, focus, and persist in the completion of challenging tasks and problems (Zelazo, Carter, & Reznick, 1997). Attaining these skills affects children's success throughout life in academics, creative arts, and interpersonal relationships (Gibbs & Teti, 1990). Children who can explore, manipulate, and play with toys; attend to a task; try out potential solutions; and persist until the problem is solved are learning how to learn. Although these skills develop throughout childhood, they begin to emerge in simple forms during the earliest years of life. Being able to track whether or not individual infants and toddlers are making progress learning problem-solving skills is essential to knowing that they are on a developmental trajectory toward school readiness (Bauer et al., 1999; Zelazo et al., 1997).

Current State of Assessment for Cognitive Functioning of Infants and Toddlers

Unfortunately, most infant and toddler assessments are notoriously poor predictors of later cognitive functioning (Colombo, 1993; Gibbs & Teti, 1990). In addition, as discussed in Chapter 2, most have limited utility for directly informing intervention because they do not measure the progress of young children toward achieving important outcomes, nor do they have sufficient sensitivity to help early interventionists detect growth in cognitive development (Bagnato, Neisworth, Salvia, & Hunt, 1999). Information gathered cannot be used formatively to reflect recent progress, help select appropriate interventions, and guide intervention decisions. Together, these limitations make it difficult to accurately identify whether young children are following a normative pattern of growth in cognitive competence (National Research Council and Institute of Medicine, 2000), as well as make it difficult to develop effective interventions for promoting growth.

EPSI

How the EPSI Addresses Deficits in Current Measurement

As is the case for all of the IGDIs, the EPSI uses a standardized format that is easy to administer, may be repeated frequently, and can be a useful tool for monitoring individual children's growth and making intervention decisions within an RTI framework (e.g., Walker, Carta, Greenwood, & Buzhardt, 2008). The EPSI can also provide information about program progress toward the general outcome and may inform programmatic decisions about curricula related to cognitive outcomes (Greenwood, Walker, et al., 2006).

What Does the EPSI Assess?

The components or key skill elements that comprise the EPSI and make up the total problem-solving indicator include looking, exploring, functions, and solutions. These skills were selected to represent the visual exploration domain (i.e., looking), the object exploration domain (i.e., exploring and functions), and the problem-solving domain (i.e., solutions), which are three skill classes of importance to infants and toddlers who are just acquiring problem-solving skills. Following testing to see which of the key skill elements were most useful, the rates of occurrence of functions and solutions were brought together to form a single indicator of total problem solving (see Figure 5.1).

EPSI Key Skill Definitions

Looks   Look is recorded when a child orients his or her body by facing or moving toward a person or a toy that is in front of him or her, held in his or her hand, or on his or her lap. For example, the infant may be holding a shape up to his or her face, looking at the shape, or facing and looking toward the toy in front of him or her.

Explores   Explore is recorded when the child touches, moves, rubs, shakes, pushes, pulls, picks up, bangs, throws, or drops the toy, or when the child puts the toy in his or her mouth. For example, an infant may attempt to put one of the stacking cups into his or her mouth or repeatedly push or turn one of the pop-up toy buttons. Another example of exploring a toy is when an infant pushes the toy off of a table and watches the toy land on the ground. When the toy is replaced, the infant may repeat this action.

Functions   Function is recorded when the child makes a toy perform a function or creates an effect for which it was designed (e.g., popping up, fitting into, taking out, sorting, making music, stacking, opening, closing, fitting pieces). For example, a toddler may push on the toy button to make the dinosaur pop up or bang the shape to make the shape go into the shape sorter.

General Outcome: Child solves problems that require reasoning about objects, concepts, situations, and people.

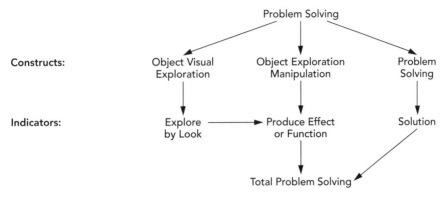

Figure 5.1. Early Problem-Solving Indicator (EPSI): Key skill indicators conceptual framework. (© Juniper Gardens Children's Project; reprinted by permission.)

Solutions   Solution is defined as a fluid sequence of skills or routines used with a toy that leads to the intended goal or objective of the toy. In contrast to a function that is a single effect, a solution occurs when the toy's end point is reached (e.g., all cups are stacked, all puzzle pieces are placed, all pieces are put into the hole at the top of the toy). The child may use any number or combination of the key skills to reach the end point of the toy (e.g., finding a toy behind a door, pushing the knob the correct way to make the toy pop up, opening the door with the key to retrieve the shape). The child may replace all of the puzzle pieces into the puzzle frame or push and pull on the door and then turn the knob to make it open in order to retrieve all of the objects placed inside.

Total Problem Solving   The total problem-solving score is the sum of functions and solutions divided by 6 minutes to form a score in terms of rate per minute. In our data collection to identify which key skill elements reflected growth toward the general outcome most accurately, it was found that functions followed by solutions were the key skills that showed the greatest growth over time (Greenwood, Walker, et al., 2006).

Research Supporting the EPSI

Technical Adequacy of the EPSI

To document the basic psychometric properties and feasibility of the EPSI, a short-term longitudinal study with 30 children was conducted (Greenwood, Walker, et al., 2006). (The psychometric information related to all of the IGDIs, including the EPSI, can be found in Chapter 11 of this volume.) In this study, we demonstrated that observers were able to become reliable in administration and coding of the EPSI (meeting the 85% criterion level), and early childhood educators were able to code

EPSI assessments with high levels of agreement (e.g., $r = .99$ and $.97$ for functions and solutions) when two independent observers coded at the same time (Greenwood, Walker, et al., 2006). When we looked at the interrelationships among the key skill elements, the strongest positive relationship was between functions and solutions. The EPSI was found to be moderately correlated to a widely used developmental assessment—the Bayley Scales of Infant Development (Bayley, 1993). The EPSI was sensitive to problem-solving growth over time when administered on multiple occasions, and it was sensitive to children who were performing at different developmental levels and who were different ages. Therefore, although the normative sample was small for this IGDI, the EPSI demonstrated sufficient technical adequacy (see Chapter 11 for more detailed technical information or visit the web site at http://www.igdi.ku.edu/measures/EPSI_Measures/EPSI_technical_soundness.htm).

Protocol for Administering the EPSI

Similar to the early communication indicator (ECI) described in Chapter 4, as well as the other IGDIs, there are options for administering the EPSI to permit for some flexibility. There are, however, standardized toys and administration guidelines that are followed when administering the EPSI so that performance may be compared over time for individual children and across groups of children. The general administration instructions used across all of the IGDIs are described in Chapter 3 of this volume, as well as on the IGDI web site at http://www.igdi.ku.edu. Figures 5.2 and 5.3 are examples of the EPSI recording form and EPSI administration checklist. The following EPSI administration protocol chart outlines the EPSI administration process.

The toys used for the EPSI were screened and selected based on the fact that each has a final end point with steps involved in reaching that end point. The pop-up toys, gumball machine, pound-a-ball, and stacking cups (round or square) are used in each administration as the standard play toys recommended for use in the EPSI (see Figures 5.4 and 5.5). These or similar toys were used for the normative sample during the development of the EPSI and represent examples of the toys recommended for each toy set.

Although the brand of the toys used for the EPSI may differ, what is most important is that each toy used has the same general characteristics as those described here and displayed on the IGDI web site. Furthermore, the adult play partner should present the toy in a manner that will make it interesting for the child and so the child knows he or she can play with the toy and make it work. For example, when the stacking cups are presented, the adult could say, "Wow, these can make a tower or fit into each other," or when the gumball or pound-a-ball toy is presented, the adult might say, "Look at this toy, I see balls in there."

For the purpose of timing the session, it is necessary to have a digital timer. It should signal when 2 minutes have elapsed and it is therefore time to rotate toys, as well as when 6 minutes have elapsed and it is time to end the session. Accurate timing of the EPSI sessions is important because progress is measured in terms of a rate per minute for a total of 6 minutes.

Child Name or #: **Miles**   Assess Date **3/20/2009** (MM/DD/YYYY)

Assessment Duration: **6** **00**   Form: **A** or B
                                         Min   Sec

Condition Change (see list below): **Speech/Language Pathologist**

Primary Coder: **Heidi Johnson**   Assessor: **Alva Smith**

Location (Circle One): **Home** Center   Other (explain in Notes)

Language of Administration: **English**

If Reliability, Reliability Coder's Name: **N/A**

Notes: *Four of Mile's cousins were at home during assessment. She seemed distracted.*

Early Problem Solving Indicator (EPSI)

Toys Form A or B (Choose only one form per assessment)	Looks	Explores	Functions	Solutions
A. Pop-up Pets A B C D* (2 Minutes) **2:00** Min Sec **B. Pop-Up Dinos** A B C D*	L ///	E /////	F //	S
A. Stacking Cups-Square (2 Minutes) **2:00** Min Sec **B. Stacking Cups-Round**	L ///	E //	F ////	S
A. Pound-a-Ball (2 Minutes) **2:00** Min Sec **B. Gumball Machine**	L ///// ///	E /////	F	S
6 min. End Total	L 14	E 12	F 6	S 0

Condition List

ABA/TEACH
Child Psychiatrist
Interpreter
Language Intervention Toolkit
Medical Intervention (e.g., Tubes)
Mental Health Consultant
Milieu or Incidental Teaching
MOD Recommendations
None
Other
Primary Care Provider
Registered Nurse
Responsive Interaction
Social Worker
Speech/Language Therapist

*These letters correspond to each of the four pop-ups. The coder may use these to track which pop-up the child has engaged. Whenever the child engages all pop-ups, a 'solution' is coded.

Figure 5.2. The EPSI recording form available on the IGDI web site http://www.igdi.ku.edu/measures/observation_forms.htm#ECI. (© Juniper Gardens Children's Project; reprinted by permission.)

Coding the EPSI

Coding procedures are designed to record the degree to which the child solves problems that require reasoning about objects, concepts, and situations. Each key skill element that is used by a child to solve a problem is tallied (see Figure 5.2). Coding of key element behaviors includes *looks, explores, functions,* and *solutions.* Each key skill element is coded separately as it occurs during a timed play session. All key skills are coded using a frequency count; that is, each instance of a behavior is counted and recorded with a tally mark. Each assessment requires three sets of

EPSI Administration Checklist

ECI Assessor: Alva   **Date:** 6/13/2009   **Tape:** 319586

This checklist may be used to score the administration tapes for the EPSI. To be certified to administer the EPSI, the adult play partner should complete the administration steps to **at least an 81% (13 of 16)** criterion level.

Setting up the EPSI Administration Situation: Materials & Positioning

	Item	Yes	No
1. Adult play partner sets up each toy for child to play with (with other toys out of sight but within reach of administrator).	1	X	
2. Each toy is arranged to attract child's attention.	2	X	
3. Adult and child are positioned so they can see and reach toys.	3	X	
4. Adult play partner and child can have eye contact.	4	X	
5. Child is positioned appropriately for his or her developmental level (head, neck, and feet supported as needed).	5	X	
6. Session is timed (2 minutes for each toy).	6	X	
7. Video camera is set up so that child can be seen for scoring.	7	X	

EPSI Assessment Administration: Play Situation

	Item	Yes	No
8. Adult play partner follows child's lead in play situation.	8	X	
9. Adult play partner comments about what child is doing with toy.	9	X	
10. Adult play partner describes what he or she is doing with toy to encourage child to play with the toy.	10		X
11. Adult play partner interacts in nondirective, friendly manner.	11	X	

Ending EPSI Session

	Item	Yes	No
12. Each toy presentation ends after 2 minutes (repeated for all 3 toys).	12	X	
13. Session ends after exactly 6 minutes.	13	X	
14. Adult play partner lets child know that it is time to stop.	14	X	
15. Adult play partner thanks child for playing.	15	X	
16. Adult play partner cleans toys (may be reported).	16		X
	Total	14 Yes	2 No

Administration Accuracy = [(Total Number of Steps Completed Correctly/16 Steps) × 100] = 87.5 % (Need 81%)

Figure 5.3. The EPSI administration checklist available on the IGDI web site http://www.igdi.ku.edu/measures/observation_forms.htm#ECI. (© Juniper Gardens Children's Project; reprinted by permission.)

toys, and each set is used for 2 minutes for a total of 6 minutes across the three sets. EPSI scoring forms have different sections for each key element and are separated into three 2-minute segments (one for each of the three toys). Additional coding information is available online at http://www.igdi.ku.edu/measures/EPSI_Measures/EPSI_scoring.htm

Coding Looks   *Looks* are coded if the infant or toddler looks at, faces, or moves his or her head toward a toy(s) that is placed near him or her or that someone gives to him or her, or if the child reaches for or manipulates a toy. *Looks* are coded if

• The child appears to gaze at or stare at the toy(s) for any amount of time, or if his or her eyes or head moves back and forth between toys presented.

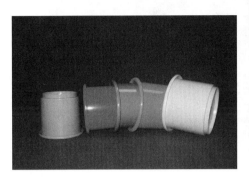

EPSI

Figure 5.4. Toy Set A as one of the two alternate EPSI assessment toy sets.

- The child looks away from the toy for 3 seconds or more, or if another key skill element occurs. For example, if the child gazes at the toy (one episode of *look* is scored), then looks at his or her shoe for 2 seconds, and then immediately returns her gaze to the toy, do *not* code another episode of *look* because he or she looked away for less than 3 seconds. If the child looked at her shoe for about 4 seconds and then looked back to the toy, two separate episodes of *look* may be scored.

- Only if the child is looking at the toy(s) presented

Look is not coded if

- The child looks toward the adult or other toys or objects in the room.

- The child is looking at his or her own body or clothes.

Coding Explore   *Explore* is coded when a child manipulates the toy with his fingers, mouth, or other parts of his body. *Explore* is coded if the child

- Touches or moves his or her fingers to manipulate the toy.

- Puts the toy in his or her mouth and bites or chews on the toy.

- Rubs fingers or another body part against the toy.

- Shakes the toy.

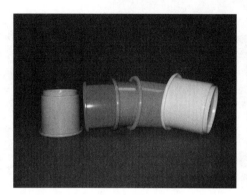

Figure 5.5. Toy Set B as one of the two alternate EPSI assessment toy sets.

- Pushes or pulls a button or another part of the toy.

- Bangs against the toy with another toy or with his or her hand or foot.

- Throws the toy and watches the toy land (may repeat this).

- Listens to the toy by putting his or her ear toward it or smells the toy by putting it up to his or her nose.

Explore is not coded if the child just looks at the toy or if he or she performs a function.

Coding Function   A *function* is coded if the child is using the toy in a manner in which it was intended; however, performing a function does not require that the child complete all of the functions of the toy that result in a solution. *Function* is coded if the child

- Uses fine or gross motor action to move one or more toy parts by manipulating the toy with his or her fingers by pushing, pulling, moving, stacking, or tapping to make the toy perform a function or to create an effect (e.g., putting some of the shapes into the opening of the toy, making one part of a pop-up toy, putting one ball into the toy).

- Pushes on the toy button to make one or two dinosaurs pop up.

- Puts one or a few cups into a larger cup, or stacks the cups but does not complete fitting all of the stacking cups into each other.

- Stacks all of the cups, but they are not nested in each other.

Coding Solution   The child may use any of the behaviors described in the previous coding sections to solve or find a *solution* to a problem (e.g., push the knob the correct way to make the toy pop up, put the balls into the gumball machine and turn the lever to have them come out). He or she may use a variety of approaches (e.g., bangs, pushes, shakes) to complete a solution to toy. Code a *solution* if the child

- Puts at least three balls into the ball machine and pushes the lever to make them come out. A solution would also be counted if the child made the same ball come out three different times (e.g., put the ball in, pressed the lever so it comes out, then repeated this two more times).

- Stacks the stacking cups in the correct order.

- Stacks or nests four to five of the stacking cups in the correct order or makes all of the toys pop up.

- Completes all of the toy actions as intended. Each time a child does this, it is counted as a solution. Therefore, if the child nests all of the stacking cups and then dumps them out and puts them all back again, a second *solution* would be recorded.

Miles: An Example of Using the EPSI for Intervention Decision Making

Miles was 20 months old when he began receiving ongoing progress monitoring along with all of the other children served in his infant-toddler program in a major metropolitan city. The program had adopted the EPSI as an outcome measure in its accountability plan and as a tool that could inform an RTI approach to the delivery of services. Alva, a family advocate who worked as part of an early intervention team who visited Miles and his family on a weekly basis, began using the EPSI to monitor Miles's cognitive development as part of her regular services. Alva and the Part C early intervention team had been working with his family for about 6 months and had reported at team meetings that Miles had very few toys at home. All of the early intervention team members who had visited his home reported that they had rarely seen his parents interacting or playing with him. When they brought toys to the home, Miles did not play with them in the manner intended.

Alva had looked for an assessment tool that would give her information about Miles's development so that she could tailor his early intervention services to his needs. Alva and the team had a very full schedule of home visits, so they needed an assessment tool that was brief. They also wanted the assessment to be useful for checking whether or not Miles was making progress. In addition, they wanted to be able to share the assessment information with the parents, as well as with their team, so they needed it to

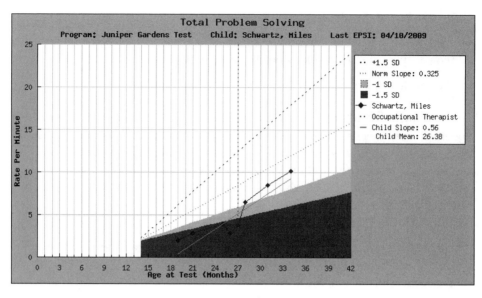

Figure 5.6. The EPSI Total Problem-Solving graph for Miles displaying EPSI total problem-solving proficiency data, slope, and time at which the intervention was implemented. The light grey-shaded region indicates total problem solving that is –1 *SD* below the mean. The dark grey-shaded region indicates total problem solving that is –1.5 *SD* below the mean. The slope line indicates the slope of growth of Miles's problem solving. (© Juniper Gardens Children's Project; reprinted by permission.)

be easily understood by others and to have features that would facilitate the sharing of information, such as reports and online data entry. Alva and the early intervention team chose the EPSI to measure Miles's cognitive skills related to problem solving because it seemed to meet their needs for a quick, effective, and reliable progress monitoring assessment, and they liked the idea that the EPSI had graphs and reports that could be printed out and shared with others.

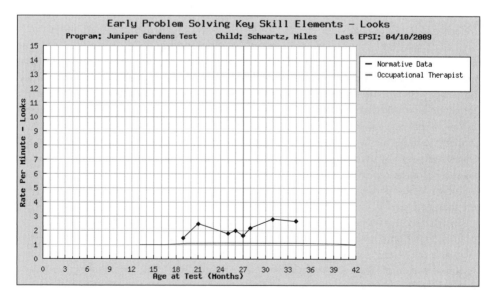

Figure 5.7. Miles's key skill element graph for look. (© Juniper Gardens Children's Project; reprinted by permission.)

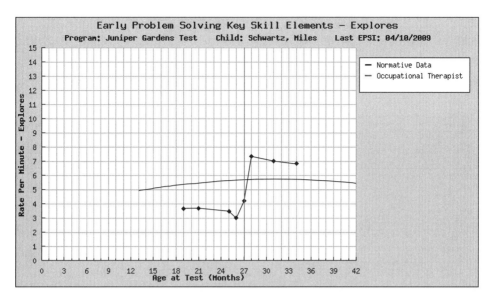

Figure 5.8. Miles's key skill element graph for explore. (© Juniper Gardens Children's Project; reprinted by permission.)

After becoming certified online at the IGDI web site to administer and score the EPSI (see Chapter 10 for certification instructions), Alva administered the EPSI to Miles in his home. When Alva had administered the EPSI three times, she printed out the EPSI individual child report (see sample individual report in appendix) along with the EPSI individual child graph for total problem solving (see Figure 5.6) and his individual key skill element graphs (see Figures 5.7–5.10) and brought them to the team meeting. The team noticed that overall, Miles's performance on the EPSI was lower than what was

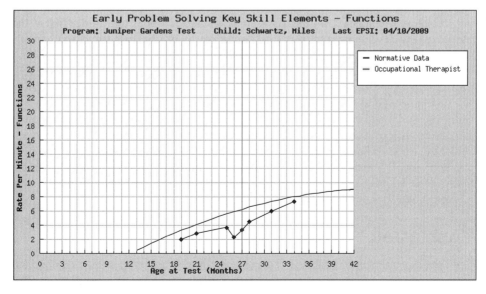

Figure 5.9. Miles's key skill element graph for function. (© Juniper Gardens Children's Project; reprinted by permission.)

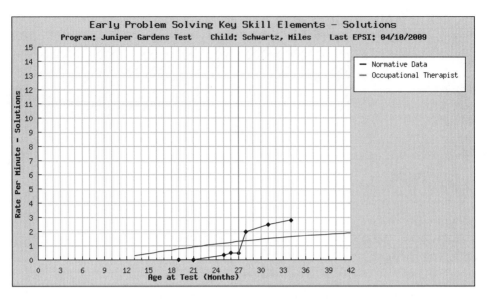

Figure 5.10. Miles's key skill element graph for solution. (© Juniper Gardens Children's Project; reprinted by permission.)

expected for his age. Miles's EPSI total problem-solving graph showed that he engaged very little with the toys, only exploring toys by banging on them or putting them into his mouth, which confirmed the team's feelings that Miles needed more intensive intervention to increase his cognitive skills. The team decided to show the graphs to Miles's parents to give them information about his development and to get their input in planning the intervention. Miles's parents were eager to work with the team after they looked at the graphs and understood that there were some simple things that could be done at home to give Miles more opportunities to explore his environment and, therefore, develop his cognitive skills. The team worked with a toy- and book-lending service affiliated with the local parents-as-teachers program to give the family some toys and books that they could use with Miles. They also gave the parents suggestions of activities that would encourage the development of Miles's play skills to promote his cognitive development. Alva developed a checklist that the parents could complete to keep track of what goals they worked on with Miles. This information could be used during home visits to keep track of how often the parents were using the intervention with Miles.

Alva continued to monitor Miles's EPSI performance, but she increased the frequency so that the team could know in a short period of time whether the intervention was having an impact on Miles's EPSI scores. Indeed, shortly after starting the intervention, they noticed differences in Miles's EPSI performance and observed differences in his play behavior. Alva and the team continued to work with the parents on ways to promote Miles's cognitive development and went back to monitoring Miles's performance on a quarterly basis after they were sure he was on the right trajectory.

Conclusion

The EPSI is a quick and reliable tool for determining whether an individual child (or group of children) is developing problem-solving skills at a rate comparable with other children his or her age. The EPSI gives early educators a basis for either altering their practices when needed or confirming their practices when children are progressing along the expected trajectory (Carta et al., 2002). Used as a progress monitoring tool, the EPSI provides guidelines to users as to how an individual child (or group of children) is progressing and when he or she may need some additional support for cognitive problem-solving skill development. The EPSI helps to inform intervention and then monitor the impact of the intervention on a child's progress toward proficiency in cognitive problem solving. Having the tools to monitor whether or not individual or groups of infants and toddlers are making progress toward learning problem-solving skills gives early educators essential knowledge that may help them ensure that children in their care have the opportunities to progress on a developmental trajectory toward school readiness.

EPSI

Administration Protocol for the Early Problem-Solving Indicator

 Materials

Digital timer

Required toys
- Pop-up toys (including four pop ups: push button, slide lever, "rocking" lever, and twist lever)
- Gumball machine (including four balls inserted in the top and released by a lever or button; batteries removed and sound switches turned off)
- Pound-a-ball (including at least four balls that are easily accessible to the child after being pounded into the holes)
- Stacking cups (round or square or other similar shapes)

Variations (each toy class has two variations [e.g., round, square, or other] assigned to sets A and B)

Toys are alternated across repeated assessments (i.e., toy set A used in May, toy set B used in June).

 Administration options

1. Two people
   - Play partner (certified EPSI administrator)
   - Certified assessor

2. One person as
   - Play partner
   - Certified assessor**

3. Two people
   - Parent as play partner
   - Certified assessor

**This option would be video recorded for later coding.

 Forms

EPSI recording form (see Figure 5.2)

 Setup

Comfortable area
- At a table
- Sitting on the floor

Arrangement of toys
- One toy is brought out at a time. After 2 minutes another toy is brought out until all three toys from a set have been presented (total time: 6 minutes).
- Present the toy in an interesting manner so the child knows he or she can play and make it work (e.g., "Wow, these can make a tower," "Look at this toy, I see balls in there").

 Time

Each toy within a set (A or B) is presented to the child for 2 minutes for a total time of 6 minutes.

(continued)

Conducting the session**

When assessing a child for the first time, spend time with the child and use toys available in the natural setting to make the child comfortable.

Assessor should be positive and enthusiastic with the child during the EPSI.

Let child know when the session has ended, assist him or her in ending play and thank the child for playing.

Offer immediate access to another toy to play with at the end of the session.

**See Chapter 3 for more detailed information.

6

The Early Movement IGDI

Early Movement Indicator (EMI)

Charles Greenwood and Judith J. Carta

T he early movement indicator (EMI) is used for monitoring growth in a child's proficiency to learn to move through his or her environment. Similar to other IGDI measures, the EMI is useful in 1) identifying children having difficulty acquiring movement skills in a program of universal screening, and 2) examining the effectiveness of movement interventions provided these children and evaluating their response to intervention (RTI).

One of the foremost developmental tasks of early childhood is learning how to move for purposes of locomotion, exploring the environment, achieving goals, and meeting basic needs (Shonkoff & Phillips, 2000). Children's early movement patterns set the stage for attainment of many other developmental and functional outcomes, including physical, cognitive, and social-emotional. This strong connection was underscored early by Piaget who theorized that children's intelligence in the first 2 years of life was founded on and evidenced by their motor actions on the environment, which was what he called the *sensorimotor phase* (Ramey, Breitmayer, & Goldman, 1984, p. 243).

For many home visitors and child care practitioners, the EMI may be the first measure of early movement developed specifically for their use. For many program directors, this may be a measure that provides them the first opportunity to report the status and progress of all children in the program in ways that could promote program improvement as well as program accountability for these outcomes. The EMI has been designed to provide unique information relevant to the needs, goals, and practices of early intervention related to children's progress in becoming mobile in natural environments. The EMI offers new capacity in support of improving children's results toward that end.

Background and Relevance of the EMI

The terms *movement* and *motor* when applied to children's development refer to different theoretical constructs but are often used interchangeably (Gallahue & Ozmun, 1995; Gilfoyle, Grady, & Moore, 1981). *Movement* commonly refers to the observable behaviors that comprise a change in posture or locomotion. *Motor* commonly refers to the neuromuscular or other nonobservable, central nervous system processes assumed to affect movement behavior. For both conceptual and practical reasons, the movement construct was used for the EMI. For example, the movement construct connects to the function of movement and, therefore, the important intervention utility that this information provides practitioners (e.g., Harris, 1997). According to Wolery, skills are functional when they "(a) are immediately useful, (b) allow a child to learn more complex skills, (c) allow a child to live in a less restrictive environment, and (d) enable a child to be cared for more easily by the family and others" (1989, pp. 488-489). Based on this functional perspective of skills, measures of movement have a greater potential of informing what early interventionists do (and need to do) because the movement construct taps the role played by environmental factors, such as parenting or movement intervention in promoting the development of movement skill. Environmental factors are often under the control of early interventionists (Thelen & Smith, 1994).

One of the most important missions of early intervention is to help children learn to "move" through their environment. Movement competence is a widely accepted and highly valued general outcome of early childhood (Priest et al., 2001). A critical goal for all children is that they become more proficient in movement and in their ability to meet their needs by using movement skills. Children's movement outcomes are reported in early intervention accountability practices. For example, the Office of Special Education Program's (OSEP; 2007) annual performance report specifically requires states to report progress information on children's functional gross and fine motor skills (OSEP Child Outcome C) and their ability to complete tasks and meet the basic goals of everyday life. A major focus of early education and early care is the promotion and development of young children's movement skills (National Research Council and Institute of Medicine, 2000). Every new type of movement very young children acquire (e.g., learning to sit independently, crawl, stand) expands their capabilities to manipulate and explore new areas of their environment (Shonkoff & Phillips, 2000).

The Developmental Course of Movement

Smith and Smith (1962; cited in Burton & Miller, 1998) proposed three broad categories for describing all movement skills: 1) postural, 2) travel or locomotion, and 3) manipulation. The function of posture is to achieve stability. The function of locomotion is to achieve mobility and exploration. The function of manipulation is to achieve object control (Goldfield, 1995). At birth, infants have little control over these movements. Most movements at this age are reflexive, and children are at the beginning of their ability to coordinate arms, legs, or chest (Mowder, 1997). They are increasingly capable of independently making transitions to a new posture within and across supine, side, and prone positions between birth and 6 months of age (Gilfoyle et al., 1981). They can typically lift their shoulders and chest, and they can roughly point to and grasp objects (Hannan, 1987).

Most infants can sit up with support between 6 and 18 months (Cratty, 1986). They are able to change positions by extending their upper extremities, pushing up, and rolling. Emerging is the ability to reach and corral objects (Gallahue & Ozmun, 1995; Goldfield, 1995). Infant movement becomes decidedly more complex and fluent as children learn to crawl, kneel, sit and stand without support, and stoop between 18 and 24 months (Burton & Miller, 1998; Gilfoyle et al., 1981). Crawling forward or backward on the belly typically advances to three- and four-point contact crawling positions (Gallahue & Ozmun, 1995). Walking first emerges as an upright, unaided gait. Forward walking is soon accompanied by sideways and backward walking.

Children are increasingly capable of hurried walk, stepping down from low objects, and jumping down from an object to land on both feet. Most achieve the ability to walk upstairs with help, and then on their own between 24 and 36 months. They also achieve the ability to walk downstairs unaided (Gallahue, 1989). Children are increasingly able to jump with both feet, engage in their first true run, throw objects such as balls with force, and chase balls. They are also able to trap or catch an object coming at them, kick with a straight leg, and swing their arms to strike an object (Payne & Isaacs, 1991).

Current State of Movement Assessment of Infants and Toddlers

There are several traditional reasons for assessing motor abilities and/or movement skills. One is to discriminate between very young children with and without potential delays in motor/movement skills. A second is that delays in movement are often the first indicator that a child may have a more general developmental disability (Harris & McEwen, 1996). Delays in movement proficiency are often more apparent early in life than those in language or cognition.

Delays in movement proficiency represent 1) a physical insult (e.g., spina bifida), and/or 2) a pervasive lack of environmental stimulation in a child's life. To learn to move and explore their environment, young children need supervised and independent opportunities (Shonkoff & Phillips, 2000). Unfortunately, cases in which a child's caregiver has restricted the child's movement, thereby unknowingly limiting opportunities to explore, practice, and develop the needed skills, are far too common (Fisher, Thompson, Ferrari, Savoie, & Lukie, 2009; Le Mare, & Audet, 2006). For example, some parents or caregivers may restrict movement by keeping children in cribs, playpens, baby seats, or highchairs for extended periods of time as a means of child management. Other parents may believe that children should be held as much as possible while they are awake, which is common in various cultures, that may or may not have an impact on the development of movement skills. In some cases, homes are simply not safe enough for children to crawl on the floor, so they are prevented from doing so for legitimate safety concerns. In extreme cases, the consequences of child maltreatment may include delayed motor development (Centers for Disease Control and Prevention, 2009; Wiggins, Fenichel, & Mann, 2007). The net effect of systematically restricted movement over time is that the child may demonstrate developmental delays in the typical pattern of adaptive behavior and movement milestones (Rosenberg & Smith, 2008).

Another reason to assess motor/movement proficiency is that early problems are often related to (associated with) developmental difficulties in other areas. Movement limitations may compromise children's abilities to communicate, interact, and explore their environments (Gallahue, 1989). Two additional important reasons to assess motor/movement proficiency are 1) to make *predictions* of a child's ability to walk at later ages, and 2) to monitor change over time as a function of intervention (Kirshner & Guyatt, 1985).

How the EMI Addresses
Deficits in Current Measurement

The EMI enables the caregiver, early educator, and early interventionist to carry out a number of tasks not available in most existing measures. It does not require special expertise as with many traditional measures for, and used by, physical therapists and occupational therapists. The EMI provides information on children's movement skills (not motor ability) that tap the class of alterable variables with relevance to early intervention, such as parenting and home visiting practices. Therefore, it has a high intervention utility compared with traditional measures. The EMI is technically sound in terms of reliability and validity, which is not the case with many traditional measures. The EMI growth charts are intuitive and easily understood by parents who are often collaborating in the intervention. Furthermore, the EMI is brief per administration (i.e., 6 minutes); easy to learn and use; and repeatable, which makes it sensitive to short-term growth over time. More traditional measures often require more time and cannot be re-administered for several months, which limits sensitivity to short-term growth. The EMI provides sensitive, timely, and relevant information in guiding practitioners' intervention and practice.

What Does the EMI Assess?

In development work leading to the EMI, a general outcome for movement was socially validated in a national survey of parents and professionals (Priest et al., 2001 (see http://www.igdi.ku.edu/measures/EMI_Measures/index.htm). The general outcome selected to guide development of the movement IGDI is *"The child moves in a fluent and coordinated manner to play and participate in home, school, and community settings."* For this outcome, it was possible to identify key skill elements of movement linked conceptually and empirically to the general outcome and appropriate for measurement of children in the birth-to-3 years age range. As illustrated in Figure 6.1, the organization of movement skills for infants and toddlers includes postural and transitional movement skills (e.g., rolling from back to stom-

General Outcome: The child moves in a fluent and coordinated manner to play and participate in home, school, and community

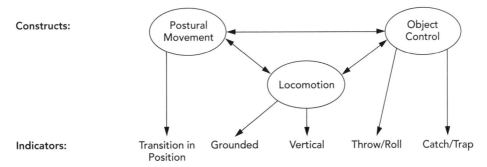

Figure 6.1. Early movement indicator (EMI) conceptual framework. (© Juniper Gardens Children's Project; reprinted by permission.)

ach, weight shifting); locomotion skills, including grounded (e.g., belly sliding, crawling) and vertical (e.g., cruising, walking, running); and gross motor manipulation or object control skills (e.g., reaching, rolling/throwing, catching/trapping). As children become more proficient, the greater functionality of these skills and skill combinations helps promote new skills and greater proficiency overall.

The five key skill elements assessed in the EMI are 1) transition in position, 2) grounded locomotion, 3) vertical locomotion, 4) throwing/rolling, and 5) catching/trapping. These skills were selected to represent the postural movement domain (i.e., transition in position), the locomotion domain (i.e., grounded and vertical), and the object control domain (i.e., throwing/rolling and catching/trapping), which are the three domains of critical importance to young children who are just acquiring movement skills (See Chapter 10 for an explanation of the procedures used to select these skills.) The occurrences of these key skills recorded by an observer are brought together in the EMI to form a single indicator of each key skill and a consolidated indicator of total movement rate per minute.

Research and Development of the EMI

The original EMI development was conducted within the context of 1 year in which a sample of 34 children in the 1- to 34-month age span were assessed monthly using the EMI (Greenwood, Luze, Cline, Kuntz, & Leitschuh, 2002). Prior to and following monthly EMI assessments, tests and parent ratings were administered measuring the children's movement. The children assessed were recruited at two child care centers serving infants and toddlers located in the inner city neighborhoods of metropolitan Kansas City.

Results indicated that 1) assessors administering and scoring the EMI were able to produce reliable data at an 85% level of agreement, 2) the EMI was valid in relationship to criterion test measures of movement, and 3) the EMI total movement score was sensitive to growth over time, as were the five key skill elements (see Chapter 11). Results indicated that grounded locomotion was a skill element that began in the early months with a linear positive acceleration over time. After 6 months of age, transition in position and vertical locomotion showed a burst of growth, clearly the most frequent and rapidly accelerating of all five skills. After rapid positive acceleration, both tended to flatten out. The most pronounced flattening occurred with vertical locomotion, whereas throwing/rolling followed by catching/trapping began to increase by 24 months (Greenwood, Luze, et al., 2002).

Administration of the EMI

Based on the generally agreed-upon principles of assessing young children discussed previously in Chapter 2, the EMI was designed to be a play-based observational measure of a child's movement occurring during a 6-minute play period with specific toys and a familiar adult as a play partner. The session is recommended to take place in a relatively sheltered, but convenient environment with few distractions. During the session, an adult play partner engages the child in play with an EMI toy, such as the School House (see Figure 6.2), the School Bus (see Figure 6.3), or the Blocks (see Figure 6.4; also IGDI web site for EMI toys and where to purchase: http://www.igdi.ku.edu/measures/EMI_Measures/emi_toys_purchase_info.htm). We recommend the addition of at least three balls (one small, medium, and large) to the House, Bus, and Blocks.

The School House toy is a flexible nylon enclosure that opens on both ends so children can crawl or walk through it. For safety reasons, there is no attached floor. It also has two see-through mesh windows on both sides. In addition to crawling through, children may stand up in the school, open and close the nylon doors, and look out the windows. We recommend adding a set of balls to the School House for children to roll or throw in and out of the house. The balls encourage movement in and around the school house.

Figure 6.2. Picture of the School House used as one of the alternate EMI assessment toys. http://www.igdi.ku.edu/measures/EMI_Measures/emi_toys_purchase_info.htm

EMI

Figure 6.3. Picture of the School Bus used as one of the alternate EMI assessment toys. http://www.igdi.ku.edu/measures/EMI_Measures/emi_toys_purchase_info.htm

Similar to the School House, the School Bus is a flexible nylon enclosure. The bus opens on one side so children can enter and exit similar to a real bus. It also has windows on all sides and two "sunroofs" on top for children to stand up and look out. The bus is light enough for children to move it to simulate a moving bus. There is no attached floor, which makes it safer for young children. As with the School House, add balls that children can throw in and out of the bus, house, or with blocks encouraging them to move.

Figure 6.4. Picture of the Blocks and Balls used as one of the alternate EMI assessment toys.

EMI Administration Checklist

ECI Assessor: _Alva_   **Date:** _6/13/2009_   **Tape:** _319586_

This checklist is used to score the administration videos for the EMI. To be certified to administer the EMI, the adult play partner should complete **at least 81% (13 out of 16)** of the administration steps.

	Item	Yes	No
Setting up the EMI Administration Situation: Materials & Positioning			
1. Adult play partner sets up the toys prior to the session.	1	X	
2. The toys have been arranged to attract child's attention (i.e., balls scattered so child can see them).	2	X	
3. Adult and child are positioned so they can see and reach toys.	3	X	
4. Child is positioned appropriately for his/her developmental level.	4	X	
5. Session is timed (may be observed or reported).	5	X	
6. Video camera is set up to follow child as child moves around during session.	6	X	
7. Video camera is set up so that session can be heard for scoring.	7	X	
EMI Assessment Administration: Play Situation			
8. Adult play partner follows child's lead in play situation.	8	X	
9. Adult play partner comments about what child is doing.	9	X	
10. Adult play partner provides support for movement when needed, but gently encourages the child to move without his/her support.	10	X	
11. Adult play partner interacts in non-directive, friendly manner.	11	X	
12. Adult play partner uses questions sparingly.	12	X	
Ending EMI Session			
13. Session ends exactly after 6 minutes have elapsed.	13	X	
14. Adult play partner lets child know that it is time to stop.	14		X
15. Adult play partner thanks child for playing.	15	X	
16. Adult play partner cleans toys (may be reported).	16	X	
	Total	15 Yes	1 No

Administration Accuracy = [(Total Number of Steps Completed Correctly/16 Steps) × 100] = _94_ % (Need 81%)

Figure 6.5. The EMI administration checklist available on the IGDI web site: http://www.igdi.ku.edu/training/EMI_Administration_Checklist-2005.pdf. (© Juniper Gardens Children's Project; reprinted by permission.)

The set of blocks include approximately 40–65 foam rubber blocks of various sizes, colors, and shapes. Using the blocks, children build structures, which they enjoy knocking down by walking through them, by throwing another block at them, or by throwing balls (sold separately) at them. In addition to the toys, a digital timer is needed to mark the beginning and signal the ending of the session after 6 minutes. Accurate timing of every EMI session is important because progress is measured by counting the rate per minute of movements during the entire 6-minute session.

The EMI administration checklist also outlines the steps for administration that should be followed (see Figure 6.5). Refer to Chapter 3 for more information on administering IGDIs including setting up and ending play sessions.

Coding the EMI

A specific set of coding procedures allows the assessor to capture how proficient the child is at moving by recording the frequency with which the child performs the key skill elements of movement. The key element behaviors include transitional movements (T), grounded locomotion (GL), vertical locomotion (VL), throwing/rolling (TR), and catching/trapping (CT). Although a child may engage in additional movement behaviors, these are the skills recorded and scored for the EMI. A child's EMI movement behaviors are recorded by the assessor or recorder every time they occur during the 6-minute assessment. Each occurrence is scored as a single frequency count of one (i.e., a tally mark) in the appropriate cell on the EMI recording form (see Figure 6.6).

The EMI recording form is a simple table with each of the five key skill elements as column headings (e.g., transitional movements, catching/trapping). There are six rows, each of which is devoted to 1 minute of recording time. The cells in this table provide space for marking tallies of single instances of each EMI behavior during each of the single minutes in the 6-minute session.

These frequencies are recorded on the paper EMI recording form using pen or pencil (see Figure 6.6). Afterward, these scores are typed into a web-based data form (see Figure 6.7). Entering the raw data in the web-based form allows rate per minute scores to be automatically calculated and the new data added to the child's growth chart, which include all data previously recorded for the child. The chart is now up to date and ready for review and use in decision making.

As part of each assessor's EMI training and certification, he or she learns the procedures for recording key skill element movements during the 6-minute session (see Chapter 9). In this preparation, they learn the basic definitions of these key movement behaviors, which are defined as follows:

1. *Transitional movements*: Transitional movements are motions used by a child to achieve a new position within a posture or to achieve a new posture. This can include movement within a stable posture (e.g., changing the primary weight-bearing surface) or movement from one distinct posture (e.g., lying in supine or prone, sitting, kneeling, stooping, standing) to another. A single episode (one occurrence) begins when a child begins moving from a stable position to a new position. The episode ends when the child has regained a stable position or begins locomotion. Examples include rolling to back from stomach, moving in and out of sitting position, standing up, and kneeling down resting on knees.

2. *Grounded locomotion*: Locomotion involves movements that transport the body forward, backward, sideways, or upward from one point in space to another. Grounded locomotion is movement horizontal to the ground and does not use upright postures when moving. An example of this movement is moving on belly from one location to the next, either forward, backward, or sideways (pivot in prone). Another example is thrusting arms forward and then subsequently flexing them in a movement that results in a slight forward or backward movement.

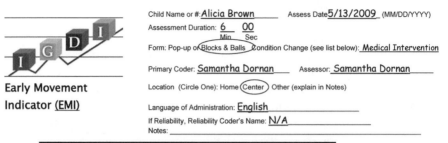

Early Movement Indicator (EMI)

Child Name or #: Alicia Brown   Assess Date 5/13/2009 (MM/DD/YYYY)

Assessment Duration: 6 (Min) 00 (Sec)

Form: Pop-up or Blocks & Balls   Condition Change (see list below): Medical Intervention

Primary Coder: Samantha Dornan   Assessor: Samantha Dornan

Location (Circle One): Home (Center) Other (explain in Notes)

Language of Administration: English

If Reliability, Reliability Coder's Name: N/A

Notes: _____

	Transitional Movements	Grounded Locomotion	Vertical Locomotion	Throwing/ Rolling	Catching/ Trapping	Condition List
Begin 0:00 Sec.	T ///	GL	VL /	TR	CT	ABA/TEACH Child Psychiatrist Interpreter Language Intervention Toolkit Medical Intervention (e.g., Tubes) Mental Health Consultant
1:00 Sec.	T ////	GL	VL //	TR //	CT	Milieu or Incidental Teaching MOD Recommendations None Other Primary Care Provider Registered Nurse
2:00 Sec.	T ///	GL /	VL ///	TR ╫╫	CT	Responsive Interaction Social Worker Speech/Language Therapist
3:00 Sec.	T //	GL	VL ╫╫	TR //	CT /	
4:00 Sec.	T //	GL /	VL ╫╫ //	TR	CT ////	
5:00 Sec.	T ///	GL //	VL ////	TR /	CT ╫╫	
6 min. End Total	T 17	GL 4	VL 22	TR 10	CT 10	

Figure 6.6. The EMI recording form available on the IGDI web site (http://www.igdi.ku.edu/training/EMI_training/ EMI_Recording_Sheet-2005.pdf). (© Juniper Gardens Children's Project; reprinted by permission.)

3. *Vertical locomotion*: Vertical locomotion is movement in an upright position that moves the child forward, backward, or sideways. Examples include walking while holding on to furniture for support (cruising) and walking without support, which involves alternating feet with one foot always on the floor.

4. *Throwing/rolling*: Throwing is propelling an object through the air. Rolling is pushing a circular object so that it rolls away from the child's body. Examples of this motion are throwing an object using an over arm, under arm, or side arm throw; and rolling an object toward another person.

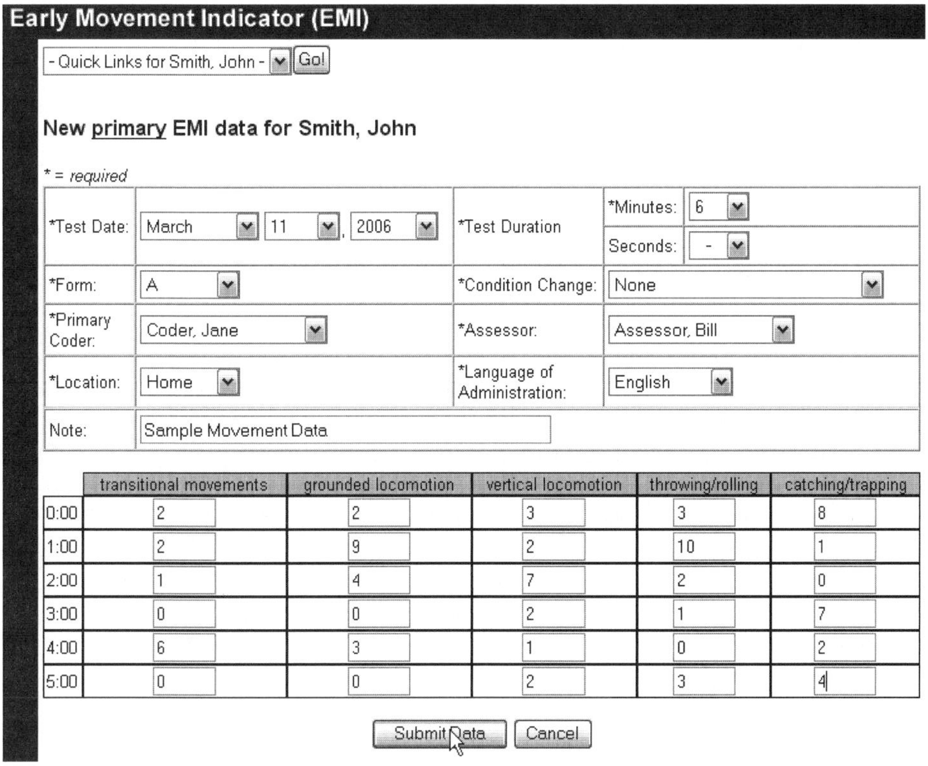

Figure 6.7. The EMI online individual child data entry form filled in on the IGDI web site (http://www.igdi.ku.edu/measures/EMI_Measures/EMI_online_data_entry_forms.htm). (© Juniper Gardens Children's Project; reprinted by permission.)

5. *Catching/trapping*: Catching is bringing an airborne object under control using hands and arms. Trapping is stopping a moving object (i.e., an object moving through the air or rolling on the ground) with hands, arms, legs, or body. Examples are catching an object with one's hands or arms or trapping it against the body.

Scoring the EMI

After completing the session and recording the child's movement episodes, scores are calculated for each of the five key skills and a for a total movement score. The key skill score (e.g., catching/trapping, vertical locomotion) is the sum of tallies in that particular column of the EMI recording form. The total movement score is the simple sum for all episodes for all skills during the session. The final scores of interest are the rate per minute of each of these skills and the total. Rate scores are calculated by summing the total episodes recorded for each skill and the total divided by 6 minutes. The rate of movement can be thought of as a fluency score in the sense that it is capable of reflecting an increase in a child's movement proficiency from one administration to the next. Note that hand scoring, charting, and reporting of EMI data can be eliminated completely by using the appropriate EMI tools in the IGDI Child Data System (online at www.igdi.ku.edu).

The Banneker Early Head Start Program: An Example for Using the EMI

The Banneker Early Head Start program has an active enrollment of 28 children. The program has been using the EMI for the past year to track the children's progress in learning to become fluent movers. There are 12 girls and 16 boys in the program, and the home language for 24 of them is English, and for 4 it is Spanish. Administration of the EMI does require a speaker of the same home language as the child. However, because EMI movement behaviors are independent of administration language, coders do not have to understand the language of administration. Funding for all of the children comes from the state. Four children have an individualized family service plan (IFSP) and are also receiving early intervention services through Part C. Three of those children are receiving services for language and early communication skills, and one is receiving physical therapy to address the delay he has been showing in movement apparently related to restricted opportunities to move in his home environment.

Since beginning to use the EMI, Gayle Moss, the program's director, has printed a full program report from the web site each month and reviewed results for all children and the productivity of the program staff. From the current program report, Ms. Moss has been tracking the management details of the EMI (e.g., those that capture the staff's effort to assess the children with the EMI). She noted that the staff had produced a total of 198 EMI assessments for the active children since starting the program. The smallest number of EMI assessments gathered per child was three (7.1% of all children), and the highest was eight (64%).

With respect to program accountability and children's outcomes, Ms. Moss was interested in examining the combined growth chart showing the children's average rate of progress over time in the program (see Figure 6.8). This chart compares the children's average (the bouncing line) with the benchmark mean (the curved line). She was pleased to see that, as a group, the children were generally following the benchmark pattern of growth in total movement rate.

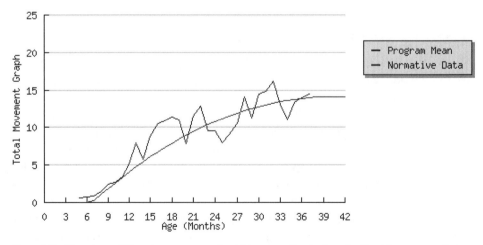

Figure 6.8. The average EMI total movement rate for children served by the Banneker Head Start program by testing age (in months). The bouncing line is the Banneker children; the curved line is the benchmark expectation. (© Juniper Gardens Children's Project; reprinted by permission.)

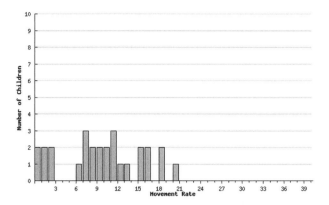

Figure 6.9. The distribution of all Banneker Early Head Start children's total movement rates. This figure shows the numbers (*N* = 28) of children with a total movement rate ranging from a low of zero to a high of 20 movements per minute based on their last EMI assessment. (© Juniper Gardens Children's Project; reprinted by permission.)

With respect to program improvement, Ms. Moss was particularly interested in how the children did in terms of total movement rate (see Figure 6.9). Because total movement rate is highly correlated with age, the general expectation is that older children will be more proficient than younger children on average. This was not true in all cases, however. Ms. Moss was very interested in individualizing services to fit children's needs as much as possible. The distribution of children's current movement rate scores shown in Figure 6.9 was helpful in identifying the numbers of children just beginning to develop movement (e.g., below three movements per minute) compared with those of greatest proficiency (e.g., 12–15 or more movements per minute). She noted that she has roughly three proficiency groupings of novice (children scoring 0–7 per minute), emerging (8–14 per minute), and fluent (15–21 per minute) movers in her program. Her interest now was to strategically assign more staff to the emerging group with larger numbers of children

Table 6.1. Children who are on target, slightly below (≤ −1.0 *SD*), or below benchmark (≤ = −1.5 *SD*) on their total movement score based on their latest EMI measurement

	Movement development status			
*Age group	On target	Slightly below benchmark	Below benchmark	Total
1–11 months	3			3
	100%	0%	0%	100.0%
12–23 months	13		1	14
	92.9%	0%	7.1%	100.0%
24–35 months	4	3		7
	57.1%	42.9%	0%	100.0%
36–47 months	3	1		4
	75%	25%	0%	100.0%
Overall	23	4	1	28
	82.1%	14.3%	3.6%	100%

*Age of children at their last observation.

Number and percentage of children in each age group whose most recent Total Movement rate is on target, slightly below (−1.0 *SD*), or below benchmark (−1.5 *SD*) as indicated by normative benchmarks. Benchmarks are based on the performance of children in previous research.

© Juniper Gardens Children's Project; reprinted by permission.

Table 6.2.   Children who are off target in movement development and who warrant special attention

Child name	Movement development status
Jasmine	Slightly below benchmark
Merle	Slightly below benchmark
Sabyn	Slightly below benchmark
Sidney	Slightly below benchmark
Asija	Below benchmark

© Juniper Gardens Children's Project; reprinted by permission.

to better serve the numbers of children at these levels of movement fluency. She is planning future professional development of staff so that children can benefit from the most effective movement activities better linked to their current levels of performance.

With respect to the number of children meeting a benchmark of age expectation, 23 of the 28 children (82%) were progressing as would be expected (see Table 6.1). However, as seen in the report, four children were flagged in Table 6.2 as "slightly below benchmark" (four children below –1 *SD*) and as below benchmark (two children below –1.5 *SD*). Several of these children who were below benchmark had been named in prior reports. Ms. Moss, therefore, noted that specific staff needed to be attending more closely to these children's individual growth charts, measuring more frequently, and recommending ways that parents can increase opportunities for their children to engage in movement activities in home routines and during play.

Conclusion

The EMI is useful for 1) identifying children who are having difficulty acquiring movement skills in a program of universal screening, and 2) examining the effectiveness of interventions provided to children and evaluating their response to intervention (RTI). The EMI is one means of checking children's growth toward the important general outcome of being able to move in a fluent and coordinated manner; play; and actively participate in home, school, and community settings. Because children's rate of growth in movement is so critical, growth on the EMI for each child and for all the children in a program becomes an important indicator of how well a program is doing in supporting children's movement proficiency. As such, the EMI can be a powerful tool for monitoring individual children's growth, evaluating RTI, and making intervention decisions. It can also provide helpful information on program progress and inform program-level decisions regarding this essential outcome.

The EMI provides unique information relevant to the needs, goals, and practices of early intervention practitioners, such as home visitors, teachers, program directors, program administrators, and parents. The EMI offers practitioners and programs a new capacity to monitor progress and act early to improve results.

Administration Protocol for the Early Movement Indicator

 Materials

Digital timer

Required toys
- Walk-in School House (see Figure 6.2) or School Bus (see Figure 6.3)
  A set of balls can be added to the toys to encourage children to roll and/or throw them in and out of the toys to encourage movement.
- Blocks and Balls (see Figure 6.4)
  Includes 45-60 foam rubber blocks of various sizes, colors, and shapes
  At least three balls of similar size (small, medium, large) should also be included.
- A rattle (for children younger than 9 months)

 Administration options

1. Two people
   - Play partner (certified EPSI administrator)
   - Certified assessor

2. One person as
   - Play partner
   - Certified assessor**

3. Two people
   - Parent as play partner
   - Certified assessor

**This option would be video recorded for later coding

 Forms

EMI administration checklist (see Figure 6.5)
EMI recording form (see Figure 6.6)

 Set-up

Comfortable area

Arrangement of toys
- Either the School House, School Bus, or the Blocks and Balls would be selected prior to the session (toys to be rotated across sessions to maintain child's interest)
- Set up the toys so that the child sees them immediately upon entering the assessment situation

 Time

6 minutes

 Conducting the session**

The play partner should stand or sit in an area that is large and comfortable enough for sustained play during the 6-minute session.

(continued)

The EMI administration checklist should be followed (see Figure 6.5).

After making the child comfortable, indicate to the child that there are fun toys to play with together.

To facilitate beginning play, comment on what child is doing (e.g., "Let's take a look in this house and see what's in there.").

During the session, interact with the child in a way that encourages the child to move and explore the toys; however, avoid directing the child to move or act in certain ways.

Let the child know when the session has ended, assist him or her in ending play, and thank him or her for playing.

Offer immediate access to another toy to play with at the end of the session.

**See Chapter 3 for more detailed information.

EMI

The Social IGDI

Early Social Indicator (ESI)

Judith J. Carta and Charles Greenwood

One of the most important missions of early intervention is to help children learn to be socially competent. Whether young children are in home-based or center-based programs, a critical outcome is to help them learn how to interact positively with peers and adults. It is also important for the interventionists in the programs to know when children are making progress in becoming more socially proficient and when they need to take action in the form of different intervention procedures when a child is not showing adequate progress. The Early Social Indicator (ESI) is one means of checking children's growth toward the important general outcomes of being able to interact with peers and adults; maintain social interaction; and participate socially at home, in school, or in the community.

The ESI is a play-based observational measure used for measuring growth in an individual child's social competence. Similar to other IGDI measures, the ESI is useful for *identification* of children having difficulty interacting with adults or peers in a program of universal screening and for *progress monitoring* the effectiveness of interventions used to foster children's social competence and to evaluate their response to intervention (RTI). For many home visitors and child care practitioners, this may be the first measure of early social competence developed completely for their use. For many program directors, this may be a measure that provides the first opportunity to report the status and progress of all children in the program in ways that could promote program improvement as well as program accountability.

Because this measure of social competence is designed for the home visitor and child care provider, instead of clinically trained staff, such as psychologists or mental health counselors, it offers a new way for early intervention practitioners to improve child outcomes. IGDIs, including the ESI, provide unique information regarding a child's progress relevant to the needs, goals, and practices of early intervention practitioners, such as home visitors, teachers, program directors and/or administrators, and parents.

Background and Relevance of the ESI

One of the most important outcomes of early childhood is becoming proficient at establishing relationships with adults and peers (see National Research Council and Institute of Medicine, 2000; Rubin, Bukowski, & Parker, 1998). Children's early interaction patterns with adults and peers set the stage for their later social competence or deviance (Kuperschmidt & Coie, 1990). Moreover, children's early social competence affects the way they evaluate their own self-worth and their views of the world as friendly or hostile (Ladd & Price, 1986). Consequently, a major focus of early education and early care has been the development of young children's social and emotional competence (National Research Council, 2001).

A critical goal for each young child is to become more competent at interacting with adults and peers in their natural environments and to have their needs met through social interaction. Social competence is a widely accepted and highly valued general outcome of early childhood (Priest et al., 2001). Similar to communication, movement, and other important outcomes, positive social interaction is reflected in early intervention accountability policies (Office of Special Education Programs, 2007).

Although social competence unfolds according to a predictable sequence for most children, by the time they reach preschool, as many as 10% of children have difficulties with social interaction that result in their rejection by peers (Asher, 1990). Among children who are socioeconomically disadvantaged, this figure may be as high as 25% (Rimm-Kaufman, Pianta, & Cox, 2000). The genesis of these delays in social competence may be factors intrinsic to the child (e.g., attentional difficulties, temperament or memory problems) or they may be related to external factors (e.g., unsupportive caregiving, limited opportunities to interact with peers) (Guralnick & Neville, 1997). When children with significant social interaction problems are not identified in a timely way nor given appropriate intervention, their problems tend to be long lasting and require more intensive services and resources over time. Moreover, when the challenging behavior of young children is not addressed in an appropriate and timely way, the future likelihood of poor academic outcomes, peer rejection, mental health concerns, and adverse effects on their families, service providers, and communities increases (Dunlap et al., 2007).

A number of interventions are available for promoting the early social interactions of young children. Some of these interventions focus on caregivers. Helping caregivers learn how to engage in warm, responsive contingent behavior toward their children in the context of daily activities and routines has been associated with favorable social-emotional outcomes for young children (Cripe, Hanline, & Daley, 1997; Landry, Smith, Swank, Assel, & Vellet, 2001). Other interventions focus on classroom-based strategies to improve social-cognitive skills (Mize & Ladd, 1990) or using peers as change agents for improving social interactions (McEvoy, Odom, & McConnell, 1992). Yet, determining when the social competence of a child younger than 3 years is deviating from the typical developmental trajectory is a challenging task. The broad variation of acceptable social behavior for children of this age makes it difficult to discriminate among individual differences within a typical range, true maturational delays, or specific social-emotional disorders. Moreover, the limitations of existing measures to assess the social behavior of very young children compounds the problem of identifying when children are not following a normative pattern of growth in social competence (National Research Council and Institute of Medicine, 2000).

The Developmental Course Of Social Interaction

Contemporary views of the early development of social competency involve the growth of both social and communicative capabilities (e.g., Goldstein & Morgan, 2002). Communication skills (verbal and nonverbal) are required to interact socially and are developed in the context of social relationships with others (Odom, McConnell, & Brown, 2008). The beginnings of social competence appear in the first few months of life. Infants remember and anticipate social interactions with their caregivers, and patterns of vocal turn-taking emerge (Tronick, Cohn, & Shea, 1986). By 2 months, babies become interested in one another and will stare intently at one another (Eckerman, Whatley, & McGehee, 1979). By 6–9 months of age, they will babble and smile at other babies, and they may try to get their attention or initiate social bids (Vandell, Wilson, & Buchanan, 1980). Before their first birthday, babies typically begin to imitate one another (Mueller & Silverman, 1989). Between ages 1 and 2 years, children's interactions become more sustained and complex. They begin to engage in simple turn-taking during play that reveals an emerging ability to understand their playmate's intent and to take on reciprocal roles (Mueller, 1972). Their growing communicative capabilities of turn-taking, sharing meaning with others, understanding others' intent, and taking on reciprocal roles all provide the groundwork necessary for coordinated play (Howes & Matheson, 1992). Between ages 2 and 3 years, children with experience interacting together usually begin to exhibit episodes of coordinated play and are capable of establishing rudimentary friendships. Children at this age have been shown to be more likely to initiate play and engage in complex interactions with familiar rather than with unfamiliar age mates (Howes, 1988; Rubin et al., 1998). Children who can communicate with their peers more clearly have been shown to be more adept at initiating play and keeping it going (Mueller, 1972).

A number of well-known taxonomies have been used to describe the play of young children in terms of increased levels of competence and increasingly sophisticated levels of interaction with peers (Howes & Matheson, 1992; Parten, 1932). Examples of play levels in these taxonomies include onlooker, parallel play, and simple social play. These measures provide important helpful information in understanding the types of interactions children have when typically engaged in play. This information can then provide the basis for interventions for advancing the play and social interaction of children who demonstrate delays in this domain. However, these taxonomies of young children's social behavior with adults, siblings, and peers are not yet capable of providing early interventionists with practical information that can be used to measure growth over the short period of time necessary for evaluating the effectiveness of interventions.

Although social competence is generally thought to unfold according to a predictable sequence as reviewed later in this chapter, in some cases, growth in social competence is uneven. For example, some children are more skilled in interactions with adults, but they have problems interacting with peers (e.g., children with speech and autism spectrum disorders) and vice versa (e.g., children with conduct and social maladjustment problems). Intrinsic factors that affect social competence include difficulty with attention, temperament, disability, or memory, whereas factors external to the child, such as unsupportive caregiving or limited access to peer social networks, are also implicated (Guralnick & Neville, 1997).

Current State of Assessment of Infants' and Toddlers' Social Interaction Skills

Determining when the social competence of a child younger than 3 years is deviating from the typical developmental trajectory and is in need of intervention support is a challenging task. This is true for a number of reasons. First, the broad variation of emerging, acceptable social behavior for children this age makes it difficult to discriminate between individual differences within a typical range and children who may be experiencing maturational delays or specific social-emotional disorders. Second, not many psychometrically sound measures exist that can help identify a child needing intervention, and almost all that exist are rating scales that rely on a knowledgeable parent or caregiver to provide accurate judgments of a child's social competence or behavior problems (e.g., *Child Behavior Checklist* [Achenbach & Rescorla, 2000]; *Brief Infant–Toddler Social and Emotional Assessment* [Briggs-Gowan, Carter, Irwin, Wachtel, & Cicchetti, 2004]).

One drawback of rating measures is that they depend on the respondents' knowledge of what is expected or socially appropriate for children of specific ages. In addition, such ratings may not have sufficient sensitivity to help early interventionists detect growth over short time periods toward a socially valid general outcome. Another concern with some measures is that the contexts in which child assessments are made are not authentic; that is, they are made by strangers in highly unfamiliar settings differing substantially from those in which adult–child, child–peer, and adult–child–peer interactions occur naturally (e.g., care and play routines). Consequently, results assessed in analogue situations may represent different aspects of social development than those of primary interest.

Collectively, these issues and limitations of existing measures make it difficult to 1) accurately identify when young children are or are not following a normative pattern of growth in social competence (National Research Council and Institute of Medicine, 2000); and 2) build suitable, effective early interventions for accelerating growth in social competence, which are both requirements of Part C of the Individuals with Disabilities Act (IDEA) of 1997 (PL 105-17). IDEA requires evaluations to determine a child's initial and continuing eligibility and his or her level of function-

ESI

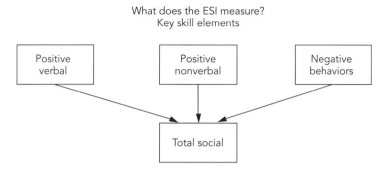

Figure 7.1.   The key skill elements of the ESI. (© Juniper Gardens Children's Project; re-printed by permission.)

ing across developmental domains. Also required is information relevant to monitoring progress toward goals contained in the individualized family service plan (IFSP) and/or individualized education program (IEP).

What Does the ESI Assess?

In development work leading to the ESI, a general social outcome was socially validated in a national survey of parents and professionals (Priest et al., 2001). The general outcome selected to guide development of the social GOM was *"Child interacts with peers and adults, maintaining social interaction and participating socially in home, school, and community."* (Priest et al., 2001). For this general outcome, we identified key skill elements of social interaction and interaction linked conceptually and empirically to the general outcome and appropriate for measurement of children birth-to-3 years of age (see Figure 7.1).

We selected these skills using the procedures described in Chapter 10 to represent the negative and positive social behavior domains important to understanding a child's current and future social-emotional adjustment across settings. In their first few years of life, children typically switch from nonverbal to verbal social behaviors and engage in relatively few negative behaviors. Social interaction behaviors occur when a child attempts to convey a message to a partner requiring one or more behavior. The key skill elements assessed in the ESI are positive nonverbal, positive verbal and negative social behaviors. Nonverbal positive social behaviors are gesture-based attempts to communicate, such as smiling, giving or showing an object, or reaching toward a person. This conceptual framework separates the refinements and expansions in positive nonverbal behaviors expected in infants, such as smiles and gestures from the positive verbal social behaviors expected of children 12 months and older (i.e., use of words in greetings, bids to play). As children get older, these positive nonverbal and verbal social behaviors are expected to be distributed differently to adults and peers, and sometimes to more than one adult and peer simultaneously (i.e., nondirected). Young children interact more frequently with adults than peers and are more likely to engage in peer interaction as they become older toddlers. For children with social difficulties who externalize be-

ESI

General Outcome: The child interacts with peers and adults, maintaining social interaction and participating socially in home, school, and community.

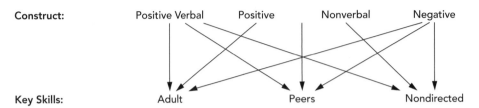

Figure 7.2. Conceptual framework for the ESI. (© Juniper Gardens Children's Project; reprinted by permission.)

havior problems, their trajectories over time may reflect more frequently occurring negative behaviors. Some children's trajectories may show a low level of age-appropriate positive social behavior due to internalizing behavior problems or delays in developing speech and/or signed communication. During an ESI assessment, an observer records occurrences of each of the key skill elements to form a total social fluency composite score that represents total positive verbal plus total nonverbal minus negative interactions (see Figure 7.2).

Technical Adequacy of the ESI

To document the basic psychometric properties of the ESI, a short-term longitudinal study with 57 children was conducted (Carta, Greenwood, Luze, Cline & Kuntz, 2004). (The psychometric properties related to all the IGDIs, including the ESI, can be found in Chapter 11.) This study examined various aspects of the reliability and validity of the measure. Reliability related to interobserver agreement was demonstrated using Pearson's r to calculate the correlation between two observers' estimates of a child's performance. Strong to very strong correlations were found for the key skill elements of adult positive (range of .91–.92 over skills), peer positive (range of .82–.84 over skills), and nondirected positive (range of .72–.73 over skills). Strong correlations were also found on measures of the same child on odd versus even assessment occasions (split-half reliability).

Tests of criterion validity were also conducted to test whether the ESI scores correlated with other measures of social competence and play. Correlations among the *Vineland Social Emotional Early Childhood Scales* (Sparrow, Balla, & Cicchetti, 1998), interpersonal and play/leisure scales, and the positive verbal key skill element were moderately large as were correlations between the Vineland and the positive total social behavior composite on the ESI. The ESI was also shown to be sensitive to change over time when administered over multiple occasions over several months, and it was sensitive children who were performing at different developmental and chronological ages. Therefore, although the normative sample was relatively small for this IGDI, the ESI demonstrated sufficient technical adequacy. (See Chapter 11 for more detailed technical information or visit the web site at http://www.igdi.ku.edu/measures/ESI_Measures/ESI_technical_soundness.htm)

ESI

How Are Social Skills Assessed?

Based on the principles of assessing young children discussed in Chapter 2, the ESI was designed as a play-based observational measure of a child's social interaction skills that occur during a 6-minute play period with specific toys and a familiar adult and peer. The session is recommended to take place in a relatively sheltered, but convenient setting with few distractions present. During the session, an adult play partner engages the child being assessed with a familiar peer of the approximate same age in one of two different sets of toys: the School House with Blocks and Balls or the Tub of Toys (see discussion of toys later in this chapter). As described in Chapter 3 and as shown in the protocol chart, three different administration options exist for administering the ESI.

1. The two person option: an adult play partner interacts with the child and a second person observes and codes the child's social behaviors onto the IGDI scoring form.

2. The video-recording option: one person interacts with the child, but records the session for later coding.

3. The familiar play partner in which a parent, teacher, or other familiar caregiver interacts while a second person video records the session for later coding.

Materials Needed for Administering the ESI   The materials needed to administer the ESI and outlets for purchasing the toys are identified on the web site at http://www.igdi.ku.edu/measures/toys.htm. The two alternate forms of toys that are currently recommended for the ESI administration are the pop-up style enclosure toys and Tub of Toys (see the protocol chart). Because toy manufacturers often modify toys, it is important to refer to the web site for updated information about recommended materials for this assessment, including additional items that might be added to the primary toys, and for information about suggested outlets for purchasing toys or replacement pieces.

The toys were selected following a process of screening and testing to identify play objects that would be highly engaging for young children and would be likely to evoke the social interaction skills of typically developing infants and toddlers (see Carta, Greenwood, Luze, Cline, & Kuntz, 2004; Chapter 10, this volume). Examples of the pop-up style enclosures recommended for Form A include the Big Burger Drive Through or the School Bus (see Figure 7.3). These are flexible nylon enclosures characterized by a door that children can walk through and windows through which children can communicate with each other and/or the adult play partner. Several balls can be added to the enclosure to encourage further interaction between children in and around the toys. (With enclosure toys such as the School Bus, some children like to lean on the structure to make it collapse. They are designed to pop back up, so this is allowable, but the play partner should not let children fall on one another or get wrapped up in the enclosure material.) The Tub of Toys recommended for this assessment is an assortment of play materials that in-

ESI

Figure 7.3. Examples of toys recommended for ESI alternate forms.

cludes a bowl, three balls, at least two people, a vehicle (e.g., a little car or truck) that the little people can move about in, and four animal figures. Although there is not a specific set of toys recommended for this toy set, the Fisher Price Little People pictured in Figure 7.3 are acceptable for the people and animal figurines. Appropriately sized vehicles that do *not* require batteries should be used to encourage children to interact with the figurines.

All toys used for these assessments should be easy to clean and large enough to avoid a choking hazard. Finally, as explained in the general administration instructions described in Chapter 3, a digital timer is needed to signal the end of the session at 6 minutes. Accurate timing of every ESI session is important because progress is measured by counting the rate per minute of social behaviors during the entire 6-minute session. Once all of the materials are in place, the ESI administration checklist (see Figure 7.4) and the protocol chart outline the steps that should be followed for carrying out the ESI.

ESI Administration Checklist

ECI Assessor: _Darian Woodrow_ **Date:** _May 3, 2009_ **Tape:** _N/A (live observation)_

This checklist may be used to score the administration tapes for the ESI. To be certified to administer the ESI, the assessor should complete the administration steps to **at least an 83% (15 out of 18) criterion level.**

Setting up the ESI Administration Situation: Materials & Positioning

		Item	Yes	No
1.	Pop-up enclosure with Balls or Tub of Toys are set up prior to session.	1		X
2.	The toys have been arranged to attract children's attention.	2	X	
3.	One or two toys from the Tub of Toys are presented at a time (mark "Yes" if using Form A, the School House with Balls).	3	X	
4.	Adult and children are positioned so they can see and reach toys.	4	X	
5.	Adult play partner and children can have eye contact.	5	X	
6.	Children are positioned appropriately for their developmental level (head, neck and feet supported as needed).	6	X	
7.	Session is timed.	7	X	
8.	Video camera is set up so that children can be seen for scoring.	8	N/A	
9.	Microphone is set up so that children can be heard for scoring.	9	N/A	

ESI Assessment Administration: Play Situation

10.	Adult play partner follows children's lead in play situation.	10	X	
11.	Adult play partner comments about what children are doing.	11	X	
12.	Adult play partner describes what he/she is doing.	12	X	
13.	Adult play partner interacts in non-directive, friendly manner.	13	X	
14.	Adult play partner uses questions sparingly.	14	X	

Ending ESI Session

15.	Session ends exactly after 6 minutes have elapsed.	15	X	
16.	Adult play partner lets children know that it is time to stop.	16	X	
17.	Adult play partner thanks children for playing.	17		X
18.	Adult play partner cleans toys (may be reported).	18	X	
		Total	16 Yes	2 No

Administration Accuracy = [(Total Number of Steps Completed Correctly/16 Steps) × 100] = __89__ % (Need 83%)

Figure 7.4. ESI administration checklist, which is also available on the IGDI web site (http://www.igdi.ku.edu/training/ESI_training/ESI_Administration_Checklist-2005.pdf). (© Juniper Gardens Children's Project; reprinted by permission.)

Coding the ESI

A specific set of coding procedures allows the assessor to capture how proficient the child is in social interaction by recording the frequency with which the child performs the key skill elements of social interaction. Scoring procedures are designed to record the degree to which the child demonstrates social behaviors with his or her peers and/or adults. Key skill elements for the ESI vary across three dimensions: 1) verbal/nonverbal; 2) target (peer, adult, or nondirected); and 3) positive/negative. Each instance of an element is counted and recorded with a tally mark in the appropriate cell on the ESI recording sheet (see Figure 7.5). Recording

Early Social Indicator (ESI)

Child Name or #: <u>Miguel Valindo</u>   Assess Date <u>6/13/2009</u> (MM/DD/YYYY)

Assessment Duration: <u>6</u>   <u>00</u>
                              Min   Sec

Form: Pop-up or Blocks & Balls   Condition Change (see list below): <u>ABA/TEACH</u>

Primary Coder: <u>Danita Frizzel</u>   Assessor: <u>Katherine Puckett</u>

Location (Circle One): Home (Center) Other (explain in Notes)

Language of Administration: <u>Spanish</u>

If Reliability, Reliability Coder's Name: <u>N/A</u>

Notes: _____

| | Positive Behaviors | | | | | | Negative Behaviors |
| | Adult | | Peer | | Non-Directed | | |
	Verbal	Non-Verbal	Verbal	Non-Verbal	Verbal	Non-Verbal	
Begin 0:00 Sec.	A_V //	A_{NV} /	P_V	P_{NV}	ND_V /	ND_{NV}	N
1:00 Sec.	A_V /	A_{NV} /	P_V /	P_{NV}	ND_V	ND_{NV} //	N
2:00 Sec.	A_V //	A_{NV}	P_V ///	P_{NV}	ND_V //	ND_{NV}	N
3:00 Sec.	A_V //	A_{NV}	P_V ЖHT	P_{NV}	ND_V	ND_{NV}	N
4:00 Sec.	A_V	A_{NV}	P_V ////	P_{NV} //	ND_V	ND_{NV}	N /
5:00 Sec.	A_V ///	A_{NV} /	P_V ///	P_{NV}	ND_V	ND_{NV} /	N
6 min. End Total	A_V 10	A_{NV} 3	P_V 16	P_{NV} 2	ND_V 3	ND_{NV} 3	N 1

Condition List

ABA/TEACH
Child Psychiatrist
Interpreter
Language Intervention Toolkit
Medical Intervention (e.g., Tubes)
Mental Health Consultant
Milieu or Incidental Teaching
MOD Recommendations
None
Other
Primary Care Provider
Registered Nurse
Responsive Interaction
Social Worker
Speech/Language Therapist

Figure 7.5.   The ESI recording form, which is also available on the IGDI web site (http://www.igdi.ku.edu/training/ESI_training/ESI_Data_Sheet-2005.doc). (© Juniper Gardens Children's Project; reprinted by permission.)

sheets have different sections for each element for each minute of the assessment. Elements can be summed into a total social score.

Social behaviors occur when a child attempts to convey a message to a partner, whether the partner is an adult, a peer, or no one in particular (nondirected). Social behaviors may be either positive or negative, and if they are positive, they can be either verbal or nonverbal. Social behaviors may last as long as a single behavior (e.g., an initiation to play) or as long as an episode or exchange of social behaviors involving several turns (e.g., responded to by a peer or by the target child). Social

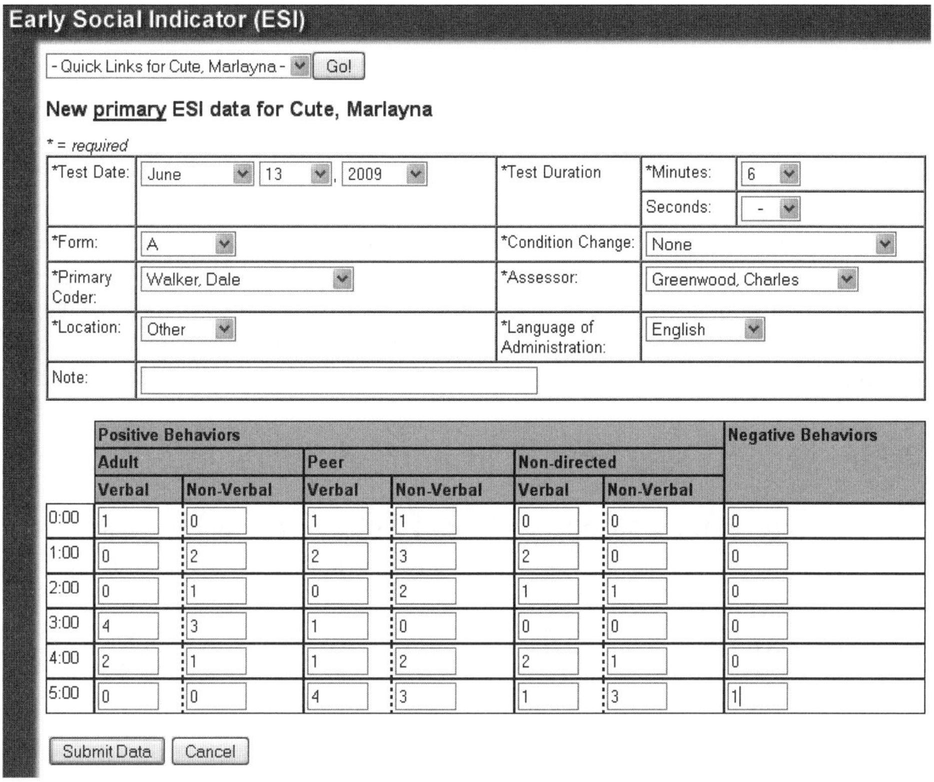

Early Social Indicator (ESI)

- Quick Links for Cute, Marlayna - ▾ [Go!]

New primary ESI data for Cute, Marlayna

* = *required*

*Test Date:	June ▾ 13 ▾ , 2009 ▾	*Test Duration	*Minutes:	6 ▾
			Seconds:	- ▾
*Form:	A ▾	*Condition Change:	None ▾	
*Primary Coder:	Walker, Dale ▾	*Assessor:	Greenwood, Charles ▾	
*Location:	Other ▾	*Language of Administration:	English ▾	
Note:				

	Positive Behaviors						Negative Behaviors
	Adult		**Peer**		**Non-directed**		
	Verbal	Non-Verbal	Verbal	Non-Verbal	Verbal	Non-Verbal	
0:00	1	0	1	1	0	0	0
1:00	0	2	2	3	2	0	0
2:00	0	1	0	2	1	1	0
3:00	4	3	1	0	0	0	0
4:00	2	1	1	2	2	1	0
5:00	0	0	4	3	1	3	1

[Submit Data] [Cancel]

Figure 7.6. The ESI individual child data entry form, which is also available on the IGDI web site (http://www.igdi.ku .edu/measures/ESI_Measures/ESI_online_data_entry_forms.htm). (© Juniper Gardens Children's Project; reprinted by permission.)

responding is considered ended after 3 seconds of no responding. For example, an episode begins when a child initiates or responds to an initiation presented by another person. The episode ends after a pause of at least 3 seconds. Thus, each social behavior or each episode separated by at least a 3-second pause is counted as one event.

The ESI recording sheet is a simple table with 6 rows in which each row is devoted to 1 minute of recording time. The recorder must identify each instance of a social behavior, identify it as positive or negative, and, if positive, determine to whom it is directed (adult, peer, or nondirected) and if it is verbal or nonverbal. Simple tallies are recorded in this way for each behavior in the appropriate cell moving down the rows in each minute for a total of 6 minutes.

The frequencies are recorded on the manual ESI recording sheet (see Figure 7.5), and then these scores are entered into an electronic data sheet (see Figure 7.6) at the IGDI web site (http://www.igdi.ku.edu/training/EPSI_training/EPSI_Recording_ Sheet-2005.pdf). Entering data on the web-based forms allows scores to be automatically calculated and these new data added to the child's growth charts, which includes any data previously recorded for the individual child.

Who Can Record ESI Social Interactions?

Only someone who has been certified as a calibrated and reliable "recorder" is qualified to record the occurrence of a child's ESI key skill behaviors. This person may also be the assessor and adult play partner. For information about how to become an assessor, see the web site at http://www.igdi.ku.edu/measures/ESI_Measures/ESI_administration.htm. For information on how to become a certified ESI recorder and/or coder, refer to Chapter 10 or see the web site at http://www.igdi.ku.edu. As part of each assessor's ESI training and certification, he or she learns the procedures for recording key skill element social interaction behaviors recorded during the 6-minute session (see Chapter 3). In this preparation, the person learns the basic definitions of the key social behaviors.

Definitions of Key Skill Elements of Social Interaction

Positive versus Negative Social Behaviors
Social behaviors are recorded as either positive or negative. Social behaviors are positive when they are greetings, offers to play, requests, and so forth. Social behaviors are recorded as negative when they involve aggression, hitting, kicking, threatening, grabbing away another's toy, or other negative behavior. Crying for children this age is considered to be an acceptable form of social communication; however, it is not recorded as a social behavior for the ESI.

Verbal Social Behavior
Verbal social behaviors are vocal (or sign language) attempts to communicate using nonword, single word, or multiple word utterances. False starts or stutters are counted as one verbalization. For example, "I think this is . . . this looks like a dog" counts as one verbalization. An episode is ended when there is a pause of at least 3 seconds without vocalizations (i.e., count to yourself, "one thousand one . . . "). Again, crying is considered acceptable, but it is not recorded. Similar to nonverbal, verbal social behaviors are recorded as directed either to the adult or peer or as nondirected when it is impossible to tell to whom the social behavior is directed. Some additional examples of verbal social behaviors are animal sounds (e.g., "moo," when looking at a cow); transportation or motor sounds (e.g., "vroom," when pushing a tractor); blows to ask for more bubbles; sequentially naming objects (e.g., "block, red, phone, girl" [tally for each word]); a vocalization in which only one word is understandable; imitation (e.g., sounds, nonsense words, sensible words); or standard sign language. Verbal behavior that should not be scored as social behavior includes involuntary noises, such as hiccups, coughing, or sneezing.

Nonverbal Social Behavior with or to an Adult, Peer, or Nondirected
Nonverbal social behaviors are gesture-based attempts to communicate. Examples include smiling at, giving or showing an object, rejecting an object by pushing it away, reaching toward, touching a partner or object that the partner is holding, pointing toward an object or person (may or may not be used to

establish joint attention), nodding or shaking head to indicate "yes" or "no," and shrugging shoulders. Nonverbal social behaviors are recorded according to the person they are directed to—the adult play partner, the peer play partner, or undirected in cases in which it is not clear exactly to whom they are directed or if they are directed to both partners. Nonverbal social behaviors do not include play behaviors, such as reaching for a toy lying on the ground, physical movements independent from social communication, and physical movements showing excitement or pleasure that are not in direct communication with the partner (e.g., waving arms when watching a ball roll away or when ignoring directions).

What Scores Are Derived for the ESI?   After completing the session and recording the child social interaction episodes, scores are calculated for *total social* by subtracting the frequency of negative behaviors from the total of the two positive behaviors (nonverbal and verbal). This frequency is divided by 6 minutes (the length of the assessment) to produce a rate of social behavior per minute. This rate of social interaction can be thought of as a fluency score in the sense that is capable of reflecting an increase in a child's positive social interaction proficiency from one administration of the ESI to the next. Scoring and reporting of the ESI data is simplified using the appropriate ESI tools in the IGDI child data system on the web site (http://www.igdi.ku.edu/measures/ESI_Measures/ESI_online_data_entry_forms.htm).

How Can the ESI Be Used to Monitor and Inform Intervention?   The ESI is one means of checking children's growth toward the important general outcome of being able to interact with peers and adults, maintaining social interaction and participating socially in home, school, and community. Because children's rate of growth in social interaction is so critical, growth on the ESI for each child and for all the children in a program becomes an important indicator of how well a program is doing in supporting children's social competence. As such, the ESI can be a powerful tool for monitoring individual children's growth, evaluating response to interaction, and making intervention decisions. It also can provide helpful information on programwide progress in moving children in a positive direction on their social interaction skills, as well as help inform program-level decisions regarding this essential outcome.

Destinee: An Example of Using the ESI

In this section, we present a case illustration of a child (Destinee) who was given the ESI as part of her Early Head Start program's three-tiered approach to providing support for children's social-emotional competence. Destinee was 13 months old when she and her young teen mother enrolled in the Early Head Start program, and, similar to all the children in the program, she began receiving quarterly ESI assessments as part of the universal screening this program had undertaken. By the time Destinee had been given the ESI three times, Wendy, her early intervention provider, noticed a pattern of a low total social interaction rate per minute. When Destinee was approximately 21 months, Wendy decided to go to the IGDI web site and print out Destinee's ESI individual child report

Early Social Indicator (ESI)

Individual Child Report for Destinee

Child: Destinee
Birthdate: 01/01/1998
Program: ESI sample data 2003
Date: 06/28/2009
□=Primary Data   ■=Reliability Data

Date	Age at Test (Months)	Positive Verbal	Positive Nonverbal	Negative	Total Social	Intervention Conditions
		Rate Per Minute				
03/01/1999	13	4	4	5	3	None
06/01/1999	16	2	3	3	2	None
09/01/1999	19	4	3	4	3	None
01/01/2000	23	3	2	2	3	None
02/01/2000	24	6	1	4	3	Responsive Interaction
03/01/2000	25	7	1	3	5	None
04/01/2000	26	8	2	4	6	None
05/01/2000	27	9	3	5	7	None
06/01/2000	28	8	3	5	6	None
07/01/2000	29	8	0	2	6	None
10/01/2000	32	8	0	2	6	None
01/01/2001	35	6	1	0	7	None
Average		6.08	1.92	3.25	4.75	
Slope						0.24

Averages and Slopes are calculated using the Primary Data Only. The Reliability data are not included in these calculations nor in the following graphs.

Figure 7.7. Destinee's ESI individual child report. (© Juniper Gardens Children's Project; reprinted by permission.)

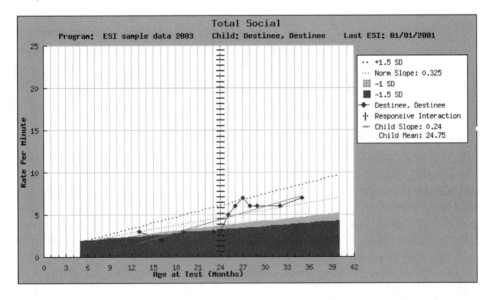

Figure 7.8. Destinee's ESI total social graph. (© Juniper Gardens Children's Project; reprinted by permission.)

(see Figure 7.7) and her ESI total social graph (see Figure 7.8). She brought them to a team staffing for Destinee and pointed out that by 21 months Destinee's total social rate per minute was more than 1.5 *SD* below the mean, which is in an area of concern.

When Destinee was 24 months, her early intervention team decided to move her into a more intensive tier of intervention (responsive interaction). This tier 2 intervention focused on providing Destinee with additional time in the classroom working in a small group with her teacher who tuned into and provided scaffolding for Destinee's play and interactions. Wendy continued to monitor Destinee's ESI performance on a monthly basis. Within a month, they noticed a rapid increase in Destinee's rate of total social behavior. By the time she was 30 months old, Destinee's total social rate on the ESI total social graph revealed that for 6 months, Destinee's total social behavior was at or above the rate typical for her age. Her team decided to move Destinee back to tier 1 in which she continued to receive a high quality classroom experience that supported her growth in social interaction.

Conclusion

Similar to other measures in this volume, the ESI is useful 1) for identifying children having difficulty acquiring social interaction skills within a universal screening program and 2) after children begin receiving more intensified social interventions, examining these interventions' effectiveness and evaluating children's responses to intervention (RTI). The ESI provides unique information about children's progress in learning to be social in natural environments relevant to the needs, goals, and practices of early intervention practitioners. The ESI offers practitioners and programs a new capacity to monitor progress and to act in a timely manner to improve results.

ESI

> ## Administration Protocol
> ## for the Early Social Indicator

 Materials

Digital timer

Required toys
- Pop-up style enclosure toys (Form A)
- Includes Big Burger Drive Through or School Bus (see Figure 7.3)
- Several balls should be added to the enclosure to encourage further interaction between children in and around the toys.
- Tub of toys (Form B)
- An assortment of play materials, including a bowl, three balls, at least two play people, a vehicle (e.g., a little car or truck that *does not* require batteries that the people can move around in), and four animal figures (see Figure 7.3).

 Administration options

1. Two people
   - Play partner (certified EPSI administrator)
   - Certified assessor

2. One person as
   - Play partner
   - Certified assessor**

3. Two people
   - Parent as play partner
   - Certified assessor

**This option would be video recorded for later coding

 Forms

ESI administration checklist (see Figure 7.4)
ESI recording form (see Figure 7.5)

 Set-up

Comfortable area
- Everyone can be sitting or standing to begin

Arrangement of toys
- Either the Form A or Form B toys would be selected prior to the session (toys should be rotated across sessions to maintain child's interest).
- Set up the toys so that the child sees them immediately upon entering the assessment situation.
- When using a camera, be sure that it is angled toward the opening of the enclosure to capture activity and communication inside.

 Time

6 minutes

 Conducting the session**

The play partner should ensure that children are comfortable with the surroundings and with each other.

(continued)

ESI

After making the child comfortable, indicate to the child that there are fun toys to play with together.

To facilitate beginning play, comment on what child is doing (e.g., "Let's take a look in this house and see what's in there").

Avoid directing the child to move or act in certain ways.

Let the child know when the session has ended, assist him or her in ending play, and thank him or her for playing.

Offer immediate access to another toy to play with at the end of the session.

**See Chapter 3 for more detailed information.

ESI

8

The Indicator of Parent–Child Interaction (IPCI)

Kathleen Baggett and Judith J. Carta

IPCI

T he Indicator of Parent–Child Interaction (IPCI) is a progress-monitoring measure that was designed for use by practitioners whose efforts are aimed at supporting parents and other caregivers in nurturing young children's positive social-emotional behavior. The IPCI was developed to meet practitioners' needs for a technically sound measure that serves as a quick and easy-to-use indicator of the quality of sensitivity and responsiveness that parents and other caregivers use with very young children. The IPCI was created to be used across the disciplines of early education and intervention, mental health, and nursing professionals who work with parents and other caregivers to support and enhance their interactions with children ranging from 2 to 42 months of age.

As discussed in Chapter 1, a key feature of IGDIs is that they make it possible for practitioners to monitor progress so that when children fall below benchmark on a particular outcome domain, intervention can be initiated or modified. In the case of the IPCI, rather than focusing on a developmental domain, it focuses on the domain of opportunities for children to be exposed to nurturing interactions with their parents or other caregivers, including child care providers. Using the IPCI can inform practitioners about the level of children's exposure to nurturing interactions known to promote positive child social-emotional behavior. Moreover it can provide practitioners with valuable information about whether or not children's exposure to nurturing interactions is occurring at levels comparable to other children their age, and, if not, how well the program or intervention is moving an individual child or group of children toward optimal exposure. For programs committed to demonstrating accountability, the IPCI can provide helpful information about program effectiveness and can help to inform programmatic decisions regarding progress toward the general outcome of children's nurturing interactions with parents and caregivers.

Background and Relevance of the IPCI

The IPCI is one of five progress-monitoring tools developed for infants and toddlers that measures progress toward socially valued outcomes and guides intervention decision making (Greenwood, Carta, Baggett et al., 2008). In a review of 17 home-based early intervention programs, one of the most highly rated outcome goals was the promotion of sensitive parenting behavior (Brooks-Gunn, Berlin, & Fuligni, 2000). This is no surprise considering that two of the most systemic federal early intervention programs, Early Head Start (EHS) and early childhood special education programs for infants and toddlers (Part C of the Individuals with Disabilities Act [IDEA] of 1997), recognize the importance of parent–child interaction in supporting child development.

This recognition is evident in the EHS performance to "promote parent–child bonding and nurturing parent–child relationships" (Administration for Children and Families, 1996). Part C, Office of Special Education, also recognizes the importance of the parent–child relationship in supporting child development as indicated through the requirement that programs report the following: "(1) the percent of infants and toddlers with IFSPs who demonstrate improved: positive social-emotional skills (including social relationships" and (2) "the percent of families participating in Part C who report that early intervention services have helped the family to help their children develop and learn" (Regional Resource Center Program, 2008).

These aims make sense in light of more than 3 decades of research demonstrating that children who are nurtured by parents and other caregivers from their earliest stages of development have the best chances of achieving school readiness and lifelong success (see Isaacs, 2008). During the first generation of such research, descriptive approaches showed that specific sensitive, responsive caregiving strategies predicted important child outcomes. For example, studies driven by both attachment and behavioral theory have shown that high levels of caregiver acceptance and warmth predict positive feedback and pro-social behavior (George & Main, 1979; Landry, Smith, Swank, Assel, & Vellet, 2001; Zanolli, Paden, & Cox, 1997). Another example is caregiver use of rich descriptive language, especially when linked to children's interests (i.e., following children's lead), predicts children's engagement and expressive communication (Hart & Risley, 1995; Tamis-LeMonda, Bornstein, & Baumwell, 2001). Two more examples of sensitive, responsive caregiving strategies include that following a child's lead and maintaining a child's interest has been shown to promote joint attention and follow through (Landry et al., 2001), and caregiver support to reduce child distress has been associated with active child engagement and less avoidant and withdrawn behavior (Field, 1994; George & Main, 1979).

Since 2005, second generation research has demonstrated that these important caregiver sensitivity and responsiveness behaviors can be supported through direct intervention to improve child outcomes and, in particular, social-emotional and language outcomes (Landry, Smith, Swank, & Guttentag, 2008; Van den Boom, 1994). Infants whose parents respond in a sensitive manner tend to display more self-calming behaviors, less irritability, more positive attachment patterns and social engagement, and more favorable social-emotional and language developmental trajectories than do infants whose parents do not (Heinicke, Fineman, Ponce, & Gutnrie, 2001; Landry et al., 2001; van den Boom, 1994). Moreover, when children are the recipients of responsive interactions beginning in early infancy and continuing through preschool, they fare significantly better in social and communication outcomes by the time they enter kindergarten as compared with children who lack consistent, high-quality interactions with their caregivers (Landry et al., 2001).

In light of the important role that sensitive, responsive caregiving plays in promoting positive child outcomes, practitioners need to have a reliable and valid indicator of when the interactions children have with parents and other caregivers put children at risk for adverse outcomes and when more intensive or structured intervention is needed to support and then monitor growth in caregivers' levels of sensitivity and responsiveness to intervention or programmatic changes. The IPCI was developed as one means of checking growth toward the important general outcome of nurturing, responsive interactions that parents and caregivers have with their children (Baggett & Carta, 2006; Greenwood, Carta, Baggett et al., 2008).

Although many measures exist to assess the quality of caregiver–child interaction, the IPCI is unique in three ways. First and foremost, it is designed to be administered by a variety of practitioners who typically provide early intervention services (e.g., early intervention teachers, family support advocates, parent aides, nurses, social workers). Second, it is designed to be quick to administer so that it can be repeated on a frequent basis for use in progress monitoring. Third, it is supported by a web site that generates automatic reports to guide intervention decision making.

What Does the IPCI Assess?

The IPCI includes a total of 14 items comprised of four domains: caregiver facilitators, caregiver interrupters, child engagement, and child distress. Figure 8.1 shows each of the key elements and their relationships to each of the four domains.

Key elements for the parent and caregiver domain were selected for their utility in predicting child outcomes based on review of the research literature and existing measures of parent sensitivity and responsiveness. For both the parent and/or caregiver and child domains, key elements reflect behaviors that were most commonly and consistently associated with important outcomes in the research literature.

For the parent competency domain, skills reflect sensitive and responsive behaviors that are associated with and have been shown to support or facilitate more positive child social-emotional outcomes (see Landry, Smith, Swank, Assel, & Vallet, 2001; Landry et al., 2008; van den Boom, 1994). Therefore, the competency domain for parents and other caregivers is called facilitators and is comprised of five key elements that include conveys acceptance and warmth, uses descriptive lan-

General Outcome: Children's exposure to nurturing, responsive interactions with parents.

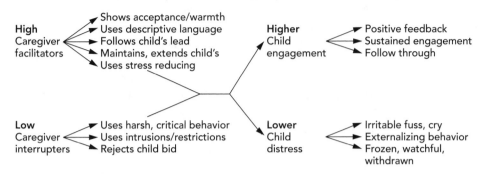

Figure 8.1. IPCI conceptual model.

guage, follows child's lead, maintains and extends child's interest, and uses stress-reducing strategies. Stress-reducing strategies include parent behaviors, such as giving a brief break from interaction when a child shows signals of frustration, or a parent using swaddling or providing a pacifier to comfort a young infant who is crying frantically at the end of a dressing routine.

The parent interrupter domain consists of behaviors that interrupt interaction and have been associated with poor child outcomes (see Appleyard, Egeland, van Dulmen, & Sroufe, 2005; Chang, Schwartz, Dodge, & McBride-Chang; 2003). The interrupters domain includes three key elements: uses harsh, critical behavior or voice tone, uses intrusions or restrictions, and rejects child bids. Restrictions and intrusions include both verbal and nonverbal prohibitions, such as a parent saying, "No, no" and pulling a large, clean, safe ring toy that the child is obviously enjoying out of an infant's hand or mouth during free play.

For children, the engagement domain is comprised of positive feedback, sustained engagement, and follow through. An example of child follow through would be observed during a dressing routine in which a parent smiles, holds open a shirt sleeve, and says, "Put your hand through this hole," and the child raises his or her hand toward the open shirt sleeve. The distress domain includes irritability and fussiness; externalizing behaviors, such as tantrums; and internalizing behaviors, such as withdrawing from interaction. An example of an internalizing behavior is a young toddler who, during free play, flinches when a parent raises her hand, pulls away from the parent, or withdraws from interaction while watching the parent from a distance with wide open eyes. When problems within these domains emerge for young children, they tend to be durable over time without intervention and to be associated with later social-emotional and behavioral problems that can interfere with school readiness (see Bricker, Schoen Davis, & Squires, 2004; Briggs-Gowan, Carter, Irwin, Wachtel, & Cicchetti, 2004; Raver, 2003).

Research Supporting the IPCI

Based on the descriptive and experimental research literature, the IPCI was developed in a program of research designed to test its technical soundness as a brief indicator of the responsiveness of parent or other caregiver interactions with children. As noted previously, the degree to which this outcome is viewed as socially valid is underscored by the many programs, including the most prominent federal early intervention programs—EHS and Part C—that stress the importance of positive parent–child relationships. Basic psychometric properties and feasibility of the IPCI have been documented through longitudinal and intervention studies conducted with highly diverse samples. To date, these samples include an EHS sample ($N = 62$), a low-risk community sample ($N = 19$), adolescents and adult mothers who did not graduate from high school ($N = 65$), and low-income mothers living in small towns and rural areas ($N = 19$). Overall, studies of the psychometric integrity of the IPCI have indicated that it is an instrument that can be reliably administered, that it is measuring what it is intended to measure, and that it is sensitive to known differences in parent and child risk characteristics (see Chapter 10 or http://www.igdi.ku.edu/measures/index.htm for a detailed discussion regarding psychometric properties of the IPCI).

Administration of the IPCI

Given that the goal of the IPCI is to capture typical caregiver responsiveness, a set of standard situations or activity contexts in which to examine ways a caregiver typically interacts with a child was developed (see protocol chart). It is important that assessors who administer the IPCI follow carefully the procedures presented in the manual for standard administration of activities while establishing and maintaining a warm, supportive relationship with the caregiver. Reliable and valid administration requires that assessors partner with parents and caregivers to help them understand the purpose of the assessment and to help put them at ease without prompting for specific interaction strategies during activities. For example, expectations about the book activity, in which caregivers select one or more books to look at with their child, are communicated by letting parents know that the purpose of the activity is "to understand how you and your child use the book together." The instruction to "read books" is specifically avoided as some parents are unable to read or simply do not engage in this activity when looking at books with their children.

How Is Parent–Child Interaction Assessed?

The IPCI is completed during a 10-minute observation period that includes a series of brief interaction episodes that can take place in a home situation between a child and parent or in a center-based program between a child and a familiar caregiver. These activities and corresponding materials are depicted in Figure 8.2. For children who are younger than 1 year, activities include 1) free play, 2) looking at books, and 3) a routine dressing task. For children who are 1 year old or older, the three activities plus a distraction task are employed. Prior to the first observation, parents (or caregivers) are provided information about the purpose of the observation and are informed about the types of activities that will be observed. At the time of the

Figure 8.2. Recommended IPCI toys. Looking at books (A); free play (B); a routine dressing task (C).

observation, rapport is established with the parent (caregiver) and information about what to expect during the observation visit and how to avoid and handle interruptions is reviewed and an opportunity for questions and discussion is provided. It is crucial that the IPCI assessor gives special attention to preparing parents or caregivers for the assessment, including the purpose, what to expect, and how to prepare. In addition, assessors need to be prepared to recognize and respond to questions, concerns, or apprehension that parents or caregivers may communicate verbally or nonverbally before, during, and after the assessment. The IPCI manual provides standard instructions for preparing parents or caregivers for visits and setting up activities at the time of assessment. In addition, the manual provides detailed suggestions for addressing individual concerns that can arise during the visit, as well as debriefing and diffusing to provide any needed support for parents or caregivers following the assessment.

Although video recording is not required, it does increase the ease and accuracy of ratings, as well as provide a useful tool for intervention. Materials provided by the assessor to conduct the observation include two board books for the book activity and a 5×7-foot blanket. A nonactivated recorder that plays prerecorded musical tunes every 7 seconds is provided for the distraction task. The recorder is attached to a bright-colored key chain with keys. The dressing activity and the free play activity do not require any assessment materials as the purpose of these activities is to observe typical play routines for the parent and child. The following are step-by-step guidelines for carrying out each of the four activities.

1. Free play

   - Materials: No materials are required for this activity; however, if the caregiver and child wish to use toys or games, these should be available before the assessment begins.

   - Set up: Remember to set the timer for 4 minutes as soon as you give the following instructions.

   - Instructions:

     - Let's get started by spending a few minutes with you and your child doing something together that you enjoy.

     - This activity should be something that you and your child are both comfortable with and used to, and something that your child loves to do.

     - Please feel free to move around as is comfortable for you and your child. You don't have to sit in one place, but I'll need to know what room you'd like to be in so that I can move along with you.

     - Sometimes parents talk or play games without toys, sometimes parents just sit with their children, and sometimes children like to play with a favorite toy.

     - Whatever you and (child's name) normally do that makes (child's name) smile, laugh, or have fun is what I want to see. Feel free to stay with an activity or change activities as you would like. Attend to any needs your child might have during this time just as you normally would.

   - Note: The purpose of this activity is to encourage the caregiver and child to engage in whatever activity they enjoy and to be as nonrestrictive as possible. It is important not to impose any structure on the parent that is above and beyond the instructions. Therefore, do not restrict the parent's and child's movement by asking them to stay in one place. Instead, encourage the parent to let you know if they would like to move simply so that you can stay with them. If the parent looks toward you during the assessment or engages in behavior that suggests he or she is concerned with being in view of the camera or needs to "look good for the camera" (e.g., pulling child's arm in an attempt to position child in front of camera or saying 'stay here so they can see you' to the child), remind the parent that it is your job to move the camera around and that you need the caregiver and child to do whatever they would like without worrying about the camera at all and to ignore the camera as much as possible.

IPCI

2. Looking at Books

    - Materials: Books (*Brown Bear, Touch and Feel Puppy, Fiesta*)

    - Set up: Give the books to the parent. Remember to set the timer for 2 minutes as soon as you give the following instructions.

    - Instructions:

        - During the next few minutes, you and your child can spend a few minutes with these books.

        - However you want to use the books with your child is fine.

        - Feel free to attend to whatever needs your child might have during this time.

    - Note: Do *not* ask the caregiver to read to his or her child. This is very important for at least two reasons. First, parents who cannot read or who are self-conscious about their reading ability may shy away from interacting with their children because of the instruction to read. Second, some parents will interpret the instruction to read literally and will do so regardless of whatever conflicting signals for readiness the child might show. Although this may happen spontaneously, the instructions were designed to avoid stimulating such an effect. If the parent gives verbal or nonverbal cues of discomfort with the task or tells you that he or she cannot read, encourage the parent that however he or she would like to use these books with the child is just fine and that you're really interested in the interaction with books, not necessarily in reading. If the caregiver appears uncomfortable and looks to you for support or confirmation as to what is expected, paraphrase instructions and maintain a supportive stance, but do not make any specific behavioral suggestions to the parent.

3. Distraction Task

    - Materials: Blanket or tablecloth, recorder with tunes (10 seconds of tunes alternating with 3 seconds of silence), and key chain

    - Set up: Lay down the blanket and then give the instructions. As soon as the instructions have been given, turn the recorder on and set it on the blanket in front of and within reach of the child. Do not give the recorder directly to the parent. Remember to set the timer for 2 minutes as soon as the parent and child are on the blanket and the recorder has been placed on the blanket and turned on. If the parent has a physical disability that makes it difficult or impossible to get down on the floor, this activity can be set up by placing the recorder and keys on the couch within reach of the child and asking the parent and child to stay on a couch rather than a blanket.

    - Instructions:

        - Sometimes there are materials around the house that are either dangerous (e.g., electrical outlets) or that may not be unsafe for children but are breakable or simply off limits, such as objects that belong to guests or other family members.

- Just as you would try to keep your child from things that are unsafe or inappropriate for young children, we would like for you to keep (child's name) on this blanket for a few minutes and not allow him or her to get this recorder.

- Normally, we would never intentionally place something in front of your child that he or she cannot have, but because there are times when such materials may be unavoidable, such as in the car, grocery store, or at the doctor's office, it's important to see how your child handles situations when there is something in reach that is not appropriate to have.

- Note: It is fine for the parent to engage the child with any materials so long as the caregiver introduces the materials. Do not make any suggestions or give the parent alternate materials with which to engage the child. If this activity is particularly stressful for the child or parent, be prepared to help the parent and child calm at the end of this activity before moving on to the final activity. Be empathetic and reflect that this was a difficult task and praise the parent for making it through. Ask the parent what he or she thinks would be most helpful at this point for unwinding and helping the child to feel better. Encourage the parent to attend to the child's needs at this time. If a short break is needed before moving on to the next IPCI activity, be sure to provide it. If the parent is unable to identify any strategies for attending to the child's need for calming or support, encourage the parent that they have made it almost all of the way through the activities and that remaining activity is very brief.

4. Dressing task

- Materials: No materials are required if the parent wishes to take a child's clothes off and then put them back on (e.g., shirt, socks, shoes). If parent wishes to put on a change of clothes, these will need to be available.

- Set up: Remember to set the timer for 2 minutes as soon as you give the following instructions. In rare cases, the dressing task, particularly with a young infant, may not last for 2 minutes. Simply note the time on the rating form, but do not tell the parent that the activity may be less than 2 minutes and do not curtail the dressing time for any reason other than the parent's spontaneous completion in less time.

- Instructions:

  - Let's spend a few minutes now seeing what it's like to get (child's name) dressed in the morning with whatever clothes and/or changing routine you use.

  - Let's focus on changing shirt, socks, and shoes or a diaper if that's needed. It's fine to simply remove and then replace the same clothing or if you'd like to use a change of clothes, that's fine too.

  - However you two normally go about dressing is what I'm interested in.

- Note: After this final activity, end on a positive note. Point out something positive that you observed during the observation. If something positive was recorded, replaying a brief section of it to point out the positive and encourage the caregiver's reflection can be helpful. If the activities were particularly difficult or stressful for the parent or child, acknowledge that and empathize with the parent. If the child is distressed, ask the parent what he or she thinks might help to soothe the child. If appropriate, explore basic needs (e.g., diaper change if this was not done during the session, bottle, food, rest, activity that child especially enjoys).

Modifications for Children with Unique Needs

In the course of using the IPCI with a wide variety of individuals, including children with and without disabilities and culturally and linguistically diverse families, several modifications to materials and administration have been explored and are recommended. For example, for children with sensory impairments, books can be purchased in Braille. For cultural appropriateness, book substitutions have been made to ensure appropriate themes. For linguistically diverse samples, books have been purchased that display both English and Spanish text or that display other multiple language texts. For children with significant hearing impairments and for those confined to restrictive seating, the distraction task is omitted.

Scoring the IPCI

A relative frequency is produced for each key element based on a scoring scale of 0–3, whereby 0 = never, 1 = rarely, 2 = sometimes or inconsistently, and 3 = often or consistently. For example, if a parent does not make any descriptive comments during the observation, a score of 0 would be assigned for Descriptive Language. For some items, level of intensity is also captured (1 = mild and 3 = severe) such that low base-rate behaviors of concern receive a higher rating). The IPCI rating sheet is shown in Figure 8.3.

After a rating is generated for each key element, a score is then generated for each domain (i.e., parent facilitators, parent interrupters, child engagement, and child distress) by summing the scores across the key elements for a particular domain and dividing the summed score by the total number possible for that domain. This yields a domain percentage score for each observation. For example, a score ranging from 0 to 100 is generated for each domain.

Both competency and difficulty domain scores are automatically graphed for each parent or caregiver and child when scores are entered in the IPCI web site database. In addition, key elements for each domain are graphed to provide detailed information about how these specific elements contributed to the overall domain score. For example, Descriptive Language and Follow Child's Lead, two of the five key elements that contribute to the facilitators domain score, are illustrated in Figure 8.4. Such reports provide important information to practitioners about the relative frequency of specific parent or caregiver behaviors and how these frequencies

Indicator of Parent Child Interaction (IPCI) Rating Sheet

Never = 0 (Never) Rarely/Mild = 1 (Once; Mild for Cg Interrupters and Child Distress) Sometimes = 2 (Inconsistently) Often/Severe = 3 (Often, Consistently; Severe for Cg Interrupters and Child Distress) No Opportunity = N/O (No Opp. to observe)	Free Play	Looking at Books	Distraction	Dressing	Overall Never = 0 Rarely/Mild = 1 Sometimes = 2 Often/Severe = 3 No Opportunity = N/O
Caregiver Facilitators (1) Acceptance/Warmth	I	I			0 1 **2** 3
(2) Descriptive Language		I			0 **1** 2 3
(3) Follows Child's Lead	II				0 1 **2** 3
(4) Maintains and Extends	I				0 **1** 2 3
(5) Stress Reducing Strategies	N/O	N/O	N/O	N/O	0 1 2 3 N/O
Caregiver Interrupters (1) Criticism/Harsh Voice					**0** 1 2 3
(2) Restrictions/Intrusions	II	II	III	I	0 1 2 **3**
(3) Rejects Child's Bid					**0** 1 2 3
	N/O	N/O	N/O	N/O	N/O
Child Engagement (1) Positive Feedback	I				0 **1** 2 3
(2) Sustained Engagement	I				0 **1** 2 3
(3) Follow Through	I				0 **1** 2 3
	N/O	N/O	N/O	N/O	N/O
Child Reactivity/Distress (1) Irritable/Fuss/Cry					**0** 1 2 3
(2) External Distress					**0** 1 2 3
(3) Frozen/Watchful/Withdrawn					**0** 1 2 3

Place an X in the gray box below for each activity observed. Then proceed to record tallies in clear boxes below each activity for each item listed at the left. After observing each activity, circle your Overall rating below for each item.

IPCI

Figure 8.3. IPCI rating sheet (copies are available at http://www.igdi.ku.edu/). (© Juniper Gardens Children's Project; reprinted by permission.)

are changing over time with intervention to contribute to growth in parent or caregiver facilitators, which, in turn, provide children with opportunities to practice and develop social-emotional competencies.

Who Can Administer and Score the IPCI   Training certification is available for administration as well as for scoring. Certification trainings for administration and scoring are generally conducted separately during two half-day trainings each. Anyone who completes each respective certification training may administer and score the IPCI. Following thorough review of the IPCI manual, administration

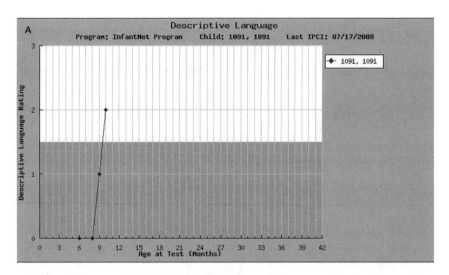

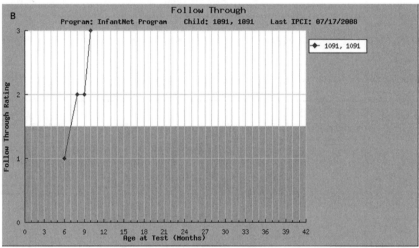

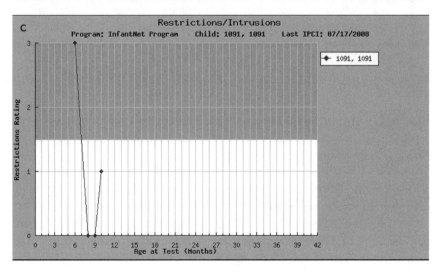

Figure 8.4. Examples of IPCI key element reports: descriptive language (A); follow through (B); restrictions/intrusions (C). (© Juniper Gardens Children's Project; reprinted by permission.)

certification training is generally conducted in one half-day training whereas scoring training requires completion of the initial half-day administration training followed by another half-day focused exclusively on scoring. Following training, individuals submit two video-recorded IPCI administrations and three scored rating sheets based on IPCI videos. Certification is completed when at least one administration and at least two scorings meet certification criterion.

The parent or caregiver facilitator and child engagement domain reports are designed to be interpreted by early childhood service providers who are certified in both IPCI administration and scoring. However, mental health consultation should be sought for interpreting and sharing the caregiver interrupter and child distress domain reports to address specific interaction challenges that a parent and child may be facing. Specifically, when scores in the domains of parent or caregiver interrupters and child distress fall within the caution or concern range, mental health consultation should be sought for guidance in intervention decision making and planning.

How Can the IPCI Be Used to Monitor and Guide Intervention?

IPCI results can be used by early intervention practitioners to make data-based decisions regarding intervention. The decision-making model, described in Chapter 2 and as applied to the IPCI, serves four purposes: 1) to monitor growth and/or change, 2) to signal the need for implementation of or modification of intervention to promote parent or caregiver responsiveness; 3) to evaluate growth and/or change in nurturing and responsive parenting or caregiving once a new intervention has been introduced or once the intervention is intensified or otherwise modified; and 4) to continue monitoring children's exposure to nurturing, responsive interactions over time (see Carta et al., 2002).

Caregiver–child interactions may veer off course for a variety of reasons, including individual child risks that present notable challenges for parenting and caregiving, such as behavioral and temperament issues associated with very low birth weight and medical or disability conditions. Parent and family experiences can also contribute to interactions in which children are exposed to low levels of nurturing and responsive strategies. For example, caregivers who did not experience nurturing and responsive strategies as children and who lack positive social relationships and support as adults may not have had opportunities to learn and use nurturing and responsive strategies with children. In addition, stressors associated with poverty, maternal depression or other serious health concerns, limited intellectual functioning, learning disabilities, and substance abuse can all contribute to caregiver–child interactions that are lacking nurturing and responsive strategies.

Data-based decision making can be especially important for very young children and their families. When early parent–child interactions veer off course, they are not likely to self-correct without intervention (Hofacker, & Papousek, 1998). Rather, when caregiver–child interactions fall outside the range of optimal levels, that is, when children, especially those who have a disability or who are at risk, ex-

IPCI

perience interactions with caregivers in which nurturing, responsive strategies are used significantly less often than with typically developing children, they have fewer opportunities to make social-emotional gains. Furthermore, discrepancies between these two groups of children's social emotional trajectories tend to widen with the disability or at-risk group falling farther behind (see Landry et al., 2001). Hence, the sooner that practitioners can identify interactions in which nurturing, responsive strategies are lacking, the sooner intervention can be provided to support more positive caregiver–child interaction, which then contribute to more positive child social-emotional trajectories over time. The IPCI provides data that can be used by multiple stakeholders, including early intervention practitioners, families, clinical supervisors and mental health consultants, program administrators, and policy leaders who are interested in seeing that children experience nurturing, responsive interactions with parents and other caregivers.

Early Intervention Practitioner   Early intervention practitioners, such as Part C early interventionists and Early Head Start family support staff can use the IPCI to identify when interactions are falling outside optimal limits. This is crucial for providing supportive intervention to caregivers before interactions become so problematic and entrenched that they require highly specialized interventions. Not only do specialized interventions tend to be more intrusive, but they are far more costly and less effective than preventive intervention. Finally, early intervention practitioners can also share IPCI videos and facilitator data with families to mutually set goals and celebrate successes in working toward those goals.

Clinical Supervisors and Mental Health Consultants   Clinical supervisors and mental health consultants can use IPCI data to engage in informed, reflective, supervisory processes with early intervention home visitors or center-based staff. By looking together at IPCI data, supervisors and consultants can provide support to staff delivering interventions to facilitate child social-emotional development through nurturing, responsive interactions with parents and caregivers. Such support may be provided in the form of encouragement and celebration when interventions are working; informed, supportive, and reflective discussions to facilitate decision making about possible intervention modifications or changes when interventions are not working; and data-based information to support referral and/or more specialized or intensive intervention when concerns are severe, protracted, or not improving in response to intervention.

Program Administrators   Program administrators can use IPCI data to summarize the level of program need for intervention to support nurturing, responsive parent–child interactions and thereby improve child social-emotional outcomes. Program administrators can also use IPCI data to summarize program gains, such as numbers of families and children who make gains in response to intervention, as well as the level of those gains.

Policy Leaders   Policy leaders can use IPCI data at the county, state, regional, or national level to describe how well children are doing in terms of their exposure to nurturing, responsive interactions with parents and other caregivers.

An Example of Multiple Stakeholders Using IPCI Data

Jesse, a program administrator for an Early Head Start (EHS) program serving diverse children and families was growing increasingly concerned about several issues. First, she was aware of the increasing demand to demonstrate program outcomes in response to accountability mandates for funding. She was, therefore, interested in being able to demonstrate that the program was making a difference with regard to the EHS performance standard to promote parent–child bonding and nurturing parent–child relationships. Second, she had recently learned about response to intervention (RTI) and understood this as a process for guiding intervention decision making to provide varying levels of intervention to children based on individual needs. Jesse viewed this approach as being particularly important because although general supportive involvement with the parents of all children was a crucial program objective, the program needed an efficient way of identifying children whose interactions with parents and other caregivers required more intensive support. To implement such an approach, she needed to identify an assessment tool that could be administered quickly and be repeated over time to monitor interactions with parents for all children. Moreover, she needed to find a reliable and valid means of identifying children whose interactions with parents were in need of higher levels of support than could be provided to all children in the program. Finally, she was well aware of the existing burden on early intervention staff of conducting multiple, time-consuming assessment measures. Consequently, it was important to Jesse that the addition of any outcome measure would serve multiple purposes and, in particular, would be useful for guiding and informing decision making about intervention. This led her to become interested in the IPCI as a progress-monitoring tool that could be used to address her concerns. She presented the IPCI to other administrative and early intervention staff, as well as to the policy council, and with their collective interest, they decided to begin implementing the IPCI programwide to monitor progress of all children's exposure to nurturing, responsive strategies in interactions with their parents.

Jodi, a home visitor, began administering the IPCI once every 3 months with each child on her caseload to monitor parent–child interaction. For some children, Jodi found that parent–child interaction domain scores were within typical limits. Jodi was encouraged by this and continued to monitor on a quarterly basis so that she could identify possible risky interactions. For another group of children, Jodi noticed that domain scores for either caregiver facilitators or caregiver interrupters were falling just outside typical limits. In these cases, Jodi decided to increase quarterly monitoring to monthly monitoring so that in conjunction with other assessment data she could get a picture of whether the atypical scores were a consistent pattern or simply reflecting an off day.

In the course of monitoring, Jodi became particularly concerned about parent–child interaction for one child, Shawna, and her mother. Consistent with other assessment data indicating concerns, IPCI results showed that during the first quarter of entering the EHS program, Shawna's results were significantly below the expected level for child engagement (see Figure 8.3). In addition, parent facilitators were significantly below the expected level, and interrupters were significantly above the expected level. Next, Jodi looked at the key elements of parent facilitators and interrupters so that she could identify relative strengths and concerns for Shawna and her mother. Jodi sought out reflective supervision with an infant mental health specialist at her agency to look at the data with her and to begin developing an intervention plan to support more positive interactions between Shawna and her mother. In addition to working with Jodi to develop an intervention plan, her supervisor was able to engage in an informed, reflective process with Jodi to celebrate intervention successes as well as to support Jodi in her efforts to modify intervention when data showed that a particular strategy was not working. With continued IPCI monitoring, Jodi and her supervisor were able to see whether modifications were actually working. The IPCI video and reports provided Jodi's supervisor with immediate data that could be used to support Jodi in her efforts with families.

Although the IPCI does not require video recording for scoring purposes, Jodi did video record IPCI assessments so that she could then use them as an intervention tool. Jodi began by sharing the video with Shawna's mother to point out strengths that were identified by the key elements graphs. This gave Jodi an opportunity not only to point out a relative strength (e.g., acceptance and warmth), but also to illustrate to Shawna's mother what she had been doing to help Shawna engage during the video and how that form of engagement is related to the important child outcome of Shawna's readiness for school.

Jodi and Shawna's mother worked out a plan whereby Shawna's mother would continue to practice the newly identified behavior between home visits. Jodi continued to conduct monthly IPCI assessments and to video record them so that she and Shawna's mother could look at them along with data reports to see target behaviors grow over time. As Shawna's mother's confidence began to grow, Jodi began to target key elements that were significantly below the expected level (e.g., following child's lead, using descriptive language). Jodi and Shawna's mother continued to look together at key element graphs and video examples of parent and child behavior during visits. In this way, Jodi was able to use IPCI reports to encourage Shawna's mother to try out specific new skills, celebrate with Shawna's mother as her nurturing and responsiveness strategies grew, or consult with the mental health specialist to modify the intervention for Shawna and her mother.

Conclusion

Programs need to know when parents and other primary caregivers are making progress in interactions that foster the social-emotional growth of their very young children. It is essential for programs to recognize and support parents and primary caregivers in their responsive roles with their children. Programs also need to know when to provide additional supports to help parents and primary caregivers respond in ways that foster positive social-emotional behaviors in their children. Checking growth in the nurturing, responsive interactions with parents and other primary caregivers is vital to understanding if and how parents and children are benefitting from early intervention aimed at promoting child social-emotional competencies through responsive interactions.

Administration Protocol for the Indicator of Parent-Child Interaction

 Materials

Digital timer

Included activities

- For children younger than 1 year (see Figure 8.2)
  Free play
  Looking at books
  A routine dressing task

- Children 1 year old and older
  Include the three activities above, plus a distraction task

Materials required
- Two board books (book activity)
- A 5 × 7-foot blanket
- A nonactivated recorder that plays prerecorded musical tunes every 7 seconds (distraction task)
- Free play and dressing task do not require materials

 Administration options

Two people
- Parent or caregiver included in assessment
- Certified assessor**

**This option would be video recorded for later coding.

 Forms

IPCI rating sheet (see Figure 8.3)

 Set-up

Comfortable area

All toys or games available before the assessment begins

 Time

10-minute observation period that includes a series of brief interaction episodes (all individually timed) in a home situation between a child and parent or in a center-based program between a child and a familiar caregiver

 Conducting the session

Prior to the first observation, provide the parents (or caregivers) with information about the purpose of the observation, types of activities that will be observed, and how to prepare for the assessment.

Discuss with parents (or caregivers) how to avoid and handle interruptions and answer any questions they may have.

See detailed instructions for step-by-step guidelines for carrying out each of the four activities.

**See Chapter 3 for more detailed information.

IPCI

Web-Based Support for Decision Making Using IGDIs

Jay Buzhardt and Dale Walker

Successful use of IGDIs programwide for purposes of quarterly screening and accountability represents a major investment in resources, professional development, and technical assistance (Walker, Greenwood, et al., 2008). The web-based IGDI system (see the Appendix) provides an important infrastructure that includes access to information, forms, procedures, training and certification, and data services needed to support large-scale adoption of early childhood progress monitoring. The additional step of implementing a response to intervention (RTI) approach to services, for example, by using multiple systems of support (e.g., 3 tiers) presents an even larger challenge.

For this RTI component, early childhood program staffs need a far greater level of training and support in RTI concepts and components, such as progress monitoring, decision making, and use of tier 2 and 3 interventions. Findings from a recent national survey of state-level preschool leaders concerning early childhood RTI indicated that their number one challenge was the need for more staff trained in the use of RTI components (Linas, Carta, & Greenwood, 2009). Other challenges in order of importance included the lack of resources to build an infrastructure, lack of knowledge about building an RTI model, lack of tier 2 and 3 interventions, and lack of progress monitoring measures.

In the absence of systematic supports for progress monitoring and RTI, Walker, Greenwood, and their colleagues (2008, July) reported relatively little implementation of tier 2 and tier 3 interventions that included increased progress monitoring. Their findings suggested that even in the context of systematic quarterly screening and professional development devoted to progress monitoring and decision making, large-scale implementation of this component was not achieved under conditions of low support. Consequently, without significant support for RTI components programwide, such as effective practices, implementation procedures, and access to needed information, implementation of data-based decision making will be effortful and haphazard in many instances, particularly for service providers with limited experience.

Data-based decision making in RTI involves individualizing the intensity of intervention strategies based on children's responses to the present intervention. Systematic monitoring of child growth using IGDIs informs the decision-making process, ensuring a timely identification of ineffective interventions and their replacement given lack of progress and continuance of effective interventions (described in Chapter 2).

One reasonable solution to overcome these challenges is the use of a web-based system that includes tools linked to the relevant progress monitoring data. For example, practitioner decision-making support tools are used in medical care and K–12 education. Reports indicate practitioners make faster and more effective decisions when they can readily access individual client information, and treatment decision-making support is easily integrated into existing workflow patterns (Fuchs & Fuchs, 1998; Garg et al., 2005).

The Making Online Decisions (MOD) tool (www.igdi.ku.edu) is an experimental, web-based support tool designed to integrate important RTI components with the Early Communication Indicator (ECI) progress monitoring to provide a standard guide for early childhood staff members working with individual children through an RTI process. (Future plans include developing MOD resources for the other IGDIs as well.) The MOD provides a child-based approach to individual decision making and RTI implementation. Current findings suggest that the MOD is a useful and effective tool for improving early childhood service providers' implementation of RTI components (e.g., more frequent progress monitoring, and intervention implementation) (Buzhardt et al., 2009). It can be used by staff in early childhood programs (e.g., Early Head Start [EHS], Part C providers, private child care centers) wherein IGDI data are collected systematically and managed within the web site's data services. In these programs, universal screening occurs quarterly to identify children that may not be making expected rates of progress. The experimental MOD guides staff members through a standard RTI process. This chapter describes the experimental MOD and its component features, including a case example of the MOD's use by a home visitor in an EHS program. The chapter concludes with a discussion of future directions and implications for research and practice.

Data-Based Decision-Making Support for Infant and Toddler IGDIs

The Infant and Toddler IGDI web site represents a step in the right direction for early childhood by providing service providers access to progress monitoring measures, benchmarks for child performance, training resources, administration forms and protocols, and individual child and group progress reports and graphs. Integrated into the web site, the MOD provides the decision rules and a user interface

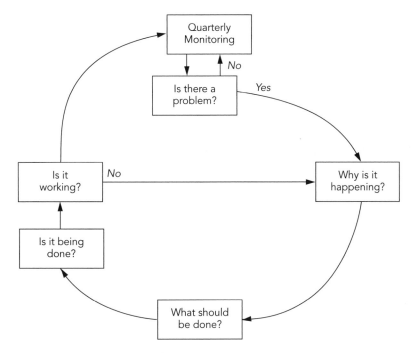

Figure 9.1. The decision-making framework for the Making Online Decisions (MOD) system tool for Infant and Toddler IGDIs. (© Juniper Gardens Children's Project; reprinted by permission.)

through which service providers work through the steps of the decision-making model for each child.

Consistent with the decision-making model discussed in Chapter 2, Tilly's (2002) model (see Figure 9.1) was selected as the practical basis for developing a web-based user interface to support data-based decision making on the IGDI web site. This interface is designed to guide an individual service provider's progress through an RTI process with an individual child, including use of a tier 2 intervention for early communication (Walker, Carta, Greenwood, & Buzhardt, 2008). As shown in Figure 9.1, the model is iterative in that procedures are repeated and decisions refined as often as needed in order to solve the initiating problem of child performance that is below benchmark. Supported by data collected from quarterly ECI screenings, the key decision-making steps are as follows:

1. Is there a problem? Are we confident that the child's performance is below benchmark?

2. Why is it happening? What might be causing low performance?

3. What should be done? What can we do that will most likely solve the problem?

4. Is it being done? Is the intervention being implemented with fidelity?

5. Is it working? Do we see acceleration in the rate of growth since starting the intervention identified in Step 3?

6. What do we do if it is not working? We cycle back to exploring new solutions, implementing a different intervention, or modifying the existing one.

Because the MOD management tools and reports are integrated into the larger IGDI data system, assessors as well as program coordinators and directors are able to monitor caregivers' progress in the MOD, including completed steps, upcoming tasks, and prompts and/or reminders to complete needed tasks.

What Decisions Does the Making Online Decisions Tool Support?

Is There a Problem?

Because of the universal ECI screening context in place, the MOD is designed to begin by alerting the responsible staff member that there may be a problem in that a particular child has just scored below age benchmark on his or her last ECI. At this point, the process begins by validating that the assessment is an accurate reflection of the child's language proficiency. The MOD seeks to determine the level of the service provider's confidence that the child's performance is truly below benchmark. Unfortunately, RTI researchers have yet to agree on one specific means of making this determination for an individual child. For example, the most prominent means recommended in the literature include use of 1) benchmarks, 2) benchmarks plus growth, 3) growth alone, and 4) educator judgment (Fuchs, Fuchs, & Compton, 2004). The IGDI research team at Juniper Gardens Children's Project has experimented with several approaches, including a low level of performance, the slope (a low rate of growth), and a combination of the two, among others. Currently, the MOD alerts service providers that there may be a problem immediately following the first score that falls more than −1 standard deviation (*SD*) below the benchmark mean on the total communication score. This is a bit liberal perhaps, but it leads to additional measurement and a means of monitoring a child who is low performing, at risk, and in need of tier 2 intervention.

Immediately after an ECI is entered into the IGDI data system that meets this criterion, the MOD alerts the service provider, showing the child's progress monitoring graph. The MOD asks the provider to confirm that the assessment was valid and that mitigating factors during assessment did not negatively influence the child's performance (e.g., illness, visitors present in the home, sibling interference). Confidence in a low score's accuracy also may be lessened if the child recently transitioned to a new child care center or if other novel sources may be mitigating factors, such as the ECI being administered in an unfamiliar setting by an unfamiliar assessor. In novel conditions, we have reason to question the accuracy of an ECI score. If the service provider indicates that the assessment may not be valid, the MOD will recommend doing another assessment within 2 weeks as a way to confirm the child's low score. If the low score is validated, the MOD recommends that the child move from receiving quarterly ECI assessments to monthly assessments. Because a problem of low performance has now been identified and an intervention is likely to begin for the child, more frequent assessment will help monitor the child's language proficiency more closely and his or her RTI.

Why Is the Problem Happening?

After the service provider confirms that the low ECI score is an accurate measure of the child's language, the MOD asks him/her to consider the likely causes of the low performance by answering questions about the child's health and current environment. Similar to the pediatrician described in Chapter 2, service providers also seek to consider as well as rule out the most likely explanations. Factors considered include current family circumstances, child's health (e.g., hearing impairment, ongoing illness), level of environmental risk and disability, and quality of the home language environment, among others. Information may be gathered from the caregiver and possibly other service providers to help identify potential causes of the problem. To further enlighten at this stage, the service provider may conduct additional assessment and/or evaluation or refer the child for assessments to obtain additional information.

If review of this information indicates that the child's low ECI performance is likely caused by a temporary condition, such as disruption in the primary language environment (e.g., ear infection, change in child care or living situation), then the MOD recommends continuing monthly monitoring to "wait and see" if improvement is made. If there are no clear causes or the service provider indicates that the cause is unknown, the MOD moves immediately to the "What should be done" stage.

What Should Be Done?

Given a better understanding of the likely causes, exploring solutions begins in earnest at this step, leading to an intervention with a likelihood of addressing the problem and accelerating the child's future progress. As in RTI, this step helps identify an appropriate evidence-based intervention where possible; one that fits the child's needs and is acceptable to caregivers and other service providers.

In cases where the problem may be linked to a caregiving environment that is not responsive or stimulating, a reasonable solution is to strengthen the home and/or child care language environment to accelerate growth in communication skill. The MOD recommends strategies for use by primary caregivers in the home or by child care providers in the child care setting. Two evidence-based, caregiver-delivered language intervention strategies are available in the MOD. These are the *Kansas Early Head Start's Language Intervention Toolkit* (Crowe, 2002) and *Strategies for Promoting Communication and Language of Infants and Toddlers* (Walker, Bigelow, Harjusola-Webb, Small, & Kirk, 2004). These strategies were developed specifically for implementation by a child's primary caregiver(s) in the child's natural environment to promote parent–child communication during daily routines. The strategies can be downloaded in their entirety as manuals or the MOD will recommend the most relevant strategies based on the child's performance. Using these MOD recommended interventions is optional; any other language intervention can be used and incorporated as either a replacement or in combination with the MOD recommendations. All intervention strategies are implemented under the leadership and direction of the practitioner and involve training the parent or other caregivers to use the strategies.

The MOD recommends sections of the two intervention strategies that are best linked to the child's communication proficiency. These strategies support communication described as 1) preverbal, 2) first words, 3) early verbal, and 4) expanding verbal. The MOD uses these patterns of performance based on a child's actual use of gestures, vocalizations, and single and multiple word skills to point to the most relevant sections of the two intervention strategies. These sections can be printed and used as the basis for teaching parents and structuring the home language environment to achieve the intended effect. As the child shows growth in communication proficiency over time, the MOD adapts its recommendations to be taught and used by parents or other caregivers.

Is It Being Done?

Is the intervention being implemented with fidelity? To support this component of RTI, the MOD provides a means for tracking the fidelity of implementation of the selected strategies. This support is in the form of an intervention fidelity checklist completed at least monthly. Among a number of indicators of implementation, one of great importance is the caregiver's reported frequency of use of the language strategies. Figure 9.2 shows the initial fidelity checklist completed by service providers. It is followed by the fidelity follow-up checklist (see Figure 9.3) completed on subsequent home visits to assess the degree to which the caregivers implement the strategies. Figure 9.4 shows the Language Strategies Checklist, which is a report of how much the caregivers used the language strategies each week. These checklists are available in English and Spanish. Information obtained from these forms helps document that the interventions are being carried out or guide the user to the next steps in addressing potential issues of nonimplementation. For example, a parent may find that he or she does not have the time available to implement the strategies. This problem needs to be overcome if the intervention is expected to have the desired benefit. All service provider fidelity checklists and weekly caregiver intervention implementation checklists are available online at http://www.igdi.ku.edu/measures/observation_forms.htm

Is It Working?

Do we see acceleration in the monthly rate of growth as a result of intervention? With the intervention and monthly progress monitoring ongoing, child data continue to inform the MOD's decision making regarding intervention delivery and its success and/or lack thereof. When three ECI observations have been completed following the intervention implementation, the MOD reports the effects on child performance. As described later in this chapter in the MOD example of Chase, the MOD considers the child's performance on the ECI in terms of the most recent score, the

<u>   </u>   <u>   </u>   <u>   </u>

    (Your Name)   (Date)   (Child Name or ID#)

Home Visitor's First Fidelity Checklist

After the ECI indicates a need for more frequent monitoring, and you have selected specific intervention strategy(s), please discuss the strategies with the caregiver(s) on the next home visit. Complete the checklist below, marking either **Yes** or **No** for each step to indicate whether or not it has been done.

<u>**Please only use this checklist the first time you go over the intervention materials. On subsequent visits, use the Home Visitor's Fidelity Follow-Up Checklist.**</u>

What strategy(s) and/or routines did you select to give to the caregiver (you can refer to the MOD for the information)? _____

Home Visitor's Implementation Support Steps	Y	N
1. Was the person with whom you reviewed the strategies the child's primary caregiver? (Select 'No' if unknown) a. Write the number hours a week this person estimates spending with the child, or mark an "x" by "Unknown." _____ Hours _____ Unknown		
2. I explained the concern to the parent/caregiver and showed them the ECI graph.		
3. I talked to them about how they can help by using the strategy across their daily routines.		
4. I helped them pick one (1) or two (2) routines in which they could do the strategies.		
5. I gave them the materials related to the strategies.		
6. I modeled/demonstrated how the parent/guardian should use the strategy.		
7. I role-played the strategies together with the parent/caregiver.		
8. I observed the parent/caregiver perform the strategy(s).		
9. I showed them where to record their usage of the strategy(s) on the routines sheet (attached to this checklist).		
10. I asked the parent/guardian how they plan on using the strategy across the routines.		
11. I suggested that they keep the routines sheet and intervention handout in a place they will see it every day.		
12. I asked if they had any questions.		
General Comments/Notes:		
	/12	/12

Figure 9.2. Home Visitor's First Fidelity Checklist. This is used for service providers to indicate steps taken to ensure that the caregiver is prepared to implement the recommended language strategies. (© Juniper Gardens Children's Project; reprinted by permission.)

child's trend before and after intervention, and the child's expected performance in 6 months based on current score and current trend.

Based on these results, the MOD will recommend 1) keeping the current intervention in place, 2) modifying the current intervention, or 3) in the case of improved and sustained progress, determining whether intervention should be removed or decreased in intensity. Based on these data, the intervention strategies and MOD recommendations are continuously updated according to the child's ECI performance. New strategies and checklists can be generated at the web site for caregivers at any time.

| _____ | _____ | _____ |
| (Your Name) | (Date) | (Child Name or ID#) |

Home Visitor's Fidelity Follow-up Checklist

After the ECI assessment indicates a need for more frequent monitoring, and you have selected a specific intervention strategy, please check either Yes or No for each step below to indicate whether or not it has been done.

Please only use this checklist after your initial home visit in which you reviewed the intervention material with the parent. On your initial visit, use the Home Visitor's First Fidelity Implementation Checklist.

What strategy(s) and/or routines did you select to give to the caregiver (you can refer to the MOD for information)? _____

Home Visitor's Follow-up Support Steps	Y	N
1. Was the person with whom you reviewed the strategies the child's primary caregiver? (Select 'No' if unknown) a. Write the number hours a week this person estimates spending with the child, or mark an "x" by "Unknown." _____ Hours _____ Unknown		
2. I asked the parent/guardian if they were able to do the strategy(s) after my last home visit.		
3. I asked the parent/guardian if they were comfortable doing the strategy(s) and asked if they noticed any improvement.		
4. I talked to the parent/guardian about how they could continue doing the strategy(s) across some additional routines.		
5. I talked to the parent/guardian about how much they have been using the strategy(s). **Please indicate how much they are using the strategy(s) by completing one or both of the sentences below. If they have been tracking their frequency of using the strategies, refer to the tracking form.** • I asked them how often they used the strategy(s), and they said (circle one): Often Sometimes Rarely Never • I saw them use _____ strategy(s) across _____ routine(s) while I was there.		
6. I left the parent/guardian with a new intervention handout(s) and pointed out where they could record how often and when they used any of the strategies (attached to this checklist).		
General Comments/Notes:		
	/6	/6

Figure 9.3. Home Visitor's Fidelity Follow-Up Checklist to indicate to what degree the caregiver is continuing to implement the recommended strategies. (© Juniper Gardens Children's Project; reprinted by permission.)

Following is an example of how a home visitor used the MOD to inform her implementation of home-based language intervention strategies and make decisions based on the data she entered into the MOD and how it used those data to inform intervention recommendations.

MOD Case Example

Is There a Problem?

Yvonne provided weekly in-home early childhood services for 18-month-old Chase and his family. Because of an IFSP, Chase received Part C services. Prior to a February 13

Language Strategies Checklists

This checklist is provided as a way for caregivers to track how often they are using recommended language strategies. Using this information can help you and your home visitor identify strategies that you are not using very often, and either find alternative strategies or identify other routines in which to use them.

Caregiver: Circle your best estimate of how often you used the strategies for each day.

Week of _____

Day	How Often You Used the Strategies			
Monday	Often	Sometimes	Rarely	Not Today
Tuesday	Often	Sometimes	Rarely	Not Today
Wednesday	Often	Sometimes	Rarely	Not Today
Thursday	Often	Sometimes	Rarely	Not Today
Friday	Often	Sometimes	Rarely	Not Today
Saturday	Often	Sometimes	Rarely	Not Today
Sunday	Often	Sometimes	Rarely	Not Today

Comments:

Child Name: _____

Caregiver Name: _____

Home Visitor Name: _____

Rev. 4.09.2008
©2008, Juniper Gardens Children's Project

Figure 9.4. Language Strategies Checklist that is completed by the caregiver to indicate how much the strategies are being implemented each week. (© Juniper Gardens Children's Project; reprinted by permission.)

home visit in which she planned to administer a quarterly ECI, she reviewed Chase's ECI progress monitoring graph to see how he scored on his last assessment. Figure 9.5 shows that although he was not yet performing 1 *SD* below benchmark on his 15-month assessment, his trend or rate of growth in communication that was not increasing indicated that he was fast approaching the benchmark indicating performance significantly (1 *SD*) below the mean. His record of progress was lower than what would have led the practitioner to conclude that he would meet or exceed in the future. Slope is a trend statistic similar to an average, so if the slope is 0 or close to zero, the trend over time is flat. If the slope is a negative value, the trend is down, and if it is positive, the trend is up and accelerating.

Yvonne recognized this by comparing his slope, indicated by the child slope of 0.13 in the legend, with the norm slope of 0.64. (For more information about ECI scoring, see Chapter 3, and refer to the Appendix for details about the reports and graphs generated by the data system.) She also referred to his performance on the key skill elements, which showed that his single words were slightly low, which, according to the single word norms, should have started showing steep growth by 18 months. Therefore, Yvonne kept this in mind throughout her home visit and during the ECI assessment.

After the home visit, Yvonne returned to her office and coded a video recording of Chase's ECI and entered his scores into the online data system. After she submitted his scores online, the MOD reported that Chase had fallen more than 1.5 *SD* below bench-

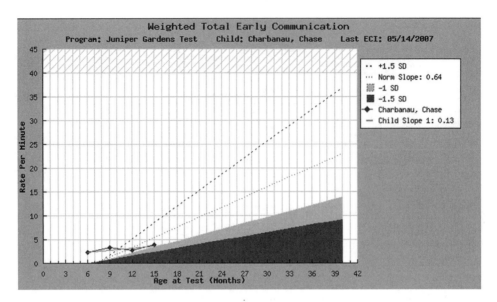

Figure 9.5. Chase's Weighted Total Communication progress monitoring graph reviewed by his home visitor before his 18-month quarterly ECI assessment. (© Juniper Gardens Children's Project; reprinted by permission.)

mark for this assessment. First the MOD wanted Yvonne to confirm that the assessment was valid. In other words, she considered whether there were unusual circumstances surrounding the administration that might have influenced Chase's performance during the 6-minute ECI assessment (e.g., was he physically or emotionally distressed; were there distractions from siblings, TV, radio, or other unusual circumstances?). She indicated that it was a valid assessment. If she had indicated that it was not valid, the MOD would have recommended that she conduct another ECI within the next 2 weeks to verify this score.

Why Is It Happening?

Because it was a valid ECI, the MOD then asked Yvonne why she thought Chase's communication was lower than would have been expected at this age, with the goal of identifying causes that may preclude the need for caregiver-delivered language intervention strategies. For example, it is important to eliminate possible causes, such as frequent ear infections that might cause hearing loss or recent disruptions in the family, school, or child care settings that might resolve themselves over time. If she had indicated that one of these factors or something else may be affecting Chase's language, the MOD would have recommended that Chase move from quarterly to monthly progress monitoring. This would provide more frequent monitoring of Chase's language, which would allow Yvonne to identify gains that resulted from medical interventions or a stabilization of the home or child care environment. Yvonne would also share this information with the primary caregiver to begin a dialogue about ways to address the challenges that may be influencing Chase's language development (e.g., notify his pediatrician that his continuing ear infections may be affecting his language and that ear tubes should be explored, discussing his language with child care providers and teachers to identify potential accommodations).

What Should Be Done ?

Yvonne indicated that the cause of Chase's depressed growth rate was unknown; therefore, the MOD recommended a set of home-based language intervention strategies individualized for Chase's proficiency on each ECI key skill element. As described earlier, these strategies are designed to be implemented by caregivers during daily routines. Yvonne reviewed the MOD recommendations as shown in Figure 9.6, and selected the most appropriate strategies and routines based on her knowledge of Chase's family and their current circumstances. However, Yvonne was unsure about their willingness to integrate some of the strategies into their daily routines, so she selected and printed them all so she could review them with his caregivers and let them choose which strategies and routines they would like to use.

Is It Being Done?

At the next weekly home visit, Yvonne took copies of the strategy descriptions, the first fidelity checklist (see Figure 9.2), and a caregiver language strategies checklist (see Fig-

---

In the *Language Intervention Tool Kit* (Linda K. Crowe, © 2002), these strategies are identified as *Preverbal* and are described on pages 13 – 21 of the *Tool Kit*. Specific strategies and activities for children who are using mostly gestures and vocalizations are suggested on the pages listed below for the following routines. Please select one or more of the routines below that you think Morgan Buzhardt's caregiver would be most likely to use:

☑ Feeding (pp. 13 - 14)
☐ Diapering (pp. 13, 15)
☑ Bathing (pp. 13, 16, & 19)
☐ Reading (pp. 13, 20)
☑ Drawing/Writing (pp. 13, 21)

☐ Feeding - Spanish (pp. 13 - 14)
☐ Diapering - Spanish (pp. 13, 15)
☐ Bathing - Spanish (pp. 13, 16, & 19)
☐ Reading - Spanish (pp. 13, 20)
☐ Drawing/Writing - Spanish (pp. 13, 21)

In the *Promoting Communication Manual* (Juniper Gardens Children's Project, © 2003-2004), suggestions are given for using strategies with children communicating mostly through gestures and vocalizations. Examples of the strategies and their use across routines and activities are provided in sections arranged by child communication level. When using this information, it may be most helpful to begin by picking a strategy or two, and then gradually adding more strategies across routines as they become easier to use. Please select one or more of the strategies below that you think Morgan Buzhardt's caregiver would be most likely to use:

☐ Following Child's Lead (pp. 14, 15)
☑ Commenting and Labeling (pp. 19, 20)
☐ Imitating and Expanding (pp. 24, 25)
☑ Providing Positive Attention (pp. 39, 40)

☐ Following Child's Lead - Spanish (pp. 14, 15)
☐ Commenting and Labeling - Spanish (pp. 19, 20)
☐ Imitating and Expanding - Spanish (pp. 24, 25)
☐ Providing Positive Attention - Spanish (pp. 39, 40)

Before your next home visit, please print these selected strategies and review them with Morgan Buzhardt's caregiver. Along with your chosen strategies, there will be a brief checklist for you to complete and enter into the MOD the next time you enter ECI data for Morgan Buzhardt.

| Previous | 1 2 **3** | View & Print All Selected Strategies | View & Print Later |

Figure 9.6. A portion of the MOD intervention recommendations that shows the strategies recommended for Chase from the *Promoting Communications Manual* (Juniper Gardens Children's Project © 2003–2004; reprinted by permission) and suggestions for incorporating strategies into daily routines from the *Language Intervention Tool Kit* (Linda K. Crowe © 2002; reprinted by permission). Clicking the "View and Print All Selected Strategies" generates a comprehensive description of each strategy, including suggestions and examples for incorporating them into daily routines.

ure 9.4) with her. The fidelity checklist can be used by service providers to guide them through the steps of explaining and demonstrating the recommendations to the caregivers, providing the caregivers with a copy of the strategy descriptions and examples, and ensuring that the caregivers keep a record of the frequency with which they use the strategies. The caregiver language strategies checklist is a simple form that the caregiver can use to indicate how frequently (i.e., often, sometimes, rarely, not today) they used the strategies each day of the week. When placed in a common area of the home (e.g., on the refrigerator), many caregivers have reported that the checklist also serves as an effective prompt to use the strategies. After reviewing the strategies and ways to use them during daily routines, the caregivers choose two strategies to begin with and three daily routines in which to use them. After the home visit, Yvonne entered the checklist items that she completed on that home visit into the MOD.

On subsequent home visits, Yvonne completed the fidelity follow-up checklist (Figure 9.3) and brought a new weekly caregiver checklist. During the follow-ups, she discussed the strategies with the caregivers, problem solved any implementation issues, and chose additional strategies and/or expanded on existing strategies that seemed to be working particularly well. Information from the follow-up checklists was also entered into the MOD, allowing Yvonne and/or her case supervisor to review at anytime the historical record of Yvonne's work with Chase's family on using language intervention strategies. This can be particularly useful to verify the intensity and duration of intervention implementation, and, because the checklists are generic, they can be used in conjunction with any caregiver-implemented intervention.

Is It Working?

Yvonne continued to administer monthly ECIs and work with the family to add new strategies, build on existing strategies, and help integrate the strategies into their daily routines. After two more monthly ECI assessments (a total of three since beginning the intervention), the MOD reported on Chase's language growth since the intervention began by considering the following three factors:

1. Is the latest ECI greater than –1 SD below benchmark rate of total communication?

2. Is the ECI's slope higher than it was before intervention?

3. Based on the slope and latest ECI, is Chase's ECI performance projected to be above benchmark 6 months from now?

In Chase's case, the MOD reported (see Figure 9.7) that his language was making progress in terms of growth (slope is higher than pre-intervention), but that he was still greater than –1 SD below benchmark and his projected progress did not have him out of this range in 6 months. Therefore, the MOD recommended that they continue monthly monitoring and using the intervention strategies. Yvonne shared the MOD report with Chase's caregivers, which served as a powerful immediate reinforcer of their intervention efforts. The report also reminded Yvonne to continue checking the recommended strategies because as Chase's performance on the key skill elements grew, the recommended strategies would change. For example, at that time he was receiving strategies that focused on improving his rate of single-word utterances. However, even if he began producing more single words, he would remain below benchmark if his rate of multiple-word utterances did not grow in later months. Therefore, the MOD would adapt to this need and begin recommending strategies that targeted multiple-word utterances.

Is it working? | View MOD details for this child |

As you can see by the graph, Chase Charbanau's language is showing improvement!

However, because the slope suggests that Chase Charbanau will not likely be out of the 'slightly below benchmark' area in at least six months, we recommend that the caregivers continue using the recommended strategies, you continue entering the follow-up checklist data, and continue conducting monthly ECI observations with Chase Charbanau.

As Chase Charbanau's language continues to improve, we will continue to recommend new strategies that will help to improve this progress. We recommend that you print these strategies and give them to the family or use them along with your regular home visiting program.

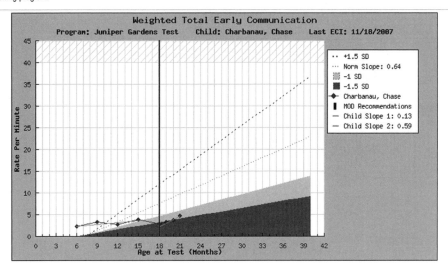

Figure 9.7. MOD report of Chase's progress since beginning the intervention. (© Juniper Gardens Children's Project; reprinted by permission.)

If all three of the progress factors were satisfied, then the MOD would recommend that the caregivers continue using the strategies and discontinue completing the checklists, which would mean that Chase could return to quarterly monitoring. However, the home visitor and caregiver can continue with any or all of the steps if they believe this is warranted based on other information (e.g., other assessments, caregiver concern). If Chase's ECI falls at least one standard deviation below benchmark, the MOD decision-making process will start again from the first step; however, information about his previous MOD steps would be available to the home visitor. For example, using the "MOD details" menu shown in Figure 9.8, at any point during or after the MOD process, Yvonne can view Chase's MOD progress, including his most recent weighted total communication graph, his current MOD step, the date each step was completed, and the number of fidelity follow-up checklists completed. Yvonne also used this menu to enter additional follow-up checklist data from her weekly home visits.

Conclusion

Web-based decision-making support can be implemented to support a practitioner's work through an RTI process for individual children. The MOD represents a major step forward for early childhood service providers to integrate progress monitoring and RTI approaches into their services for parents and caregivers. The MOD brings

Step	Complete?	Completed on
Step 1 - Is there a problem?	Yes	02/16/2009
Step 2 - Why is it happening?	Yes	02/16/2009
Step 3 - What should be done?	Yes	02/16/2009
Step 4 - Is it being done?		
Step 4 - Home Visitor's First Fidelity Checklist View/Print First Checklist (for observation done on 08/15/2007)	Yes	02/16/2009
Step 4 - Home Visitor's Fidelity Follow-up Checklist View/Print Follow-up (for observation done on 08/15/2007)	Yes	02/16/2009
Step 4 - Home Visitor's Fidelity Follow-up Checklist View/Print Follow-up (for observation done on 08/15/2007)	Yes	02/16/2009
Step 4 - Home Visitor's Fidelity Follow-up Checklist View/Print Follow-up (for observation done on 09/16/2007)	Yes	02/16/2009
Step 4 - Home Visitor's Fidelity Follow-up Checklist View/Print Follow-up (for observation done on 10/17/2007)	Yes	02/16/2009
Step 4 - Home Visitor's Fidelity Follow-up Checklist View/Print Follow-up (for observation done on 11/18/2007)	Yes	02/16/2009

Add new follow-up checklist for observation done on: -Select- ▾   Add checklist

Step 5 - Is it working?

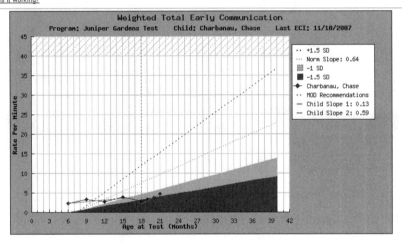

Figure 9.8. Summary of Chase's progress through the MOD with links to details about each step. (© Juniper Gardens Children's Project; reprinted by permission.)

together progress monitoring with decision making in step-by-step procedures for intervening, including two evidence-based language promotion strategies linked to child performance. It also enables monitoring of RTI work by program coordinators and directors.

A functioning prototype of the MOD is currently available to individuals with an account on the IGDI online data system (www.igdi.ku.edu), which can be created by contacting the authors. A randomized trial of the MOD's effectiveness in improving the use and quality of data-based decision making practices of early childhood service providers is in progress. It is important to realize that the MOD uses the same procedures, follows the same steps, and uses the same data in its decision process as would be used by a knowledgeable and skilled RTI practitioner. The potential value of a tool such as the MOD is its support of relatively untrained staff who through using it learn the knowledge and skill needed to conduct data-based decision making without technology support should they choose to do so. As such, the MOD appears to overcome a number of challenges to RTI implementation.

The MOD is still in its infancy, and there is much to learn about the many ways early childhood service providers can integrate it into their programs. As programs from other states and with varying service delivery models begin to use tools such as the MOD, additional features will be added and existing functions will be revised to optimize its use in a variety of settings.

There are some potential additional features that could make the system more usable and accessible for early childhood decision making. One of the most obvious extensions of the MOD will be to make it available for use with the other IGDIs in addition to the ECI. Developing the MOD for use with these measures will require consideration of the relevant questions service providers should consider when deciding whether or not a child needs an intervention and the types of interventions, if any, to make available in the MOD for these outcome areas. Indeed, each of these measures has a unique set of circumstances to consider when adapting the MOD for their use. For example, the Early Social Indicator (ESI) requires identification of a same-age peer to engage with the child and adult play partner during the session. So, when determining the validity of a low ESI score (i.e., Is there a problem?), the service provider will need to consider the appropriateness of the peer and whether or not a different peer would evoke social engagement from the target child that is more reflective of his or her typical interactions. For the Early Movement Indicator (EMI), the assessor would need to consider whether or not the child had a recent physical injury that might temporarily affect his or her ability to demonstrate motor skills that are reflective of his or her true ability.

Currently, infant and toddler progress on IGDIs is reflected in monthly increments, even though they can be administered more frequently (e.g., weekly). Early work with infant and toddler programs suggested that monthly monitoring would be the optimal frequency for progress monitoring within their service delivery models. Nonetheless, some early childhood programs request the ability to display weekly progress monitoring graphs, and it is expected that as progress monitoring and data-based decision making become more widespread in early childhood, the need for this level of progress monitoring will also increase. In addition, advancements in web technology make it more feasible to allow users to customize graphic displays of dynamic data.

Additional technology supports for practitioners using IGDIs, the MOD, and similar approaches are envisioned. These include PDA devices capable of IGDI data entry, communication with the IGDI web site, and point-of-care decision making. Providing the opportunity for service providers to collect data, complete checklists, and receive intervention recommendations on wireless portable devices would streamline the decision-making process, further reducing the delay between the identification of a problem and intervention implementation.

Informed by psychometrically sound measures of child growth toward socially valid general outcomes, the MOD informs service providers' intervention services for caregivers to identify when and how intervention strategies should be implemented for children performing below expected benchmarks, assesses fidelity of intervention implementation, and reports on the child's RTI. In an era when time and resources are limited and time intensive data-based decision making is frequently recognized as a recommended practice for early childhood service delivery, the MOD represents a bold step toward providing the support necessary for early childhood service providers to implement immediate, individualized intervention strategies for young children performing below their peers on important outcomes.

III

Technical Information

General Guidelines for IGDI Training and Certification

Jay Buzhardt and Dale Walker

The Individual Growth and Development Indicators (IGDIs) for infants and tod-dlers share some common training certification procedures. Implemented within a trainer-of-trainers model wherein one or more certified individuals at a program may train others, the certification process accommodates the needs of both novice and experienced assessors. Therefore, although no prior experience is required, all IGDI coders and assessors must successfully complete three certi-fication steps to ensure that sessions are administered with high fidelity and child behaviors are reliably coded. The three steps to IGDI certification include the following:

1. Learning about the IGDI measure

2. Successfully scoring two certification videos to criterion

3. Administering the IGDI assessment with high fidelity or integrity

The usefulness of the information provided by an observational assessment is directly related to its implementation fidelity, coding, and scoring accuracy. An as-sessment's psychometric properties and the data collected are rendered irrelevant if the assessment is improperly administered or child behaviors are inaccurately coded. Therefore, one of the fundamental challenges in developing an assessment is establishing a system that supports and promotes a high level of sustained admin-istration fidelity and coding reliability, as well as ensures that the system is efficient, usable, scalable, and provides meaningful information. In addition, it is important to articulate the purpose of the assessment and ensure that assessors have a clear understanding of who should use it and when it should be used. A critically impor-tant aspect of IGDI assessment is articulating how these measures are used for progress monitoring and data-based decision making. This chapter describes how assessors are certified to use infant and toddler IGDIs, who should be trained, how technology has been used, and how a trainer-of-trainers model should be used to maintain rigorous training standards while allowing for scalability.

The training model adopted for IGDIs is loosely based on an experiential learning model in which trainees learn by performing the skill and receiving immediate feedback about their proficiency throughout training. This requires a trainee who actively engages in the skills to be learned, receives individualized and immediate feedback on errors, and demonstrates progress toward mastering those skills. Consequently, this also requires a system for providing individualized feedback and determining mastery. For IGDIs to be effective, it is necessary to ensure sufficient understanding of how to use them, as well as how to maintain high levels of scoring reliability and administration fidelity.

Who Should Be Certified?

After deciding to use the infant and toddler IGDIs, often one of the first questions asked is "Who needs to be certified?" Achieving and maintaining implementation of IGDIs, particularly for frequent progress monitoring and decision making, requires that the program consider how they will implement IGDIs, including who will administer and score them, how many children will be assessed and how frequently, and who will enter and manage the data. Developing this plan from the outset improves the likelihood that training targets those staff who need it most.

The use of IGDIs within a decision-making framework has broad, programwide implications, and some staff may be unfamiliar with how to use assessments in this way. Therefore, it is recommended that any staff involved in using IGDIs for monitoring and/or decision making about child progress, either directly or indirectly, have a clear understanding of the purpose of the IGDIs and how to use them within this framework. For example, consider a small, home-based Early Head Start program that has a director, staff coordinator, data manager, and five home visitors who use the Early Problem-Solving Indicator (EPSI) to measure their children's proficiency in problem solving. At the beginning of the week, the staff coordinator logs into the IGDI data system to identify children due for an EPSI observation and notifies home visitors of which children need an EPSI that week. The home visitors administer and video record the EPSI in the home with the parent as the play partner after they have given the parent some information about how to be an engaging play partner. After each EPSI, the home visitor scores the video-recorded administration at his or her office, and the data manager enters the scores into the online data system. Before the next home visit, the data manager gives the home visitor an individual child report to share with the parent(s), which includes graphs of the child's progress and interventions currently being used (see the Appendix). For their quarterly meetings with state coordinators, the director generates a program report that provides children's aggregate EPSI performance, a list of children falling below benchmark, interventions used, and other important child and staff information. In this scenario, it is clear that it would be helpful if most of the intervention staff had a working knowledge of the assessment's purpose and how to fit it into their organization's daily operations. For this reason, it is recommended that all staff participate in Step 1 of the certification process (learning about the IGDI measure). This ensures that all staff understand the purpose of the EPSI, what it measures, how it differs from other norm-referenced early childhood problem-solving or cognitive measures, and how to interpret the progress monitoring reports and graphs.

The next two certification steps, which involve scoring model administrations to criterion and administering the EPSI with high fidelity of implementation, may be reserved for staff who will administer and score the observations (e.g., the home visitors). Although certified home visitors can certify future home visitors, in some cases, a program may want at least one upper level staff member to be fully certified who can then manage future certification training should there be staff turnover.

Figure 10.1 illustrates how the trainer-of-trainers model would operate for an organization that coordinates services for a large region. At the top level, IGDI staff at the Juniper Gardens Children's Project facilitate the initial training, certification, and support to regional technical assistance (TA) staff (either through a face-to-face workshop or by providing access to materials from the IGDI web site). These individuals can then certify at least one person at each Local Education Agency (LEA) who will subsequently certify the remaining staff in their program. A key milestone in reaching programwide implementation of an IGDI measure is fully certifying at least one person in the program, either through regional support or through support

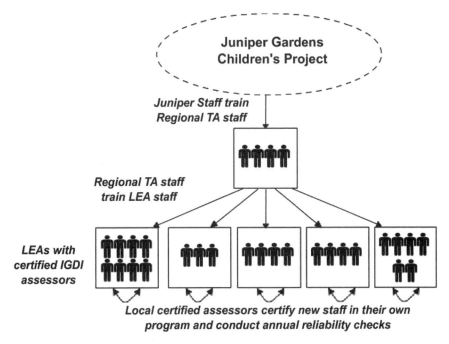

Figure 10.1. The IGDI trainer-of-trainers model for certifying assessors and maintaining annual reliability checks. (© Juniper Gardens Children's Project; reprinted by permission.)

from the IGDI staff at the Juniper Gardens Children's Project. Additional members of the program are more likely to become certified when local support is available.

Steps to Becoming a Certified Assessor

There are three primary steps for certification across all IGDI measures: 1) learning about the measure by attending a workshop or reading online materials, 2) learning the IGDI's scoring definitions and coding two videos of model assessments, and 3) reviewing the IGDI's administration procedures and administering the assessment with high fidelity. Table 10.1 provides an overview of these steps. The last two steps are criterion referenced in that a certified assessor scores the trainee's performance relative to a master scoring sheet and an administration fidelity checklist. Each of these steps leads the trainee to a better understanding of how to use infant and toddler IGDIs and mastery of coding and administration fidelity.

Step 1: Learning the Purpose of the Assessment and How to Use It
The first step of the certification process gives trainees a broad understanding of IGDIs, describes their purpose, explains how IGDIs differ from other standardized assessments, and describes how they can be used for progress monitoring within a decision-making or Response to Intervention (RTI) framework to inform intervention and individualization of treatment. Without this foundation, staff may struggle to understand why it is helpful to measure a general outcome, why IGDIs are administered more frequently than other standardized assessments, and how to use the progress monitoring graphs. Because states and LEAs vary considerably in the degree of professional development they provide on data-based decision making, information is included on the use of the IGDIs within an RTI framework, including case examples and potential challenges and limitations. Although a comprehensive review of RTI and the issues surrounding data-based decision making is not included, the training resources offer a basic understanding of how to use IGDIs for progress monitoring and data-based decision making. Also recommended during this step is for trainees to practice scoring video-recorded assessments with feedback from trainers. This has been found to reduce the number of attempts that trainees need to achieve reliability when scoring the certification videos.

Programs can complete this training step by having a staff member attend a workshop at Juniper Gardens Children's Project or by having a staff member review the PowerPoint presentations available on the web site. Attending a workshop provided by the Juniper Gardens Children's Project staff is primarily for those programs that do not have an onsite certified assessor. Those programs may also download the presentations from the web site.

Following the trainer-of-trainers model (Figure 10.1), once a program or regional site has at least one certified assessor, that person is authorized to certify others and lead workshops as necessary. Table 10.2 lists the resources available on the web site to support certification efforts, including links to the presentations needed for this first certification step.

Table 10.1. Summary of steps for IGDI certification

Step 1: Learning about IGDIs and the scoring definitions
View IGDI presentations either via the web or at a workshop
Learn scoring definitions for IGDI key skill elements
Practice scoring (optional)
Materials needed:
- PowerPoint presentations from IGDI web site
- Space and technology for group presentation in group trainings

Step 2: Score certification videos to at least 85% agreement with master coding
Access certification videos online
Score videos using standard coding form
Certified assessor calculates agreement between trainee coding and master coding and provides feedback on disagreements
Repeat coding until 85% agreement is achieved
Materials needed:
- Certification videos from IGDI web site
- Observation forms from IGDI web site
- Calculator to calculate reliability and/or agreement
- Master coding and video transcripts (*for trainers only*)

Step 3: Administer an assessment, achieving at least 81% fidelity of implementation
Certified assessor observers trainee's administration live or via video
Certified assessor administration fidelity according to administration checklist
If needed, trainee repeats administration until criterion is achieved
Materials needed:
- Caregiver consent to assess the infant or toddler
- Space to conduct the assessment
- Administration checklist from IGDI web site
- Video equipment if certified assessor cannot view administration live

© Juniper Gardens Children's Project; reprinted by permission.

Step 2: Reliably Coding the Certification Videos

Attaining coding reliability with the certification videos available through the web site is important to ensure the accuracy of IGDI codings. Establishing coding agreement with the IGDI calibration videos improves the likelihood that assessments will be coded accurately within and across individuals and programs. Imprecisely coded assessments may not only result in an inaccurate assessment of a child's communication performance, it may incorrectly indicate that a child is above or below benchmark. Such coding imprecision might result in failing to recommend intervention for children who need it. For children who are already receiving intervention, inaccurate assessment may not reflect the effectiveness of the intervention or may fail to indicate when changes in the intervention are needed.

After learning an IGDI's coding definitions by reviewing the coding instructions available for each IGDI on the web site and conducting practice coding recommended during Step 1, trainee observation and coding proficiency is developed through observing and coding calibration videos. Trainees may view the certification videos via the IGDI web site and code them using the standard coding forms also available on the web site (see Table 10.2 for links to these materials). After coding a video, a trainee may enter scores into the trainee section of the web site (if

Table 10.2. Training resources available on the IGDI web site

---

Overview of certification steps: This page summarizes certification requirements and provides links to online materials that support certification efforts.

- http://www.igdi.ku.edu/training/Assessor_Training/certification_steps.htm

Links to online resources: These resources are needed to complete certification requirements for each IGDI.

- http://www.igdi.ku.edu/training/onsite_training.htm

Downloadable PowerPoint presentations: This page provides links to presentations that provide overviews of IGDIs, how they are administered, how to interpret data, and how to use the online data system.

- http://www.igdi.ku.edu/training/power_point_presentations.htm

IGDI scoring definitions: This page provides links to each IGDI's scoring definitions, which trainees need to learn before attempting to score the certification videos.

- http://www.igdi.ku.edu/measures/scoring.htm

IGDI scoring and observation forms: This page provides links to observation forms used to score the certification videos.

- http://www.igdi.ku.edu/measures/observation_forms.htm

Certification videos: This page provides links to videos for all IGDIs that trainees will need to score to at least 85% agreement with a master scoring key. Master scoring keys for an IGDI are only available to assessors certified for that IGDI.

- http://www.igdi.ku.edu/training/index.htm

Administration checklists: This page provides links to all administration checklists, which list the required administration procedures for each IGDI. A certified assessor must verify that the trainee administers these procedures to criterion either by watching a live or recorded administration by the trainee.

- http://www.igdi.ku.edu/measures/admin_checklists.htm

---

they have requested a temporary trainee account on the web site), and their calibration scores will be automatically figured by the online system.

Online Training Most of the certification process is facilitated through online tools and resources. The professional development literature is rich with examples of the efficiencies realized by integrating online instruction into training in business (e.g., Newton & Doonga, 2007; Strother, 2002) and education environments (e.g., Buzhardt & Semb, 2005; Jung, 2005). The first two steps of the certification process are well suited for online training; therefore, tools and materials were developed to allow trainees to complete these two steps through the web site and online data system. The presentations and coding definitions for Step 1 are accessible on the web site. For Step 2, the online data system automatically grades the trainees' coding of the IGDI certification videos, providing immediate feedback on overall agreement and agreement for each key skill element. Trainees are given three opportunities to reach 85% agreement on the certification video. A trainee who does not achieve 85% after three attempts must contact the trainer for additional feedback, and the trainer can reset his or her scores for additional attempts. If a certified trainer is not available onsite, trainees may contact the Juniper Gardens Children's Project staff for feedback (http://www.igdi.ku.edu/contactus.htm) related to specific misunderstandings about the coding definitions. Program directors and coordinators can also access the results of trainees' scores on the certification videos. (Note: As of this writing, online certification agreement checks are only available for the Early Communication Indicator. Future work is planned to develop this resource for the other IGDIs.)

Pen-and-Paper Certification

After a trainee enters scores onto a standard IGDI coding form, a certified assessor may calculate the trainee's reliability against a master coding using the reliability calculation form (shown in Figure 10.2). As indicated by the form, reliability is calculated using a standard interobserver reliability formula, which is (agreements/[agreements + disagreements]) × 100. For each key skill element, agreements are the number of behavior counts that correspond between the trainee and the master coding. For example, if Jenny counted 15 "looks" for the entire assessment, and the master coding form has 17 "looks" recorded, then she had 15 agreements and two disagreements for "looks": (15/[15 + 2]) × 100 = 88% reliability for "looks." This calculation is repeated for each key skill element. The final step is to sum all agreements and disagreements using the same formula to calculate Jenny's overall reliability. If Jenny's *overall* reliability is equal to or above 85%, then she has reached criterion and can move on to the next video or the final certification step.

Master coding keys for the certification videos are available only to certified assessors. After becoming certified, assessors who certify others can obtain a master key from their trainer, the online data system if they have the appropriate access level, or by contacting the IGDI staff at the Juniper Gardens Children's Project (http://www.igdi.ku.edu/contactus.htm). To maintain the integrity of a program's IGDI training, it is important to limit access to these scoring keys to staff who are actively involved in training. However, to ease the burden on trainers, it is recommended that the online certification process be used instead of having certified assessors calculate the accuracy of certification video scoring.

Depending on how well the trainee understands the coding definitions, experience with other observational assessments, prior knowledge of the assessment area, and other factors, trainees may need a few attempts to achieve 85% agreement for each certification video. Prior to each attempt, the trainee should review the key skill element scoring definitions, particularly those for which they had agreement below 85%. Another way to identify misinterpretations of coding definitions is to examine the reliability calculation sheet to determine whether or not the trainee over- or under-coded key skill elements. For example, if the trainee coded too many "gestures" for the ECI, he or she is likely counting a behavior that is excluded from the ECI's definition of gesture (e.g., eye contact, reaching for toys that the play partner is not holding). The trainer should share this information with the trainee without divulging the exact count of gestures needed. Because the scoring key describes each occurrence, what the behavior was, and when it happened, and the coding sheet provides a minute-by-minute record of each key skill element coded by the trainee, the trainer should be able to give a general account of what should be coded and what the trainee might be missing or coding too frequently during the session. Comparing the master with the trainee's coding in this way helps quickly identify erroneous scoring patterns (e.g., for the EPSI, scoring "looks" when the child looks at

	Looks	Explores	Functions	Solutions	TOTALS	
Primary Coder					PC$_{TOTAL}$	Overall % Agreement
Reliability Coder					RC$_{TOTAL}$	
Agreement					A$_{TOTAL}$	A/A+D=
Dis-agreement					D$_{TOTAL}$	
Percent						

Determining Reliability:
1. Record Primary coder scores in first line
2. Record Reliability coder scores in second line
3. Record the number on which they agreed on the third line
4. Record the number on which they disagreed on the fourth line
5. Calculate Percent Agreement for each Key Element category
6. Calculate Overall Percent Agreement using total scores
7. Calculate Average Percent Agreement across categories (add agreements and disagreements in the third and fourth lines across key skill elements)

Formula for determining percent agreement:
$$\frac{\text{Agreements}}{\text{Agreements} + \text{Disagreements}} \times 100$$

Figure 10.2. The reliability calculation form for the EPSI. (© Juniper Gardens Children's Project; reprinted by permission.)

her clothes; scoring "functions" in conjunction with "solutions") and prepare to explain how to correct them. Again, the easiest way to calculate agreement with the master codings of the certification videos is to use the online system available on the IGDI web site.

Step 3: Administering the Assessment with High Fidelity To complete the third and final step of certification, the trainee administers the assessment with a child whose age falls within the specified age range for the IGDI. The criterion for completing this step is accurately administering at least 81% of the tasks on the assessment's administration checklist during the assessment (83% for the ESI). Because the certification videos from Step 2 show model administrations of the assessment, the trainee will have closely observed examples of assessments implemented with high fidelity prior to administration for Step 3. However, the videos do not show all of the administration steps (e.g., setting up the assessment and cleaning the toys), nor do they describe some of the subtle behaviors required of play partners during the assessment (e.g., following the child's lead, keeping the child engaged with the toys, appropriate positioning for a child with a physical disability) that might be overlooked. Therefore, it is recommended that during training, trainees review the assessment's administration instructions and administration checklist (available on the IGDI web site for each IGDI) prior to conducting the assessment and have them available during the assessment until they are comfortable with the administration process.

The administration checklist serves both as a tool for determining a trainee's level of administration fidelity and as a summary of assessor tasks and expectations for each session. Each checklist is divided into three categories: 1) setting up the session, 2) administration, and 3) ending the session. Although all IGDIs have these three categories and the administration items are similar, there is some variation across the IGDIs. Therefore, it is important to refer to each IGDI's respective administration checklist for specific guidelines (see Table 10.2 for a link to the checklist for each IGDI). Figure 10.3 shows the EMI checklist as an example of an administration checklist. (See Chapter 3 for more comprehensive information about general IGDI administration procedures.)

Other Training Considerations

Group or Self-Paced Training   Although most of the certification process is individualized, if time and space permit, it is recommended to conduct the first step (learning about the IGDI measure) didactically in a group setting. This ensures that all trainees are exposed to the information and have an opportunity to clarify concepts as a group, thus preventing the trainer from answering similar questions multiple times. In addition to completing the first certification step, trainees can also begin step two (reliably coding the certification videos) in a group format by practicing coding. This requires access to a video of an assessment (do not use the online certification videos) that is administered with a high level of fidelity, includes examples of all key skill elements, has an accurate coding of the assessment, and is shown in a setting in which all trainees can clearly see and hear it. (Note: Signed parental or guardian consent must be obtained for the use of any video that involves children.) The trainer has two options for practice coding in a group format. They are: 1) stopping the video at each occurrence of a key skill element to describe it and why it should be coded as such, or 2) asking trainees to code the video in 1-minute intervals and reviewing each interval with the group to provide corrective feedback and explain common errors. This preliminary work on the fundamentals of coding will result in less repetitious feedback.

Annual Recertification   Once a trainee is certified, it is important to maintain a high level of reliability across observers. As the amount of time increases since an observer's last reliability assessment, coding accuracy may decline. One way to alleviate this problem is for observers to "recalibrate" themselves occasion-

EMI Administration Checklist

EMI Assessor: _Yolanda Mayvery_   Date: _7/2/2009_   Tape: _176_

This checklist is used to score the administration videos for the EMI. To be certified to administer the EMI, the adult play partner should complete at least 81% (13 out of 16) of the administration steps.

Setting up the EMI Administration Situation: Materials & Positioning	Item	Yes	No
1. Adult play partner sets up the toys prior to the session.	1	X	
2. The toys are arranged to attract child's attention (i.e., balls scattered so child can see them).	2	X	
3. Adult and child are positioned so they can see and reach toys.	3	X	
4. Child is positioned appropriately for his or her developmental level.	4	X	
5. Session is timed (may be observed or reported).	5	X	
6. Video camera is set up to follow child as child moves around during session.	6	X	
7. Video camera is set up so that session can be heard for scoring.	7	X	
EMI Assessment Administration: Play Situation			
8. Adult play partner follows child's lead in play situation.	8	X	
9. Adult play partner comments about what child is doing.	9	X	
10. Adult play partner provides support for movement when needed, but gently encourages the child to move without his or her support.	10	X	
11. Adult play partner interacts in nondirective, friendly manner.	11	X	
12. Adult play partner uses questions sparingly.	12	X	
Ending EMI Session			
13. Session ends after exactly 6 minutes have elapsed.	13	X	
14. Adult play partner lets child know that it is time to stop.	14		X
15. Adult play partner thanks child for playing.	15	X	
16. Adult play partner cleans toys (may be reported).	16	X	
	Total	14 Yes	1 No

Administration Accuracy = [(Total Number of Steps Completed Correctly/16 Steps) × 100] = _94_ % (Need 81%)

Figure 10.3. The Early Movement Indicator (EMI) administration checklist. (© Juniper Gardens Children's Project; reprinted by permission.)

ally. Observers commonly accomplish this by coding the same observation and calculating interobserver reliability with each other. Therefore, recertification of all IGDI assessors should occur at least annually.

Annual recertification simply requires that an assessor conduct an observation with another certified assessor. Reliability is calculated between these two codings using the calculation described in Step 2 of the certification process. If there is less than 85% agreement between the two sets of IGDI scores from the observation, the assessors should discuss their disagreements and refer to the coding definitions when necessary. After resolving disagreements, another reliability check should be conducted until 85% agreement is achieved on the first coding.

To streamline the recertification process, the online data system calculates reliability automatically between two observations. After entering observation scores into the data system, the reliability observer also enters his or her scores into the data system but designates them as a "reliability" assessment on the online form. After both observations are entered, the system displays the percent agreement below the reliability total communications score in the child's data view. Reliability observations are clearly marked as such in the child's data view and are not included on progress monitoring graphs. An assessor's completion is also tracked on the program report, which provides the date of each assessor's certification and most recent reliability check. This helps program directors or coordinators identify who is due for an annual reliability check.

Often when observers do not follow the specified protocol for coding, similar patterns are observed across assessors within the same program or center. For example, an observer is mistakenly told to stop coding gestures when a child shows an object to the play partner. This error then spreads to other observers, until eventually most observers within the center no longer code this behavior as a gesture. Subsequent reliability checks do not identify this as an error because the observers are reliably scoring incorrectly. To avoid this problem, it is recommended that observers from other programs serve as reliability observers to identify program or sitewide coding errors. Unfortunately, this is not logistically possible for all programs because, among other reasons, there may not be another local center that administers the IGDI. In these cases, programwide observer "drift" can be avoided by briefly reviewing scoring definitions annually during regular staff meetings or other professional development activities.

Conducting Annual Reliability Checks   There are two primary options for conducting reliability checks. Two assessors (a primary and reliability assessor) can either 1) score a live assessment together, or 2) score the same video-recorded assessment at different times. Either of these options is appropriate. Choosing one depends on the program's resources and staff availability. When scoring for reliability during an ongoing session, the reliability observer must be in a position to see and hear the child while remaining inconspicuous and not interfering with the session. For this reason and because it is typically easier to score video-recorded sessions, scoring for reliability from video is recommended; however, for some programs, scoring in person may be the only option. Figure 10.4 shows a primary and reliability assessment entered into the online data system and the results of the reliability calculation. Notice that the reliability assessment is visually differentiated among the child's list of assessments with a shaded area. Reliability assessments are not plotted on the child's graph, nor are they considered in any other way by the data system regarding the child's outcomes.

Coding a session for reliability does not require a special coding form. The only difference is that the reliability coder must write his or her name in the designated area. A name in this space indicates to the person who enters the assessment into the online data system that it is a reliability observation. Prior to entering a reliability assessment into the data system, the primary assessment *must* be entered first. After the primary assessment is entered, the assessor selects the primary assessment within the data system and clicks "Add Reliability Data" (see Figure 10.5). This

Early Communication Indicator (ECI) Data

Child: Cute, Jacob
Birthdate: 08/29/2000
Program: Juniper Gardens Test
Date: 10/25/2009
              ☐ =Primary Data
              ▨ =Reliability Data

Select	Observation Date	Form Type	Coder	Location	Assessor	Condition Change	Total Communications	Total Minutes	Weighted Total Communication
○	05/09/2002 (20 months)	Barn	Cathy Small	Center	Walker, Dale	None	26	6	6.50
○	08/01/2002 (23 months)	House	Montagne, Debra	Center	Buzhardt, Jay	None	50	6	14.33
○	08/01/2002 (23 months)	House	McConnell, Libby	Center	Buzhardt, Jay	None	44 (88% agreement)	6	12.67

Figure 10.4. A reliability check entered into the online data system (grey highlighted assessment) and scored for reliability. (© Juniper Gardens Children's Project; reprinted by permission.)

will bring up an online data entry form such as that shown in Figure 10.6. This form is identical to that for primary assessments except that the contextual information will be filled in based on what was entered for the primary assessment. If the session is video-recorded and the reliability observer scores the assessment at a later date, the date in which the reliability observer scored the assessment should be the date entered into the online form. This is important because this date will be used to determine when the assessor should conduct his or her next annual reliability check. After entering the reliability data, the system will calculate and display the

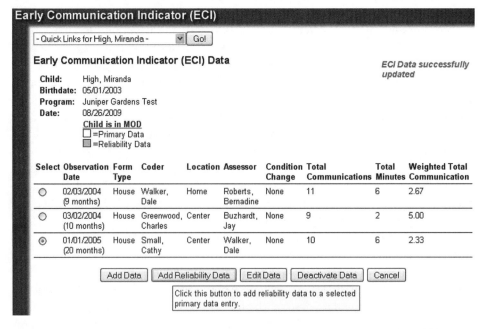

Figure 10.5. Adding a reliability assessment to an existing primary assessment. (© Juniper Gardens Children's Project; reprinted by permission.)

Edit Reliability ECI data for Cute, Jacob

* = required

*Test Date:	08/01/2002		Test Duration	Minutes:	6
				Seconds:	0
Form Type:	House		Condition Change:	None	
Assessor:	Buzhardt, Jay				
Location:	Center		Language of Administration:	English	
Note:	INT began 7/25/02				
*Reliability Coder:	McConnell, Libby ⌄		*Reliability Coding Date:	September ⌄ 01 ⌄ , 2002 ⌄	

The below values are the raw data values entered directly from the child's data sheet. These values are not "weighted" values. Weighting will be applied after these data are submitted.

	Gestures	Vocalizations	Single Word Utterances	Multi-Word Utterances
0:00	2	3	1	2
1:00	1	3	3	4
2:00	2	3	0	0
3:00	2	0	3	2
4:00	2	3	0	3
5:00	1	1	3	0

[Submit Changes] [Cancel]

Figure 10.6. An online reliability assessment form with the assessment's contextual information at the top predefined from the primary assessment. (© Juniper Gardens Children's Project; reprinted by permission.)

overall percent agreement as shown in Figure 10.4. The date of this reliability check will also be reported in the organization's program as the last reliability check for that assessor, which helps coordinators or others monitoring assessments to know which of their staff have current certifications and who needs to conduct a reliability check.

Conclusion

The training procedures described in this chapter have been used to certify hundreds of IGDI assessors. These certification procedures are consistent across all IGDIs. The only variation in procedures among IGDIs is in the scoring definitions, and there are slight variations in administration procedures. Although the methods for presenting and providing access to the training materials may vary slightly among programs depending on the organization's resources and staff preferences, all organizations who administer and score IGDIs for infants and toddlers must ensure that their assessors complete the three certification steps for each IGDI they use.

Following certification, programs can ensure accurate and consistent coding across assessors by having all assessors conduct annual reliability checks to at least 85% agreement. Having these procedures in place ensures that outcomes are assessed reliably and increases staff confidence in decisions made based on the assessments. Although the online data system provides materials and tools to support training and recertification efforts, each step of the certification process is designed to provide ample opportunity for trainers to engage with trainees, provide immediate feedback specific to their needs, and identify and problem solve misunderstandings during and after the training process. Ultimately, this helps ensure that the data generated from the IGDIs are reliable, valid, and used appropriately.

Development
and Validation of IGDIs

Charles Greenwood and Dale Walker

T his chapter describes the approach used to develop and validate each of the IGDIs. The goal in developing the IGDIs was to demonstrate that each measure was capable of collecting data that were sensitive, accurate, and capable of informing early interventionists, parents, and policy makers on the myriad of decisions concerning practice. "Before an assessment instrument or test is used for making decisions about children, it is necessary to have evidence the assessment does what it claims to do, namely that it accurately measures a characteristic or construct (or outcome)" (National Research Council, 2008, p. 182). The technical soundness of any measure is demonstrated by the weight or accumulation of available evidence showing it capable of meeting high measurement standards.

Technical Standards Used for Developing Progress Monitoring Measures

Each IGDI was developed using a common program of research designed to test its soundness, and thus, the trustworthiness of decisions that would be based on it (Early Childhood Research Institute on Measuring Growth and Development, 1998b). The general outcome measurement (GOM) approach to progress monitoring (see Chapter 2) was used for this purpose. In addition, plans for collecting the desired evidence needed were influenced by three relevant measurement standards: 1) the National Center on Student Progress Monitoring technical standards (2006), 2) the American Educational Research Association's (AERA) *Standards for Educational and Psychological Testing* (1999), and 3) The Division for Early Childhood's (DEC) *Recommended practices: A Comprehensive Guide—Standards for Assessment* (Sandall, Hemmeter, Smith, & McLean, 2005). Review of these standards showed that in many cases they overlapped, and many quality indicators were included in more than one set of standards. Each of the standards, however, addressed unique technical perspectives. Each set of standards is discussed in this chapter with a focus on those that provided a unique influence on IGDI development.

Measurement Standards

National Center on Student Progress Monitoring   The attributes of high quality progress monitoring measures are linked to both foundational psychometric standards and recent developments in progress monitoring standards (NCSPM, 2006). *Reliability* and *validity* are the psychometric standards (American Educational Research Association, 1999). *Reliability* refers to evidence that the collected data are accurate and comparable within and across individual children. *Validity* refers to evidence demonstrating that collected data do in fact measure the skill or skill domain of interest.

Attributes particularly relevant to progress monitoring measurement include the following:

1. *Alternate test forms:* Alternate test forms are important in progress monitoring because this evidence rules out the effects of memorization—a common concern when measures like IGDIs are frequently administered. Different but equivalent forms of the test were developed using research comparing alternative materials and items and identifying those that produced equivalent score estimates for individual children.

2. *Sensitivity to student improvement:* This is demonstrated by evidence that children grow in proficiency over time and age.

3. *Reports of annual yearly progress (AYP) benchmarks:* AYP benchmarks are expectations for the amount of yearly progress children demonstrate at particular ages (i.e., 2 to 3, 3 to 4 years of age).

4. *Rates of progress:* Rates of progress are specified based on local and/or representative, normative data used as age benchmarks to define the pattern of typical progress expected of children within a year.

5. *Improvement of student learning and/or teacher planning:* This is demonstrated by evidence that rate of progress improves coincidentally with changes in intervention practice or by use of the measure itself in the measurement of progress with caregivers, home visitors, interventionists, and teachers adjusting intervention and/or instruction based on results.

Use of a progress monitoring measure is also expected to result in better teacher planning and more frequent changes in intervention based on children's response to intervention (RTI) (Fuchs & Fuchs, 2007). Meeting technical standards for progress monitoring measures involves accumulating research evidence that addresses these issues.

AERA Educational Testing Standards   The AERA standards that add and complement those of progress monitoring just described include the following:

1. *Domain specification:* This is demonstrated by linking what is measured conceptually to a socially desired general outcome with key skill elements reflecting proficiency in attaining that outcome over an age span.

2. *Review of relevant literature:* A review of relevant literature specifies behaviors of interest to ensure that both conceptual and empirical evidence supports the selection of key skills.

3. *Item development and refinement:* Item development is informed by the literature review followed by a process of developing and testing key skill definitions so that multiple assessors can readily understand and apply them in practice.

4. *Content validation:* This is demonstrated when items are shown to represent the larger domain or universe of skills of interest.

5. *Practicality and utility review:* The proposed administration formats and scores to be used are demonstrated through a product development sequence of incremental trial, revision, and retrial leading to improvement in the usability of the measure.

6. *Initial field or pilot testing:* This testing is demonstrated through initial trial and applications of the measures to test feasibility and identify the need for refinement.

7. *Item analysis and refinement or selection:* This is demonstrated by comparison of item quality and difficulty, such that poor and redundant items are deleted or improved.

8. *Predictive utility evaluation:* This evaluation is demonstrated by research examining the measure's ability to forecast future performance based on present performance.

9. *Bias analysis:* Bias analysis for demographic and regional variables is demonstrated through research that examines how quality of measurement is adversely affected by sociodemographic variables, such as differences in first language or disability conditions.

DEC Recommended Assessment Practices   The assessment of young children according to *DEC Recommended Practices: A Comprehensive Guide* (Sandall, Hemmeter, Smith, & McLean, 2005) is expected to do the following:

1. Point to behavioral objectives for change that are judged important and acceptable.

2. Guide change in treatment activities.

3. Incorporate several instruments, informants, and scales, including observation and interviews.

4. Incorporate input from parents.

5. Be used on multiple occasions.

DEC's recommendations uniquely reflect issues relevant to young children, children with disabilities, and the values and forms that measurement should take with these populations (Sandall, Hemmeter, et al., 2005).

The DEC recommended criteria for evaluating the appropriateness of assessment practices are as follows:

1. Acceptability: Measurement materials and approaches should share evidence of consensus among families and professionals.

2. Authenticity: Contrived tasks and persons unknown to the young child should be avoided to prevent reactivity influencing the assessment process. Reactivity may be reduced by having the parent present and by the professional assessor (e.g., occupational therapist, physical therapist, school psychologist) spending enough time with the child to overcome the "strange person" effect.

3. Collaboration: The methods used should engage teamwork between families and professionals in the collection and use of the information.

4. Convergence: Reliable data collected on everyday behavior in natural environments by multiple informants can be pooled; that is, where differences or unique information is obtained it is used to provide a more comprehensive set of information.

5. Equity: This measure is able to accommodate individual differences.

6. Sensitivity: This measure is capable of reflecting short-term, small increments of progress so that all children, including those with severe disabilities, can be included and accurately represented.

7. Congruence: Materials and approaches are designed for and field-validated with the children to be assessed.

Although each of these standards brings a somewhat different focus to measurement development, taken together they provided a strong basis for IGDI development and validation. The combined standards require that assessment formats meet generally accepted standards of reliability and validity and measure developmentally appropriate skills and address the attention levels of young children. They require that appropriate accommodations are considered from a universal design perspective, and that methods are appropriate for diverse students including English language learners. These standards provided both shared and unique requirements and thus, a systematic approach for development of measures for young children with and without disabilities (McConnell, McEvoy, & Priest, 2002).

Methods Used to Develop and Validate IGDIs

The approach used to develop and validate GOMs for infants and toddlers employed an iterative process linking product development, empirical research, and improvement. This involved multiyear activities and multiple studies designed to create the necessary measures, test and improve them, and retest to establish usability. Reports of this work for each IGDI published in peer-reviewed journals, books, and other sources can be found in Table 11.1. Support for this work came from grants[1] from the Office of Special Education Programs (OSEP), Administration for Children and Families (ACF), the National Center for Special Education Research (NCSER), and the states of Kansas and Missouri. IGDIs were developed using a sequence of methods designed to advance knowledge concerning an IGDIs feasibility, utility, and validity based on the standards previously discussed. This sequence included 1) literature review and synthesis, 2) national social validation survey, 3) pilot testing/initial trial, 4) toy forms identification and selection, 5) administration feasibility and user testing, 6) cross-sectional study design validation, and 7) longitudinal study design validation.

Literature Review and Synthesis

Extensive literature reviews for each measure were conducted to identify both the conceptual and empirical knowledge, as well as the existing measures relevant to IGDI development. Logical analyses of this literature supported development of a list of 15 general outcome statements, two to four general outcomes per domain, that were subsequently evaluated as to their social importance in a national survey of parents and professionals (Priest et al., 2001).

Based on the literature review, a conceptual framework linking each general outcome to a small set of key skill elements to be used as indicators of growth in the age range was developed. Skill selection was guided by the GOM principle that indicator skills sample a selection of those to be learned over a specific age range. In the case of infants and toddlers, the time period from 6 months to 42 months of age (with minor exception) was used for this purpose. Additional criterion for skill selection was judgment that each could be readily measured by early childhood practitioners (Early Childhood Research Institute on Measuring Growth and Development, 1998a). Using the key skills, a composite indicator was created for each IGDI based on the several skills elements whose combination and incremental attainment over time would reflect increasing proficiency (Deno, 1997; Fuchs & Deno, 1991). Selection of these key skill elements was a precursor to the design and evaluation of new data collection formats to be used for sampling children's behavior. Skill selection was also a precursor to future efforts to identify interventions likely to accelerate the learning of these skills.

For example, in the case of the Early Social Indicator (ESI), the literature review conducted indicated that the function of social interaction is to achieve a response from another person ranging from proximity, to simple reciprocity, to coordinated action to achieve a common outcome, to friendship and/or acceptance of peers (Eckerman & Didow, 1996; Warren, Yoder, & Leew, 2002). Furthermore, it is

[1]H024S60010 to the University of Minnesota, and H324C040095, H327A060051, 90-YF-0052, and R324C080011 to the University of Kansas.

Table 11.1. Infant and toddler IGDIs research and development citations

Communication (ECI)

Luze, G.J., Linebarger, D.L., Greenwood, C.R., Carta, J.J., Walker, D., Leitschuh, C., & Atwater, J.B. (2001). Developing a general outcome measure of growth in expressive communication of infants and toddlers. *School Psychology Review, 30*(3), 383–406.

Greenwood, C.R., Dunn, S., Ward, S.M., & Luze, G.J. (2003). The Early Communication Indicator (ECI) for infants and toddlers: What it is, where it's been, and where it needs to go. *The Behavior Analyst Today, 3*(4), 383–388.

Greenwood, C.R., Carta, J.J., Walker, D., Hughes, K., & Weathers, M. (2006). Preliminary investigations of the application of the Early Communication Indicator (ECI) for infants and toddlers. *Journal of Early Intervention, 28*(3), 178–196.

Movement (EMI)

Greenwood, C.R., Luze, G.J., Cline, G., Kuntz, S., & Leitschuh, C. (2002). Developing a general outcome measure of growth in movement for infants and toddlers. *Topics in Early Childhood Special Education, 22*(3), 143–157.

Social (ESI)

Carta, J.J., Greenwood, C.R., Luze, G.J., Cline, G., & Kuntz, S. (2004). Developing a general outcome measure of growth in social skills for infants and toddlers. *Journal of Early Intervention, 26*(2), 91–114.

Problem Solving (EPSI)

Greenwood, C.R., Walker, D., Carta, J.J., & Higgins, S. (2006). Developing a general outcome measure of growth in the cognitive abilities of children 1 to 4 years old: The Early Problem-Solving Indicator. *School Psychology Review, 35*(4), 535–551.

Parent–Child Interaction (IPCI)

Baggett, K., & Carta, J.J. (2006). Using assessment to guide social-emotional intervention for very young children: An Individual Growth and Development Indicator (IGDI) of parent–child interaction. *Young Exceptional Children Monograph Series, 8*, 67–76.

Concept and methodological issues

Kaminski, R.A., McEvoy, M.A., Greenwood, C.R., Carta, J.J., McConnell, S.R., Priest, J.S., et al. (1998). *Theoretical foundations of the Early Childhood Research Institute on Measuring Growth and Development: An early childhood problem solving model* (No. 6). Minneapolis, MN: Early Childhood Research Institute on Measuring Growth and Development, Center for Early Education and Development, University of Minnesota.

Early Childhood Research Institute on Measuring Growth and Development. (1998). *Research and development of individual growth and development indicators for children between birth and age eight* (No. 4). Minneapolis, MN: Center for Early Education and Development, University of Minnesota.

McConnell, S.R. (2000). Assessment in early intervention and early childhood special education: Building on the past to project into the future. *Topics in Early Childhood Special Education, 20*, 43–48.

Priest, J.S., McConnell, S.R., Walker, D., Carta, J.J., Kaminski, R., McEvoy, M.A., et al. (2001). General growth outcomes for children between birth and age eight: Where do we want young children to go today and tomorrow? *Journal of Early Intervention, 24*(3), 163–180.

McEvoy, M.A., Priest, J.S., Kaminski, R., Carta, J.J., Greenwood, C.R., McConnell, S.R., et al. (2001). General growth outcomes: Wait! There's more! *Journal of Early Intervention, 24*(3), 191–192.

McConnell, S.R., McEvoy, M.A., & Priest, J.S. (2002). Growing measures for monitoring progress in early childhood education: A research and development process for Individual Growth and Development Indicators. *Assessment for Effective Intervention, 27*(4), 3–14.

Applications

Carta, J.J., Greenwood, C.R., Walker, D., Kaminski, R., Good, R., McConnell, S.R., & McEvoy, M. (2002). Individual Growth and Development Indicators (IGDIs): Assessment that guides intervention for young children. *Young Exceptional Children, 4*, 15–28.

Carta, J.J., Greenwood, C.R., & Walker, D. (2003). Monitoring children's growth and developing using general outcome measurement: A model for estimating child progress through frequent brief measures. In B.F. Williams (Ed.), *Directions in early intervention assessment* (pp. 161–175). Spokane, WA: Spokane Guild's School and Neuromuscular Center.

Greenwood, C.R., Luze, G.J., & Carta, J.J. (2002). Assessment of intervention results with infants and toddlers. In A. Thomas & J. Grimes (Eds.), *Best practices in school psychology IV* (Vol. 2, pp. 1219–1230). Washington DC: National Association of School Psychology.

Greenwood, C.R., Carta, J.J., & Walker, D. (2005). Individual Growth and Development Indicators (IGDIs): Tools for assessing intervention results for infants and toddlers. In B. Heward, H.E. Heron, N.A. Neef, S.M. Peterson, D.M. Sainato, G. Cartledge, et al. (Eds.), *Focus on behavior analysis in education: Achievements, challenges, and opportunities* (pp. 103–124). Columbus, OH: Pearson/Prentice Hall.

Greenwood, C.R., Carta, J.J., Baggett, K., Buzhardt, J., Walker, D., & Terry, B. (2008). Best practices in integrating progress monitoring and response-to-intervention concepts into early childhood systems. In A. Thomas, J. Grimes, & J. Gruba (Eds.), *Best practices in school psychology V* (pp. 535–548). Washington, DC: National Association of School Psychology.

Walker, D., Carta, J.J., Greenwood, C., & Buzhardt, J. (2008). The use of Individual Growth and Development Indicators for progress monitoring and intervention decision making in early education. *Exceptionality, 16*(1), 33–47.

Review and synthesis

Greenwood, C.R., Walker, D., & Utley, C.A. (2001). Relationships between social-communicative skills and life achievements. In S.F. Warren & M.E. Fey (Series Eds.) & H. Goldstein, L.A. Kaczmarek, & K.M. English (Vol. Eds.), *Communication and language intervention series: Vol. 10. Promoting social communication: Children with developmental disabilities from birth to adolescence* (pp. 345–370). Baltimore: Paul H. Brookes Publishing Co.

established that social interaction in infants typically develops first with adults and second with peers (Didow & Eckerman, 2001; Eckerman, Davis, & Didow, 1989). Thus, detailed behavioral definitions were developed for each key skill so they could be reliably recorded by observers (Kennedy, 2005), followed by selecting an observational recording format and a procedure for administration, which would all be used in subsequent pilot and longitudinal studies. This step was repeated for each IGDI.

National Survey for Social Validation

An evaluation of the social validity of the general outcome statements was completed (Priest et al., 2001). A principle of GOM is that the measure reflects progress attaining a socially desired general outcome. Thus, the overall question addressed in the survey was "Which of these statements is the most important outcome of early childhood? To answer this question, a national survey of parents of young children with disabilities, educators, and other professionals who serve young children and their families was conducted. In the survey, parents and professionals were asked to rate each general outcome statement according to three levels of importance in a child's successful development: 1) critically important, 2) very important, or 3) somewhat important.

Parents and professionals surveyed were encouraged to provide suggestions and recommendations for improving the content and clarity of each general outcome statement. To ensure that parents receiving the survey had, in fact, had recent experiences with young children on which to report, only those indicating that they

Table 11.2.   General outcomes social validation findings

Outcome	Statement	Importance		Illustrative citation
		Parents	Professionals	
	Child outcomes			
Communication	The child uses gestures, sounds, words, or sentences to convey wants and needs or to express meaning to others	100%	100%	(Goldstein, Kaczmarek, & English, 2002)
Movement	The child moves in a fluent and co-ordinated manner to play and participate in home, school, and community settings	96%	72%	(Burton & Miller, 1998)
Social	Child interacts with peers and adults, maintaining social inter-actions and participating socially in home, school, and community	98%	98%	(Warren, Yoder, & Leew, 2001)
Problem Solving	Child solves problems that require reasoning about objects, con-cepts, situations, and people	93%	84%	(Zelazo, Carter, & Reznick, 1997)
	Parent outcome			
Sensitivity parenting	Parents facilitate their child's posi-tive social behavior	—	—	(Brooks-Gunn, Berlin, Fuligni, & Sidle, 2000)

Note: Percentage reflects the portion of respondents rating the outcome as "very" and "critically" important.
© Juniper Gardens Children's Project; reprinted by permission.

had a child 12 years or younger were asked to complete and return a survey. The overall return rates of completed surveys were 351 parents (32%) and 672 (53%) professionals (Priest et al., 2001).

From these results, the highest rated general outcome statements per domain were used to guide the next steps on the development of one IGDI per outcome. Because all were highly rated, final selection was a judgment call wherein relative critical importance, breadth, and the unique age range of 6–42 months were considered. The selected general outcomes can be seen in Table 11.2.

Pilot Testing/Initial Trial

Based on literature review related to the socially validated general outcomes and their key skills, development of administration formats that could be used by practitioners was completed. This step was followed by small-scale testing to determine feasibility. A key principle was to create a standard format for administering, recording, and scoring child performance so that data collected on any one child over time and between any two or more children of the same age could be reasonably compared.

Toy Forms Identification and Selection

In addition to identifying key skills, documenting that the skills could be reliably recorded by observers, and creating an observational recording method for data collection, toy-play testing situations were identified that could be used with each IGDI. A set of toys and natural situations with a high potential of evoking the key skill elements in children in the desired age range was needed. The goal was to identify and select the play situations, materials, and procedures needed to conduct authentic but standard child assessments. For example, a number of puzzles were found to evoke sitting and engagement in handling puzzle pieces—a very good situation for the problem-solving IGDI, but a very poor situation for evoking the active movement assessed by the movement IGDI. Therefore, rather than puzzles, the Play House toy that children could crawl inside, stand, and jump out of proved to be an effective situation for evoking movement.

The key skill elements of each IGDI were used to help define the needed stimulus features and functions of the toys likely to work well. Initial efforts in this work explored the suitability of using natural classroom play situations compared with those of a standard play situation with a familiar caregiver and select toy sets (Luze, Greenwood, Carta, Cline, & Kuntz, 2002). Results indicated that the natural classroom situation was generally unsatisfactory because children consistently produced lower and/or more variable counts of key behaviors than those produced by a standard toy situation (e.g., Luze, 2001). The greater variability in the occurrence of key skills of interest in natural settings was heavily influenced by natural variations in equipment, toys, and ongoing teacher–student interaction within classroom centers. Thus, the more structured toy sets were selected for use in subsequent research and development studies for each IGDI because they offered the best opportunity for evoking the optimal level of key skill elements for a child during the assessment (Greenwood, Carta, & Walker, 2005).

Initially, a list of logically appropriate toys thought most likely to evoke the key skill elements of interest were screened for each IGDI. Toys were tested and compared for their probability of evoking the key skills. The toys selected displayed an observed potential for engaging the interest of infants and toddlers and evoking the key skills of interest (Luze, 2001). Additional criteria guiding this selection were considerations of safety and developmental appropriateness for children this age, as well as their typical availability in child care settings.

A short list of toys ranked in order of demonstrated ability to evoke the children's social skill elements, for example, included Tub of Toys (TT), Window House (WH), and Kitchen with Dishes (KD) with enhancements added to each, including squeaky food items, blocks that pop together, and the Fun Sounds Garage (FSG). Deleted from this list were toys such as the Fire Engine, Ball Tower, Car Mat, and Blocks that had failed to engage children for the entire session and/or that promoted parallel play or imitation of the adult's behavior instead of the key skill elements. Toys passing this screening were tested further with a small sample of children stratified in age across the first, second, and third years of life. Involved in this test was the use of the observational recording protocol from which it was possible to test each individual toy's equivalence (i.e., alternate forms) evoking social behavior. From these several small-scale studies testing and revising toy items, it was typically possible to generate toys and toy sets with similar stimulus properties from which to create alternate forms of the same IGDI. These alternate forms were employed in subsequent studies of sensitivity to growth over time and technical adequacy.

Administration Feasibility and User Testing

The standard administration protocol was now used to ensure that each IGDI was administered in an equivalent way on each occasion by each assessor. The general administration set up that emerged involved an individual toy-play activity in a controlled, quiet setting with a familiar adult. Each testing session lasted for only 6 minutes (with the exception of the IPCI at 10 minutes' duration) after a number of trials at longer durations indicated no significant differences in scores at 6 minutes compared with longer administration times.

The adult assessor's role was to facilitate play and follow the child's lead. Additional duties included timing the session duration and ending the session after exactly 6 minutes. The assessor was also responsible for selecting and setting up the testing situation and cleaning up and putting away all toys and equipment used following the session. A second adult was responsible for video recording the child's behavior for later observational recording. Observational recording of the child's performance was guided by definitions of key skill elements developed for each IGDI (e.g., the ECI recording form [see Figure 4.5] in Chapter 4).

Cross-Sectional Study Design Phase 1 Validation

After development, pilot testing, and refinement, the IGDI was ready for its first opportunity to demonstrate evidence that it measured an important aspect of a child's performance and its potential for further study. Cross-sectional studies of children of different ages at one point in time were conducted as a relatively quick test of an IGDI's sensitivity to age differences in children within the age span of interest. These studies set out to compare children from three or more age groups (e.g., 1, 2, and 3 years) on IGDI data collected on just one occasion using the measure as developed to that point. The primary question addressed was "Is the IGDI sensitive to differences in child age? Also asked was "Do we see continuity in greater proficiency for children in the older group compared with the younger group?"

An IGDI was considered promising if statistically significant differences were detected between age groups, which indicated that the IGDI was 1) sensitive to group performance differences between younger versus older children, and 2) differences were incremental with age group. The oldest children were expected to have the higher scores. Although important initial evidence of validity, this finding among groups of children of different ages was no guarantee that the measure would also be sensitive to growth within individual child measurement over time on multiple occasions. This became the next test of IGDI sensitivity.

Longitudinal Study Design Phase 2 Validation

Year-long, repeated-measures longitudinal studies were conducted in order to test each IGDI's sensitivity to individual growth. In addition, questions were addressed that included evidence of validity with respect to other criterion measures of the outcome and reliability of IGDI measurement. The general design called for collecting criterion validity measures of each outcome (i.e., tests and parent ratings of communication, movement, social, problem solving) that occurred before and, where possible, after 5–9 repeated monthly measures using the IGDI. However, because of time limitations in some cases, this timeline was accelerated from monthly to every 3 weeks across IGDIs.

In each of the longitudinal studies (one for each IGDI), purposive sampling of children within community-based child care centers was used. Because of the frequent and intensive repeated measurement in each study, it was not economically possible to recruit large, representative samples at this stage in research and development. Thus, purposive sampling was used to obtain small samples comprised of participants ranging widely in socioeconomic status (SES), cultural and linguistic diversity, and functioning level (i.e., children with individualized family service plans [IFSPs]). The number of child care centers participating in each original longitudinal study ranged from two to five, with child sample sizes ranging from 27 to 57 across IGDI studies. In each case, however, the participating samples of children were racially and socioeconomically diverse and included children with disabilities.

Using these development and study methods with each IGDI, results began to emerge that enabled the IGDI development team to observe results, refine and improve, replicate, and further develop the sensitivity and validity of each measure. Findings are now reported from each step of development.

Results

Were the General Outcomes Socially Valid?

The general outcomes selected to guide work developing IGDIs are reported in Table 11.2. Social validity was established using a combination of literature review and survey. As seen in Table 11.2, importance percentages that combined both critically and very important ratings for communication, movement, social, and problem solving were generally above 84%, ranging from 100% (communication) to 72% (movement). Based on these results, parents and professionals agreed on the importance of communication (parent = 100%, professional = 100%) and diverged most on the critical importance of movement (parent = 96%, professional = 72%). The social validity of the IPCI's sensitive parenting outcome, a more recent development, is currently supported by literature review only (see Table 11.2).

What Are the Relevant Key Skill Elements, Skill Definitions, and Most Appropriate Observational Measurement Procedures?

The five IGDIs and their associated key skill elements are shown in Table 11.3. Although each IGDI was purposely planned to uniquely reflect increasing proficiency toward its general outcome, the final indicator score used for each was different based on results. In common however, this score proved to be most valid in refer-

Table 11.3. Indicator and key skill elements for infants and toddlers

IGDI	Scores	Key skill elements				
		1	2	3	4	5
Early Communication Indicator (ECI)	Total weighted communication rate	Gesture	Vocalization	Single word	Multiple words	
Early Movement Indicator (EMI)	Total movement rate	Transition in position	Grounded locomotion	Vertical locomotion	Roll/trap	Throw/catch
Early Social Indicator (ESI)	Total social rate	Negative	Positive nonverbal	Positive verbal		
Early Problem Solving Indicator (EPSI)	Total problem-solving rate	Look	Explore	Functions	Solutions	
Indicator of Parent–Child Interaction (IPCI)	Parent facilitation	Acceptance/warmth	Descriptive language	Follows child's lead	Maintains/extends	Stress-reducing strategies
	Parent interrupt	Criticism/harsh voice	Restrictions/ intrusions	Rejects child's bid		
	Child engagement	Positive feedback	Sustained engagement	Follow through		
	Child reactivity	Irritable/fuss/cry	External stress	Frozen/watchful/ withdrawn		

© Juniper Gardens Children's Project; reprinted by permission.

ence to criterion measures and sensitivity to growth over time. For example, work on the early problem-solving indicator (EPSI) found that two key skills, *functions* (defined as using a toy in a way consistent with its purpose), and *solutions* (defined as the frequency of task completions) were most sensitive to growth across the total infant-toddler age range. So they were combined to provide a single composite Total Problem Solving score. In the case of the early social indicator (ESI), the most parsimonious, sensitive, and valid composite was a combination of positive *nonverbal* and *verbal* behaviors minus *negative* behaviors used to define the Total Social Score. In the case of the EMI, a composite of five key skill elements best served this purpose. In the case of the ECI, research indicated that none of the key skill elements uniformly reflected growth over the entire age range, in fact gestures and vocalizations after increasing over time declined in 2 and 3 year olds, while at the same time single and multiple word communications were beginning to grow. Consequently, to form a single Total Communication Score sensitive to growth over the age range, these skills were weighted in a composite score (gestures and vocalizations each = 1 per occurrence, single words = 2, multiples words = 3).

What Toys Readily Evoked the Key Skill Elements?

The final validated toy forms for each IGDI are displayed in Table 11.4. For all of the IGDIs, several different but similar toys were identified that evoked nearly equivalent rates of performance (Greenwood, Luze, Cline, Kuntz, & Leitschuh, 2002). In the case of the EPSI, two parallel toy sets consisting of three similar toys within each set was developed. For example, pop-up dinosaurs and pop-up pets were different toy forms that had similar parallel functions. As were square stacking cups and round stacking cups, as were the DropNCatch and the PullNPop toys (see Table 11.4).

Were Results Reliable?

Early interventionists and others will want to know that an IGDI produces data on children's movement that is reliable and valid. Reliability and validity reflect the

Table 11.4. Alternate toy forms

| | Equivalent toy forms | |
	A	B
Early Communication Indicator (ECI)	House	Barn
Early Movement Indicator (EMI)	Window house with blocks/balls	School bus with blocks/balls
Early Social Indicator (ESI)	Tub of toys	Window house
Early Problem-Solving Indicator (EPSI)	Pop-up dinosaurs Stacking cups (square) Dome (DropNCatch)	Pop-up pets Stacking cups (round) Dome (PullNPop)
Indicator of Parent–Child Interaction (IPCI)	Book reading Frustration task Dressing	

© Juniper Gardens Children's Project; reprinted by permission.

trustworthiness of the data produced and indicate that important decisions may be appropriately made based on the EMI data. A measure such as the EMI, for example, is reliable when two observers simultaneously recording a child's performance return the same, or very nearly the same, score (i.e., interobserver agreement). A measure is also reliable when a child's score on one occasion is comparable with another obtained on another occasion separated by only a very brief period of time, such as several days (i.e., test–retest reliability). In this case, the same form of the measure (test–retest reliability)—or an equivalent form of the measure (alternate forms reliability)—may be administered. Reliability indicates that the EMI data obtained by multiple assessors in the same or in different programs are comparable.

Results for ECI, EMI, ESI, EPSI, and IPCI

Interobserver agreement and reliability analyses indicated that each IGDI produced reasonably high indicators of reliability. As displayed in Table 11.5, interobserver reliability estimates on each indicator ranged from 90% (ECI) to 95% (EPSI), which indicated that observers could agree on key skill definitions and record similar frequencies of behavior. Measurement reliability indices were also respectable. Test-retest reliability was completed by forming two groups of odd versus even observation occasions and comparing the scores. Results reported finding that mean frequencies of behavior recorded were highly similar with reliability correlations ranging from 0.85 (ESI) to 0.89 (ECI). Thus, similar estimates of behavior frequency and high correlations resulted. Alternate form score reliabilities (e.g., barn versus house scores) also produced respectably high reliability correlations across IGDIs. These ranged from a low of 0.57 on the ESI to high of 0.90 on the EPSI. Taken together, these findings indicated acceptable levels of sensitivity, validity, and reliability.

Were Results Valid?

A measure is valid when it is shown that it measures what it is supposed to measure. Several validity tests were conducted with the IGDIs. Criterion validity examined an IGDI's correlation to a commonly used test of the general outcome. Sensitivity to growth over age and time was another important validity demonstration.

Criterion Validity Results for the Five IGDIs

For each infant and toddler IGDI, it proved possible to demonstrate significant, positive correlations with commonly used and recognized criterion measures (see Table 11.5). The criterion measures were selected because they measured the developmental domain and outcome of interest, covered the age range birth to 3, and were widely used in the assessment of young children. With the exception of the EPSI, criterion measures included two different measures, each administered by different test agents (i.e., a professional observer or tester or a parent). These criterion validity correlations were highest in the case of the EMI, ranging from 0.77 to 0.86, that indicated that the EMI measured movement in ways similar to the professional

Table 11.5.   IGDI validity and reliability statistics

| IGDI | Validity | | Reliability | | |
	Criterion measure	Pearson *r*	Interobserver agreement	Split half	Alternate form
ECI weighted total communication rate	PLS-3	0.62	90%	0.89	0.72
	CCM	0.51			
EMI total communication rate	PDMS-2: Locomo	0.86	93%	0.88	0.84–0.91
	PDMS-2: Station	0.77			
	CAMS-GM	0.85			
ESI total social rate	Vineland–Interpersonal	0.65	92%	0.85	0.57–0.71
	Vineland–Play/Leisure	0.62			
	Howes–Simple Social Play	0.47			
	Howes–Composite	0.34			
EPSI total problem-solving rate	Bayley (MDI)	0.48	95%	0.88	0.90
IPCI parent or caregiver facilitators	HOME Total	0.60	84%	93%	
	HOME: Acceptance	0.29			
	AAPI-2: Inappropriate Expectations	−0.38			
	AAPI-2: Lack of Empathy	−0.38			
	AAPI-2: Role Reversal	−0.48			
	AAPI-2: Oppresses Power and Independence	−0.39			
IPCI parent and caregiver interrupters	HOME Total	−0.41	86%	82%	
	HOME: Acceptance	−0.24			
	AAPI-2: Inappropriate Expectations	0.36			
	AAPI-2: Role Reversal	0.36			
	AAPI-2: Oppresses Power and Independence	0.41			
	CES-D	0.42			
Child engagement	IPCI Parent/Cg Facilitators	0.77	83%	77%	
	IPCI Parent/Cg Interrupters	−0.49			
Child distress	BITSEA Problem Score	0.43	99%	37%	

Key: PLS-3, Preschool Language Scale-3 (Zimmerman et al., 1992); CCM, Caregiver Communication Measure; PDMS-2, Peabody Developmental Motor Scales-2 (Folio & Fewell, 2000); CAMS-GM, Caregiver Assessment of Movement Skills–Gross Motor (Kuntz, 2001); Vineland Adaptive Behavior Scales (Sparrow et al., 1998); Howes Play Scale (Howes & Stewart, 1987). MDI, Bayley Mental Development Index (Bayley, 1993); HOME, Home Observation for Measurement of the Environment (Caldwell & Bradley, 1984); AAPI-2, Adult-Adolescent Parenting Inventory-2 (Bavolek & Keene, 2001); CES-D, Center for Epidemiologic Studies Depression Scale (Radloff, 1977); BITSEA, Brief Infant Toddler Social-Emotional Assessment (Briggs-Gowan & Carter, 2006).

© Juniper Gardens Children's Project; reprinted by permission.

and parent informed measures (see Table 11.5). Similarly, the ECI was correlated 0.62 and 0.51 to professional-administered (Preschool Language Scale [PLS-3]) and parent-administered (Caregiver Communication Measure [CCG]) measures of early communication. The ESI was similarly positively correlated, although much more so to the Vineland Adaptive Behavior Scales measure completed by the parent than to the Howes Play Scale completed by an adult observer. Finally, the EPSI correlated 0.48 to the Bayley Mental Development Index (MDI).

Benchmarks for IGDIs

Benchmarks: Meaning and Use

In progress monitoring measures like IGDIs, benchmarks are used as a standard for purposes of comparison. The average (50th percentile) normative trajectory on the pediatrician's height and weight chart is commonly used as a basis for visually comparing any one child's growth rate at a month of age (e.g., 18 months) with that of the average growth rate for other children at that same age (see Figure 2.1). We use similar IGDI charts with similar benchmarks to aide our visual comparison of a child's monthly progress in the same way as the pediatrician to answer questions such as, "Is the child above or below the normative average for their age?" "Is the child radically lower (–1.0 SD below the mean) than other children the same age?"

Benchmark Results for the IGDIs

The growth charts in Figure 11.1 provide benchmarks for four of the five IGDIs. In this case, the mean and the +1 and –1 SD trajectories above and below are shown plotted over age at test. Any one child's trajectory based on an IGDI may be compared with these benchmarks to reveal how the child compares in age-expected levels of behavior and rate of growth over time (see Figure 2.3, the shaded areas a –1.0 and (1.5 SD below the mean trajectory). More detailed benchmarks are provided in numerical format in Table 11.6. Here one can see the IGDI values (e.g., cut points) above and below which a child could be determined to be in need of tier 1, 2, or 3 tier intervention based on deviation from the IGDI average at 12, 24, and 36 months of age.

Conclusion

The initial development and validation of each of the IGDIs described in this chapter was a thorough and carefully implemented process. Technical standards, such as those from the NCSPM, AERA, and DEC, guided the design, testing, and improvement of the measures. This ensured that each measure was 1) appropriate for use with young children with and without special needs, and 2) capable of collecting sensitive and accurate data for use by early interventionists, parents, and other stakeholders who are needing to make the myriad of practice decisions about individual children, intervention, and program improvement.

Since the initial work on these measures, additional work continues plowing new ground. For example, an extensive study is underway extending the size and representativeness of the ECI's norms and benchmarks, as well as examining the issue of its predictive utility; that is, the extent that infant/toddler scores predict success or failure (progress) in terms of preschool language and early literacy outcomes (Greenwood, Anderson, Little, Walker, & Buzhardt, 2009). Another example is work that is exploring the effects of data-based decision making on changes in intervention, planning, and individual child outcomes (Buzhardt, Greenwood, Walker,

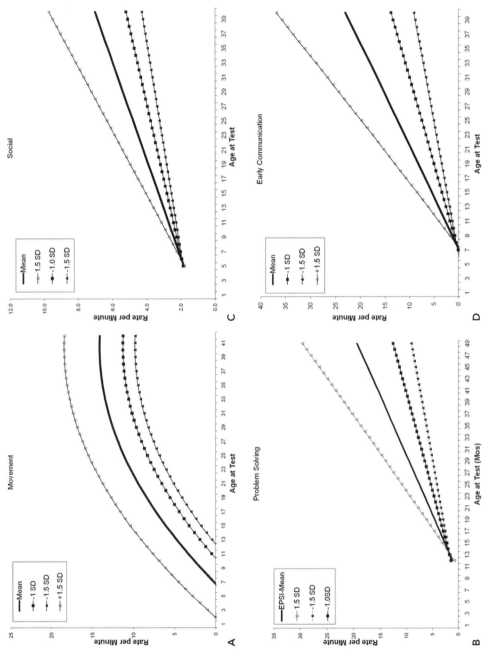

Figure 11.1. Benchmark growth curves (the mean, −1.0 SD and +1.5 SD) for movement (A), problem solving (B), social (C), and early communication (D). Data are rate per minute over age at test (months of age). (© Juniper Gardens Children's Project; reprinted by permission.)

Table 11.6. Yearly fluency benchmarks by child IGDI, age, and tier

	Age (months)											
	12				24				36			
		Tier 1	Tier 2	Tier 3		Tier 1	Tier 2	Tier 3		Tier 1	Tier 2	Tier 3
IGDI	Mean	GT	EQ or LT	EQ or LT	Mean	GT	EQ or LT	EQ or LT	Mean	GT	EQ or LT	EQ or LT
ECI	3.3	2.1	2.1	1.5	11.8	7.1	7.1	4.8	20.2	12.1	12.1	8.1
EPSI	1.5	1.4	1.4	1.1	7.0	5.0	5.0	4.0	13.0	8.6	8.6	6.4
ESI	2.9	2.5	2.5	2.4	4.7	3.7	3.7	3.2	6.4	4.8	4.8	4.0
EMI	4.1	1.2	1.2	-0.2	10.8	7.9	7.9	6.5	13.9	11.0	11.0	9.6

	Age (months)											
	2–12				13–24				25–43			
			EQ or LT	EQ or LT			EQ or LT	EQ or LT			EQ or LT	EQ or LT
IPCI	Mean	GT			Mean	GT			Mean	GT		
Parent/Cg facilitators	90.3	66.6	66.6	55.2	92.0	74.1	74.1	65.2	89.0	69.2	69.2	59.3

Benchmarks are based on local normative data samples. Cut points are based on –1.0 and –1.5 SD below the mean.

Key: GT, greater than; EQ, equal to; LT, less than; Cg, caregiver.

© Juniper Gardens Children's Project; reprinted by permission.

Carta, Terry, & Garrett, 2010). A third example is examination of the quality of IGDI implementation in two statewide implementations in Early Head Start programs with children if IFSP's are included (Walker, Greenwood, & Buzhardt, in press). Thus, IGDI research and development continues to be a work in progress. As a result, IGDI users can be assured that the data and decisions made based on these tools will be sound and trustworthy, and that additional work is continuing to expand knowledge and support use in early childhood.

IV

Other Applications for IGDIs

Early Literacy and Language IGDIs for Preschool-Age Children

Kristen Missall and Scott McConnell

Individual Growth and Development Indicators (IGDIs) were, in a broad sense, developed and tested to meet rigorous psychometric and practical standards, allowing repeated assessment over time and showing growth toward a long-term outcome or goal. Similar to infant and toddler IGDIs, preschool IGDIs for children between the ages of 30 and 66 months of age were developed in the mold of general outcome measurement (GOM). However, in addition to developing measures to meet GOM requirements, the development of preschool IGDIs brought two additional challenges: 1) creating measures with conceptual and empirical links to birth-to-age-5 developmental assessments generally and infant and toddler IGDIs specifically; and 2) creating measures with conceptual and empirical links to more academically focused K–12 assessment.

As might be expected with a charge for developmental assessment from birth to age 5, initial expectations for preschool IGDIs included assessments of all early childhood domains (i.e., language, social, cognitive, adaptive, and motor) (Priest et al., 2001). However, the additional charge of attending to more achievement focused K–12 assessments required consideration of several issues relevant to the preschool to kindergarten transition, as well as academic success after kindergarten.

Historical Relevance for Preschool IGDI Development

Since the mid to late 1990s, there have been increased enrollments in preschool and sharpened focus on preschool quality and outcomes (National Center for Education Statistics, 2003). This change may be attributed to expanded state-funded services and movement toward universal preschool in some locations (e.g., Georgia, Oklahoma, Florida) or federal focus on the importance of early development (e.g., Early Reading First grants from the No Child Left Behind Act of 2001 [PL 107-110]), but one important result has been interest in the impact of preschool participation and preschool quality on school readiness. Whereas children were once considered "ready for school" by default of maturation (e.g., age 5 or 6), definitions of "school readiness" have shifted to include an explicit pre-academic skill focus and alignment with K–12 outcomes, particularly in the area of literacy development (Dickinson & Neuman, 2006).

In short, recent years have seen increased focus on child performance and program accountability prior to and beginning with kindergarten. Specifically, it has become critical to have child-specific information about early literacy skill development that is predictive of later academic success. Although the significance of early literacy development for later reading success (see Snow, Burns, & Griffin, 1998; Whitehurst & Lonigan, 1998) has been well-documented, measures for producing reliable, valid estimates of early literacy skill that allow for data-based decision making and growth modeling have not been available.

The combined effect of increased preschool enrollments, enhanced focus on school readiness, and the urgent need for assessment tools to inform literacy development in preschool and early elementary resulted in a clear need for preschool IGDI research and development efforts. One of the primary outcomes from research on preschool IGDIs since the late 1990s is a suite of early literacy GOMs for preschool-age children collectively termed *Early Literacy IGDIs* (EL IGDIs). The purpose of this chapter is to provide an overview of the administration and psychometric support for EL IGDIs; provide information about web-based support for EL IGDIs; discuss connections between EL IGDIs and other GOMs of literacy; and present ongoing research and new directions with EL IGDIs and other GOMs for preschoolers in the broad area of literacy.

Overview of EL IGDIs

Development of EL IGDIs was grounded in a prominent model of early literacy development that conceptualizes literacy acquisition and competence as three primary components: outside-in skills, inside-out skills, and language (see Whitehurst & Lonigan, 1998). A graphic representation of Whitehurst and Lonigan's model is presented in Figure 12.1.

Outside-in skills represent children's capacity to direct basic knowledge and life experience to the understanding, recall, and interpretation of information presented in text. Inside-out skills are those that help children discern awareness of *sound units*—relationships among letters, phonemes, and syllables presented aurally—and *print units*—knowledge of letter–name and letter–sound correspondences. In reference to school-age children who are readers, outside-in skills essentially represent comprehension skills whereas inside-out skills demonstrate decoding. In the model, these primary elements of early literacy development are connected by language, which encompasses both knowledge and production of

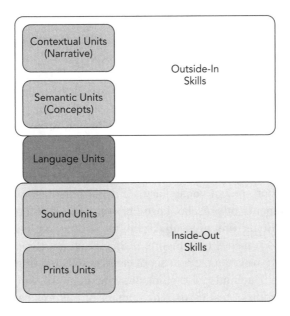

Figure 12.1. Model for emergent literacy. (From Whitehurst, G.J., & Lonigan, C.J. [1998.] Child development and emergent literacy. *Child Development, 69*[3], 848–872; adapted by permission.)

words (e.g., expressive and receptive vocabulary). These authors contend that children must develop competent early literacy skills in each of the three components of the model in order to be successful readers. Because preschool-age children do not read in a traditional sense, a primary goal in EL IGDI development has been to develop measures with GOM properties that also cover the key components of early literacy development.

Description of Measures

Similar to other standardized measures, EL IGDIs have scripted instructions and should be administered in a quiet environment that encourages child participation and engagement. Unlike other standardized measures, however, administering EL IGDIs does not require special training or credentials. Training guides to help preschool teachers and others learn to administer the measures and fidelity checklists for each EL IGDI are available at http://getgotgo.net/. Although each of the EL IGDIs has a slightly different administration procedure, each of the measures produces a raw score that is simple to calculate (e.g., total administered items minus incorrect items) and interpret. In accordance with GOM, scores produced by EL IGDIs are useful for screening early skill development and monitoring changes in skill development.

Scores from the EL IGDIs can be interpreted at multiple levels. As was the purpose of early GOMs (see Deno, 1985; Fuchs & Deno, 1991), the intended and primary purpose of EL IGDIs is to assess and monitor growth and development at the individual level. EL IGDIs were developed as screening tools to identify preschool children with low levels of critical early literacy skills and as progress monitoring tools to assess effects of intervention on skill development (see McConnell, Priest, Davis, & McEvoy, 2002; Ziolkowski & Goldstein, 2008). However, other applications also have proven useful. For example, EL IGDIs can be used for individual children in comparison with their classroom, center, or school district. The scores for individuals can be examined as aggregate, such as groups of children from a class or center in reference to some larger group (e.g., a school district). As with other GOMs, some areas have developed local norms (Reschly & Missall, 2005), and work on national norms has begun (Roseth & Missall, 2008).

Picture Naming   The Picture Naming IGDI (PN IGDI) is a measure of expressive language or spoken vocabulary. PN IGDI items are objects found commonly in environments of preschool-age children (e.g., food, transportation, animals, clothing). Items are presented one at a time on cards that measure approximately 8 × 5 inches (see Figure 12.2A). Each PN IGDI contains approximately 150 cards; however, a random set of cards is selected from the pool for each administration. Each administration includes four standard sample cards followed by a random selection of test cards. The number of pictures named correctly in 1 minute is the score.

To begin administration of the PN IGDI, the four sample cards are modeled for the child. The administrator says, "I'm going to look at these cards and name these pictures. Watch what I do." The administrator identifies the pictures on the cards and asks the child, "Now you name these pictures." The child then identifies the pictures. If the child is unable to identify the sample cards successfully, administration is discontinued. Moreover, if a child cannot successfully complete the PN IGDI, the Rhyming (RH) and Alliteration (AL) IGDIs are not administered. If the child is able to accurately identify PN sample cards, the administrator says, "Now we're going to look at some other pictures. This time, name them as fast as you can!" The first test card is presented as the administrator starts timing. Items are presented as quickly as the child responds. If a child lingers on an item for 3 seconds, the administrator prompts, "What's that?" After 5 seconds on that item, the examiner moves to the next test card. The examiner discretely creates a pile of cards to which the child responds correctly and a pile of cards that receive an incorrect response. The task continues for 1 minute. Any responses not registered within 1 minute are counted as incorrect (e.g., an item shown with a correct or incorrect response registered after the 1-minute mark).

Rhyming   The Rhyming IGDI (RH IGDI) is a measure of phonological awareness. Each RH IGDI item includes four objects presented on 8 × 5-inch cards (see Figure 12.2B): one target picture at the top and three pictures of possible rhyming items along the bottom. Cards are presented one at a time, and items on each card are always labeled aloud by the administrator. The RH IGDI has two standard sample items, four random sample items, and many test items that are selected randomly from a shuffled set of cards prior to administration. The number of rhymes from test items identified correctly in 2 minutes is the score.

Picture Naming card (A)

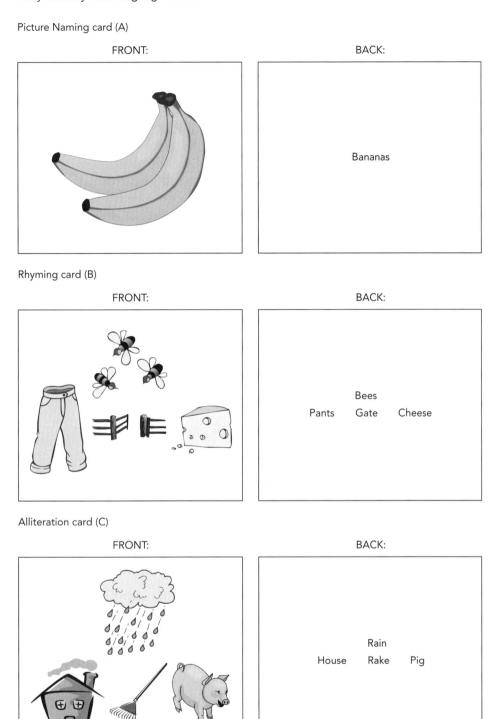

Figure 12.2.   Examples of Picture Naming card (A), Rhyming card (B), and Alliteration card (C).

The RH IGDI administration directions for the four sample items are similar. The administrator tells the child, "We're going to look at some pictures and find the ones that sound the same. They rhyme." For the first two standard sample items, the administrator models the task by naming the items and providing the answer. For example, the administrator says, "My turn: bees, pants, gate, cheese. Now I will find two that rhyme. Bees. Cheese. These two sound the same. They rhyme. Bees. Cheese." For the second two sample items, which are selected randomly from the entire set of RH IGDI cards, the procedure shifts a bit as the administrator asks the child to provide the answer. For example, the administrator says, "Let's do one together. First, it's my turn [the administrator names the pictures]. Now it's your turn. Point to the one that rhymes with or sounds the same as [administrator names the top picture]." On these sample items, the administrator may offer corrective feedback if the child answers the item incorrectly. The final two sample items selected randomly from the larger set of cards function just like test items; the administrator offers no corrective feedback. On the final samples, the administrator says, "Let's do some more. Remember, you point to the picture that rhymes with or sounds the same as the top picture." If the child correctly identifies two of the final four samples, the test items are administered. Otherwise, administration is discontinued. For each test item, the administrator names all of the pictures on the card and asks the child to "Point to the one that sounds the same as [the top picture]." Test items are administered for exactly 2 minutes.

Alliteration

Similar to the RH IGDI, the Alliteration IGDI (AL IGDI) is a measure of phonological awareness. The RH and AL IGDIs are also similar in presentation, administration, and scoring. Each AL IGDI item presents four objects on an 8 × 5-inch card (see Figure 12.2C): one target picture at the top and three pictures along the bottom, one of which begins with the same sound as the target picture. Cards are presented one at a time, and items on each card are labeled aloud by the administrator. The AL IGDI has two standard sample items, four random sample items, and many test items that are shuffled prior to administration so that each administration yields a different set of test cards. The number of alliterations from test items identified correctly in 2 minutes is the score.

Administration of the AL IGDI is the same as the RH IGDI. The one modification is that the directions ask the child to "Point to the picture that starts with the same sound as [the target picture]." The procedures for presenting sample and test items are the same as with the RH IGDI.

Segment Blending

The Segment Blending IGDI (SB IGDI) is a measure of phonological awareness. Items are words presented aloud in segmented form. Words are segmented between the compound words (e.g., cow-boy), syllable (e.g., d-og), or phoneme (e.g., g-o) level with a one-half second pause between segments. Although the SB IGDI has proved useful in research applications (Missall, 2002) and in application settings where a high degree of training and support is available to IGDI administrators, it also has been somewhat difficult to implement in less-resourced settings.

The SB IGDI has three standardized sample items. Test items are distributed across 20 alternate forms. Each form has approximately 44 items that are administered in order. Test items are administered for 2 minutes, allowing a total of 5 seconds per item for response (3 seconds before a quick prompt by the administrator followed by 2 more seconds of wait time). The child's score is the number of correct blends identified in 2 minutes.

Administration of the SB IGDI begins with standard sample items. The first sample item is fully demonstrated by the administrator who says, "I'm going to say a word in a funny way and I want you to listen closely. B-A-T. I said bat." The administrator then says, "Now let's do another one, and you tell me what word I say. SAND-BOX. What word did I say?" If the child provides the correct blend (i.e., sand-box), the administrator continues to the third sample item by saying, "I-T. What word did I say?" If the child provides the correct blend (i.e., it), test items are administered. If the child provides the incorrect response to either the second or third sample, the administrator provides the correct response. Incorrect responses, however, do not prevent administration of test items. To start test items, the administrator says, "Now let's do some more. Remember, I'm going to say a word in a funny way and you tell me what it is." Time is started as the first test item is presented.

Get It, Got It, Go!
Web-Based Support for EL IGDIs

From the outset, IGDIs were developed specifically to assist classroom teachers and others who serve young children in assessing children's developmental progress over long periods of time. As one part of our research and development effort, we wanted to ensure adequate attention to effective dissemination of background information, samples, and procedures for collecting IGDIs, as well as resources for managing, reporting, and acting on the data produced by these measures. In the late 1990s, with initial support from the U.S. Department of Education, we developed a web site that gathers and makes available a range of information for teachers and others considering using IGDIs or already using IGDIs in their early childhood practice.

Get it, Got it, Go! (http://getgotgo.net) provides access to general information, as well as high-level support for teachers and others using IGDIs to assess children's development. The web site includes both general access resources that anyone can use (primarily in the *Get it* and *Go!* sections of the web site) and password-protected, secure resources for maintaining individual, private data. Resources provided by *Get it, Got it, Go!* (or G3) continue to develop over time and are available and may be of interest to possible IGDI users. Specifically, G3 currently provides access to the PN, RH, and AL EL IGDIs, as well as more general information about IGDIs and GOM.

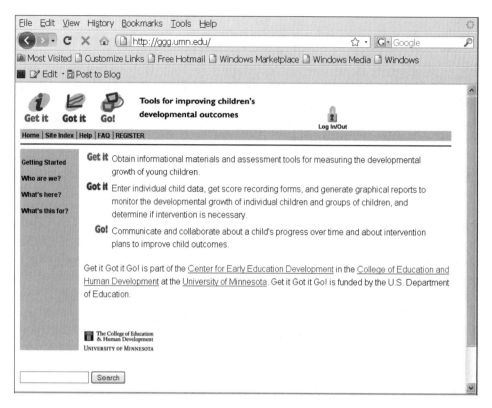

Figure 12.3. *Get it, Got it, Go!* home page. (© 2001–2006 by the Regents of the University of Minnesota; reprinted by permission.)

General Structure and Intended Audience

Figure 12.3 provides a view of G3's "front page." As may be apparent, the site has been designed specifically to be visually compelling, simple to navigate, and easy to use, which reflects the assumption that the site's primary users will be preschool teachers and paraprofessionals who have specific interests and needs and want their web-based work to be as efficient as possible.

Although anyone can use all features of the web site, many of the resources were designed with three groups of "users" in mind. First, and foremost, the site is used by preschool teachers and others who work directly with young children and who are interested in collecting GOMs of language and early literacy development and who want to use these measures to describe children's progress and plan additional interventions. Second, managers and administrators at the program, district, or state level may be interested in using G3 to gather and review information for large groups of children (e.g., in quarterly reporting programs for public school readiness programs). Last, some parents may be interested in resources provided by G3, either to better understand information they are receiving from their child's teacher or school or to actually assess their own child's developmental progress. Although some moderate level of expertise and skills related to assessing children and interpreting results is assumed, it is also known that some parents are highly motivated to monitor their own children and have (or can acquire) the skills necessary to do so.

Several common functions of assessment for G3 users were also assumed: first, that teachers would be primarily interested in monitoring the growth and development of individual children. Thus, for these reasons, much of the site's data management and reporting resources initially focused solely on individual children. With time, however, it was discovered that many users also want to administer IGDIs to groups of children on a periodic basis (e.g., quarterly) and to review results of these assessments both to monitor progress for accountability purposes and to identify individuals in need of more intensive intervention. Last, some researchers have used the site to access measures of child development and to manage the data that come from their research efforts.

Get It   The web site is organized in three functionally distinct sections. *Get it* is, in many ways, the entry point for many G3 users, providing access to information, assessment protocols, stimulus materials, and technical reports. Indeed, this section is named "get it" because it is the part of the web site where many new and returning users will gather information and resources that will enable them to implement IGDIs in their own program.

Figure 12.4 presents the *Get it* section's home page. For individuals new to IGDI assessment, or perhaps considering the possibility of adding IGDIs to their professional practice, *Get it* provides a wealth of information. *Getting Started* provides practical advice about the possible uses of IGDIs and the data they produce, as well as overviews of the assessment and data collection systems.

Background information of *Get it* provides users with information at a variety of levels. First, hyperlinks provide access to information about GOMs generally and IGDIs specifically that should be accessible to many education practitioners. This portion of *Get it* also provides links to a series of technical reports, research reports, and professional presentations that provide more detailed information on the assumptions, methods, and analyses that evaluate the rigor and quality of IGDIs for a range of possible applications. Between the general information and technical reports provided here, G3's developers hope to provide information to potential users (and consumers of IGDIs) with information that allows them to make an informed and independent assessment of the measures' utility for their particular purpose.

Finally, the *Procedures and Materials* section of *Get it* provides interested professionals with direct access to assessment formats, stimulus materials, and other resources needed to conduct IGDI assessments in preschool programs. In the near future, this section will also provide online training resources to better illustrate how to administer IGDIs with fidelity.

Got It   As the development of this web-based dissemination and technical assistance site was considered, users of other GOMs made it clear that it is essen-

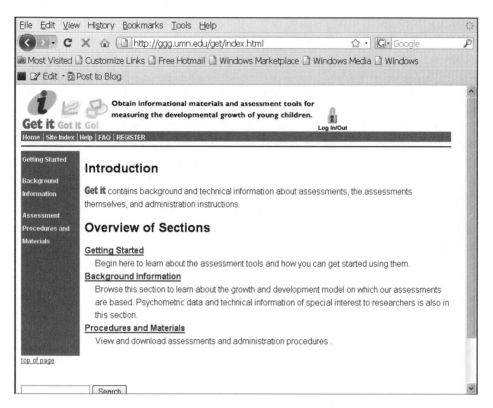

Figure 12.4. *Get it* section home page. (© 2001–2006 by the Regents of the University of Minnesota; reprinted by permission.)

tial that teachers and other consumers of GOM data have ready, easy-to-use resources for managing and reporting assessment data. This immediately raised issues of privacy and protection of confidentiality; to retain data for individual children so that teachers could assess child progress over time, it was essential to create a secure, password-protected part of the web site where these data could be kept. In other words, once teachers have "got" child assessment data, they need resources to manage and use it.

Figure 12.5 presents an image of the *Got it* part of G3. This section of the web site is perhaps the most complex and in some ways the most useful. Here, teachers can register and create their own secure storage area and register individual children in their classrooms. In both instances, registration collects simple information (e.g., name, birth date, demographic information) that will allow the teacher and others to identify and use any future data. Once registered, scores for individual IGDIs or sets of IGDIs can be entered for one child or for a group of children. In addition, some resources allow for "batch uploading" of child assessments to ease data entry burden.

Got it also provides a range of reporting formats for collected and entered data. Whereas current reports emphasize individual growth and performance (both for the individual and for the individual compared with other children), ongoing refine-

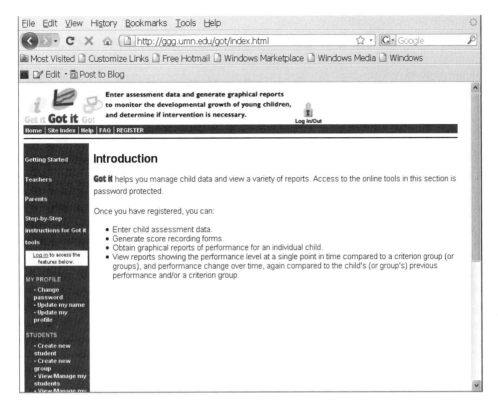

Figure 12.5.   *Got it* section home page. (© 2001–2006 by the Regents of the University of Minnesota; reprinted by permission.)

ment is adding report formats that describe groups of children over time and that are adapted for specific applications (e.g., response to intervention [RTI] screening assessments). *Got it* also provides resources for downloading entered data so that additional analyses and reports can be completed, when needed, by local users.

Go!   The third portion of G3 is designed for users who have collected information for an individual or groups, have reviewed reports and analyzed those data, and have concluded that a change of some sort is needed. In other words, that user is ready to "go!" Figure 12.6 provides a view of the *Go!* section home page. Currently, *Go!* offers two types of resources. First, more detailed information is provided to assist professionals in interpreting IGDI scores. Many users want to answer questions such as "Is this child's language growing at an acceptable rate?" or "Is this child on track to be a successful reader in second grade?" Information presented here helps users deepen their understanding of IGDI assessment and make more specific and detailed decisions about what, if anything, to do next. The second resource that *Go!* offers is descriptions and links to resources for additional intervention support in language and early literacy development. This information is intended to help teachers consider a range of scientifically based curricula, practices, and recommendations to alter current intervention for young children.

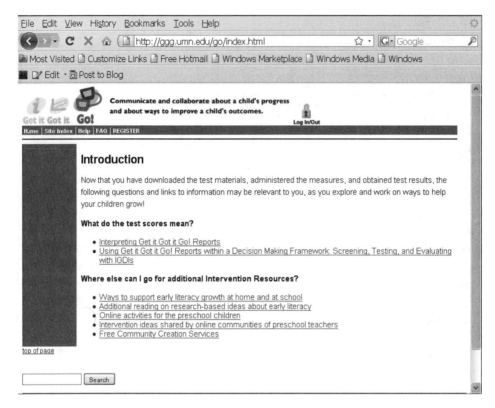

Figure 12.6. *Go!* section home page. (© 2001–2006 by the Regents of the University of Minnesota; reprinted by permission.)

In the near future, resources will be added to *Go!* to support implementation of an RTI model. These future developments will include various methods of describing and analyzing IGDI scores by group, recommendations for additional intervention for specific children, and recommendations and adapted resources for monitoring the progress of those specific children. "Wiki"-type resources that will allow individual practitioners to share their promising analyses and intervention procedures, tested with IGDIs, that others may be able to use are also being planned.

Many definitions of "assessment" indicate that the act is not simply the collection of data, but rather the intentional collection of specific data that is analyzed in a particular way to make one or several distinct decisions. *Get it, Got it, Go!* is designed to assist preschool teachers and others in using IGDIs as part of a comprehensive assessment system.

Technical Adequacy of EL IGDIs

Information on the psychometric properties of EL IGDIs is available from two primary sources. First, during research and development of EL IGDIs, each measure was evaluated rigorously in a longitudinal study. Second, since the initial development of the measures, each measure has been used in a variety of ways in multiple studies. Data from both sources are summarized here with population parameters to assist in understanding application.

Picture Naming

During development, the Picture Naming IGDI (PN IGDI) was investigated longitudinally with approximately 90 children from 30 to 66 months of age (see McConnell, Priest et al., 2002 and Priest, McConnell, McEvoy, & Shin, 2000 for more details on the following data that represent one study). The sample included children with disabilities, children living in poverty, and children without identified risk factors. One-month alternate-form reliability coefficients ranged from $r = .44$ to .78. Test–retest reliability across 3 weeks was $r = .67$. Moderate to high correlations supporting criterion validity were found between the PN IGDI and the Peabody Picture Vocabulary Test, Third Edition (PPVT-3; Dunn & Dunn, 1997) ($r = .56$ to .75) and the Preschool Language Scale-3 (PLS-3; Zimmerman, Steiner, & Pond, 1992) ($r = .63$ to .79). A correlation of $r = .41$ was also found between PN score and chronological age for the full sample; the correlation between PN score and age was $r = .63$ for children without identified risks, $r = .32$ for children living in poverty, and $r = .48$ for children with disabilities. More specifically, hierarchical linear modeling (HLM) results centered at 66 months of age showed an average PN score of 26.9 with an average gain of .44 pictures per month for children without identified risks, 19.0 with an average gain of .28 per month for children living in low income environments, and 16.9 with an average gain of .36 per month for children with identified disabilities.

In a study of 69 preschool children, HLM results centered at 59 months of age showed an average PN score of 22.2 for children without identified risks, 18.9 for children with speech-language disabilities, and 7.2 for Spanish-speaking children learning English (Missall, McConnell, & Cadigan, 2006). In a different study of 11 children with autism spectrum disorders (ASD), HLM results centered at 56 months of age produced a mean intercept of 15.7 and average growth of .12 pictures every 2 weeks; test–retest correlations ranged from $r = .65$ to .97, and PN correlated with the PPVT at $r = .80$ (Cadigan & Missall, 2007). Finally, another study examining connections between the Early Communication Indicator (ECI) for infants and toddlers (Luze et al., 2001) and the PN IGDI provided evidence for predictive validity for the ECI ($r = .65$) (Greenwood, Carta, & Walker, 2004).

Intervention studies employing the PN IGDI as a measure for monitoring the development of children have demonstrated that the PN IGDI is sensitive to intervention effects. In one multiple baseline study with three boys between the ages of 4 years 11 months and 5 years 1 month receiving speech-language and other special education services under the category of developmental delay, the PN IGDI was used twice per week during a 2-month, peer-mediated language intervention. Results showed that all children responded positively to the intervention as evidenced by qualitative observation and significant increase in PN slope (McConnell, Priest et al., 2002).

Rhyming

In initial research and development, the Rhyming IGDI (RH IGDI) was investigated in a longitudinal study of 90 preschool-age children from 30 to 66 months of age that included children with and without disabilities and those living in poverty (see McConnell, Priest et al., 2002 and Priest, Silberglitt, Hall, & Estrem, 2000 for more details on the following data). Test–retest reliability across 3 weeks was $r = .83$ to .89. Correlations with the PPVT-3 ($r = .56$ to .62), Concepts About Print (CAP; Clay, 1985) ($r = .54$ to .64), and Test of Phonological Awareness (TOPA; Torgesen & Bryant, 1994) ($r = .44$ to .62) provided evidence for criterion validity. A moderate correlation was found between RH score and chronological age $r = .46$. More specifically, HLM centered at 53 months of age showed an average RH score of 7.6 with an average growth rate of .38 rhymes per month for children without identified risks, 6.5 with an average growth of .95 rhymes per month for children living in low income families, and 5.1 with average growth of .40 per month for children with identified disabilities.

In a different longitudinal study, HLM analyses centered at 59 months of age showed an average RH score of 12.0 for children without identified risks, 6.8 for children living in poverty, 5.8 for children with speech-language disabilities, and .3 for Spanish-speaking children learning English (Missall et al., 2006).

A 2008 multiple baseline experimental intervention study used the RH IGDI with 13 children with language delays from low-income environments between the ages of 4 years 2 months and 5 years 4 months to monitor effects of an embedded phonological awareness intervention within shared book reading (see Ziolkowski & Goldstein, 2008). Results indicated that the RH IGDI was an effective progress monitoring tool across the 13-week intervention study. Participants increased their average correct score from less than one rhyme (.8) to 6.8 rhymes in 13 weeks, an effect size of $d = 2.87$ (Ziolkowski & Goldstein, 2008).

Alliteration

The Alliteration IGDI (AL IGDI) was investigated in a longitudinal study of 90 preschool-age children between 30 and 66 months of age that included children with and without disabilities and those living in poverty (see McConnell, Priest et al., 2002 and Priest, Silberglitt, Hall, & Estrem, 2000 for more details). Test–retest reliability across 3 weeks was $r = .62$ to .88. Correlations with the PPVT-3 ($r = .40$ to .657), CAP ($r = .34$ to .55), and TOPA ($r = .75$ to .79) provided evidence for criterion validity. A moderate correlation was found between RH score and chronological age $r = .61$. More specifically, HLM centered at 53 months of age showed an average AL score of 5.2 with an average growth rate of .38 alliterations per month for children without identified risks, 4.3 with an average growth of .25 alliterations per month for children living in low income families, and 4.4 with average growth of .36 per month for children with identified disabilities.

In a different longitudinal study, HLM analyses centered at 59 months of age showed an average AL score of 9.0 for children without identified risks, 4.4 for children living in poverty, 4.6 for children with speech-language disabilities, and 3.8 for Spanish-speaking children learning English (Missall et al., 2006).

A recent multiple-baseline experimental intervention study used the AL IGDI with 13 children with language delays from low income environments between the ages of 4 years 2 months and 5 years 4 months to monitor effects of an embedded phonological awareness intervention within shared book reading (see Ziolkowski & Goldstein, 2008). Results indicated that the AL IGDI was an effective progress monitoring tool across the 13-week intervention study. Participants increased their average correct score from less than one alliteration (.4) to 3.8 alliterations in 13 weeks, an effect size of $d = 2.20$ (Ziolkowski & Goldstein, 2008).

Segment Blending

The Segment Blending IGDI (SB IGDI) was investigated in a longitudinal study of 90 preschool-age children that included children with and without disabilities and those living in poverty (see McConnell, Priest et al., 2002). Correlations with the PPVT-3 ($r = .49$), CAP ($r = .35$), and TOPA ($r = .47$) provided some evidence for criterion validity. A low correlation was found between SB score and chronological age $r = .30$. The sample in this study covered the full range of 30–66 months, and it was hypothesized that the measure may be too difficult for young preschool children (30–48 months), thereby producing floor effects and suppressing correlations. Given these early results with the SB IGDI from research and development, it has been the least used of the IGDIs in the suite of literacy and language IGDIs.

Connection Between EL IGDIs and Curriculum-Based Measurement for Older Children

EL IGDIs were developed in the mold of GOM. As a result, they demonstrate conceptual connections to GOM tools for other populations that have many more years of research and application to support their use. In particular, a well-established base of information exists for GOM tools for children in kindergarten and early elementary school, namely the Dynamic Indicators of Basic Early Literacy Skills (DIBELS) (Good & Kaminski, 2003; Kaminski & Good, 1996) and Reading Curriculum-Based Measurement (R-CBM) (Deno, Mirkin, & Chiang, 1982).

Dynamic Indicators of Basic Early Literacy Skills

The DIBELS (Good & Kaminski, 2003; Kaminski & Good, 1996) were developed to evaluate children's acquisition of key early literacy skills in early elementary environments to regularly monitor progress toward early reading competence. DIBELS is comprised of several individually administered measures designed to uniquely assess different areas of literacy development. The most recent version of DIBELS (Good & Kaminski, 2003) includes the following measures: Initial Sound Fluency

(ISF) and Phoneme Segmentation Fluency (PSF), both measures of phonemic awareness; Nonsense Word Fluency (NWF), a measure of alphabetic principle; Letter Naming Fluency (LNF) and DIBELS Oral Reading Fluency (DORF), measures of accuracy and fluency; Word Use Fluency (WUF), a measure of vocabulary; and Retell Fluency, a measure of comprehension. Each DIBELS measure takes less than a few minutes to administer, is repeatable, has evidence of reliability and validity, and is sensitive to intervention effects. The measures, along with comprehensive information about each, are available at http://dibels.uoregon.edu.

Grounded in conceptual connections based on GOM principles and theories of literacy development, studies have been designed to look at empirical connections between EL IGDIs and DIBELS (see McConnell, Priest et al., 2002; Missall, 2002). In these studies with preschool-age samples, including children with and without disabilities and those living in poverty, the PN IGDI has correlated with the DIBELS measures of LNF (r = .32 to .37) and Onset Recognition Fluency (OnRF) (r = .44 to .49). In the sixth edition of DIBELS (Good & Kaminski, 2003), OnRF is called Initial Sound Fluency (ISF). The RH IGDI has correlated with LNF at r = .48 to .59 and with OnRF at r .44 to .68. The AL IGDI has correlated with LNF at r = .39 to .71.

Reading Curriculum-Based Measurement

One prominent GOM task designed to measure reading achievement in school-age students is Reading Curriculum-Based Measurement (R-CBM) (see Deno, 2003; Deno, Mirkin, & Chiang, 1982; Fuchs, 2004). R-CBM is a 1-minute measure of oral reading fluency scored as the number of words read correctly. R-CBM is appropriate for use with elementary-age students once they can read independently, or typically at first grade. A significant amount of research has examined the utility and technical adequacy of R-CBM because unlike other tests of reading achievement, R-CBM is quick to administer, has evidence of reliability and validity, is repeatable, does not require special training for administration, and is highly sensitive to intervention effects (see Deno, Fuchs, Marston, & Shin, 2001; Fuchs, Fuchs, Hamlett, Waltz, & Germann, 1993; Good & Jefferson, 1998; Good, Simmons, Kame'enui, 2001; Jenkins & Jewell, 1993). Accordingly, R-CBM has emerged as a measure commonly used in public schools.

Because of the strong conceptual connections between R-CBM and EL IGDIs, both in terms of construct (e.g., reading) and measurement properties (e.g., GOM), studies have begun to examine empirical connections between the measures. One longitudinal study followed children from age 4, when they were administered the PN, RH, and AL IGDIs, through first grade when they were administered R-CBM (Missall et al., 2007). R-CBM data from first grade were used to create a group of readers and a group of nonreaders using a criterion of 60 words read correctly per minute. Although the sample in the study was too small to identify specific IGDI scores predictive of first grade reading, analysis did determine that performance on the PN IGDI at age 4, specifically, was able to predict reading success with 73% accuracy. Sample sizes were too small for similar analyses with the RH and AL IGDIs.

Assessing Growth and Development from Preschool to Elementary School

More recently, research has begun to explore whether a "suite" of measures might be identified that describes individual children's development of early literacy and reading skills from age 3 to third grade. Utilizing samples of children with and without disabilities across the last 2 years of preschool and the first 3 years of elementary school, Wackerle and McConnell (2007) administered a large set of GOM tasks, including the EL IGDIs, DIBELS, R-CBM, isolated word reading, and other measures, and evaluated measures' performance within each age group. In simple terms, Wackerle and McConnell's (2007) analyses suggested an array of measures for describing children's progress over time, starting with PN-IGDI and RH-IGDI, moving to DIBELS, isolated word reading, and then R-CBM. Further research should clarify this suite and set empirical "cut points" to suggest when assessment can move from one measure to another.

Ongoing and Future Directions

The research group of faculty, staff, and graduate students at the University of Minnesota and elsewhere has been conducting IGDI research, development, and dissemination activities since the early 1990s. To date, we see work conducted by our group and others falling into one of two major categories: 1) *tools studies* in which investigators have developed, evaluated, and improved the available pool of IGDIs (e.g., Missall et al., 2007); and 2) *applications studies* in which investigators have used IGDIs and other measures to describe program effectiveness or conduct descriptive research (e.g., Missall et al., 2006). Furthermore, we have learned more about factors that promote or inhibit adoption and use of IGDIs in applied settings.

Based on available research on GOM for young children (summarized in Greenwood, Carta, Baggett et al., 2008; McConnell & Missall, 2008), ongoing program development in the United States and abroad, and our work with practitioners and program managers, as well as emerging federal and state education initiatives, we see several major areas for future research and development for IGDI assessment with young children.

Conceptual Developments

Assessment of developmental achievement within a GOM framework fits well with many of the core assumptions of early childhood education (McConnell, 2000). To date, GOMs for young children have been seen by developers and others as close, conceptually and procedurally, to curriculum-based measurement and other GOMs used with older children (see Deno, 1997; Fuchs & Deno, 1991). However, as work with young children has progressed, it has become clear that in future endeavors some further development and articulation will be needed of the core principles of GOM in early childhood.

Early childhood education has only recently begun to consider specific goals and objectives that might result from intervention in preschool that may in turn set the occasion for later achievement in elementary and secondary education. To date, outcome expectations for young children have been either nonexistent or described in broad and general terms (e.g., "The child shows interest in literacy materials and enjoys learning."). With the dual development of increased understanding of language and literacy development among preschool children (Dickinson & Neuman, 2006; Snow, Burns, & Griffin, 1998) and higher standards for demonstrated reading proficiency among early elementary students (largely contained within the No Child Left Behind Act of 2001 [PL 107-110]), it appears that more clearly articulated performance standards and programs designed to help children achieve these standards will become more common in coming years.

As this program approach develops, there is a need to develop a better understanding, conceptually and methodologically of the "outcomes" for preschoolers that are most closely associated with later reading proficiency. This, however, raises some important questions for preschool GOM tasks. For instance, available descriptive research suggests that phonological awareness and letter naming are most closely associated with reading performance in the earliest grades (when decoding is the primary task), whereas vocabulary and store of knowledge may be more closely associated with reading in third grade and later (when comprehension becomes more central to reading proficiency) (Snow, 1991; Snow et al., 1998; Whitehurst et al., 1999). Furthermore, some early literacy tasks that are targeted in widely adopted interventions (e.g., O'Connor, Notari-Syverson, & Vadasy, 1996) may be learned over short periods of time, rendering GOM tools sensitive to their development relatively less useful. Finally, many GOM tools of early literacy and language, including EL IGDIs and DIBELS (Good, Gruba, & Kaminski, 2002), assess more narrow ranges of child performance and may seem more like intervention targets to classroom teachers rather than indicators of development across a broader and more multidimensional skill set.

To address these and other issues that represent both the ongoing development of GOM and its application in early childhood settings, further refinement of theoretical models of development (e.g., the relation between "early literacy" development as described by Whitehurst & Lonigan, 1998, and "reading" as described by Adams, 1990) will be needed. We also may need work that helps situate indicator-level assessment within early education settings, helping practitioners distinguish between assessment activities (e.g., naming pictures on cards) and intervention needs based on knowledge and performance (e.g., expressive vocabulary).

Research

Without question, a good deal more research is needed to fully realize the promise of GOM with preschool children. To date, we have developed somewhat reasonable measures of language development and three or four aspects of phonological awareness. There are some data that allow us to assess the treatment validity of these measures, as well as their predictive validity for later reading. However, there is relatively little information about normative standards of growth on these measures and the possible benefit of measures in these domains (e.g., more sensitive, long-lasting measures of phonological awareness) or other domains (e.g., comprehension). There is only tentative information about how these measures relate to later reading performance, and relatively little information about the long-term utility of these measures with non-English–speaking children. All these topics need to be addressed in future research.

Two areas of current research hold some promise. First, several investigators have started exploring normative age- and grade-based levels and growth rates and the ways in which these levels and growth rates vary by group (Roseth & Missall, 2008). Extending Missall and colleague's (2007) sensitivity and accuracy analyses and Roseth and Missall's (2008) normative growth rates, practitioners will soon have more extensive normative information for evaluating individual children's performance.

Second, following the lead of elementary researchers (Krall, Krall, & Christ, 2006), other researchers are beginning to explore applications of Item Response Theory (IRT) to the design, evaluation, and improvement of IGDIs. Unlike many other GOM tools, EL IGDIs have features—individual stimulus cards—that function somewhat like traditional items. Researchers are now collecting data and reviewing assumptions to evaluate IRT's promise for improving the specificity and sensitivity of IGDIs at particular levels of achievement or development.

Application

As research continues to improve existing EL IGDIs and add more measures to the available set, research and program developers are also exploring new ways to use EL IGDIs to improve the efficiency and/or effectiveness of early education programs. To date, EL IGDIs have been used as measures within descriptive studies (Missall et al., 2006); to evaluate child progress and program effectiveness in Early Reading First, a U.S. Department of Education–funded program to support the development of early childhood centers focused on school readiness; and with special populations of children (Cadigan & Missall, 2007). One of the most promising future applications, however, may be to add EL IGDIs as a central feature of RTI models in early childhood education (Greenwood, Carta, McConnell, Goldstein, & Kaminksi, 2008; McConnell, 2008). In one emerging model (Greenwood, Carta, McConnell, et al., 2008) (see also http://www.crtiec.org), EL IGDIs will be used to periodically screen all children in preschool programs to identify those who are most likely to benefit from ongoing general education services (e.g., tier 1 in RTI models) and those who might require more intensive (e.g., tier 2 or tier 3) services to make adequate progress toward a long-term goal. Children engaged in tier 2 and tier 3 services will also complete EL IGDIs regularly, most likely every 2 weeks, to monitor their progress, evaluate the success of their current level of intervention, and identify times to move each child to more or less intensive levels of service based on observed growth. Existing EL IGDIs are being adapted, and new IGDIs developed, to fully operationalize assessment needed for an RTI model, with feasibility and initial effectiveness testing expected in coming years.

Developing Online Resources

In addition to expanding conceptualizations supporting EL IGDIs, improving and adding to existing measures, and developing new applications based on these measures, improvements in online resources that support teachers and others learning about, accessing, managing, and interpreting IGDIs are forthcoming. Working from the *Get it, Got it, Go!* web site, enhancements are expected that include additional online video and asynchronous chat training and technical support for new and ongoing users; report formats and specialized data management resources for teachers, administrators, and researchers; and ready access to improved stimulus materials and formats as researchers make them available.

Rapid expansion through technological innovations is also on the horizon. Some have explored administration and scoring of EL IGDIs on handheld and desktop computers, and further refinements are expected in this area. As IRT-based IGDIs develop in coming years, computer-assisted testing formats (in which item sets are tailored for an individual child and scoring is automated) can be expected. Developers are also exploring significant expansion of intervention recommendations and resources, including possible open-source solutions that would encourage teachers to share effective interventions with colleagues around the globe.

Conclusion

Preschool IGDIs were developed to assess a variety of developmental domains, assess effects of services for individuals and groups of children, align conceptually and empirically with GOM tools for infants and toddlers and older school-age children, and support effective services for young children. As early development of these measures occurred, interest intensified in development and application of tools for language and early literacy development. EL IGDIs, in particular, emerged from initial research efforts in preschool GOM because of important conceptual, empirical, political, and practical aspects supporting focus on early language and literacy development.

To date, EL IGDIs have provided focused and intentional work in language and literacy assessment from a GOM perspective. Continued efforts to develop and refine measures have produced improved tools, with additional work ongoing. Research has also focused on the needs of community-based preschool programs by focusing on conceptual and empirical links with measurement in infancy and early elementary school. Adoption and use of the measures suggest that parents and professionals who work with young children are interested in the tools. Both Ohio and New Mexico have adopted use of EL IGDIs statewide as evaluation and/or progress monitoring tools. The Pre-Elementary Education Longitudinal Study (PEELS; http://www.peels.org/Assessments.asp) adapted the EL IGDIs for its national evaluation of young children. In addition, more than 75,000 preschool-age children were registered in G3 as of 2008. There is a clear need for EL IGDIs.

In future work, research and development of EL IGDIs must thoroughly cover the various domains of early literacy and reading development (e.g., Whitehurst &

Lonigan, 1998). Early reading development clearly requires more than vocabulary and phonological awareness skills, and it will be important to have EL IGDIs of those areas of development (e.g., comprehension). Studies must continue to attend to predictive validity estimates of current and new tools. Given the primary goal of developing measures related to outcomes of importance, any progress with EL IGDIs specifically and preschool IGDIs broadly will be predicated on predictive validity for these outcomes. Similarly, forward motion will require attention to translation of research for effective practices and intervention.

A significant amount of work remains in producing a comprehensive suite of language and literacy GOM tools for preschool-age children, as well as similar measures in other domains. At the same time, substantial progress has been made since the late 1990s in developing GOM tools for preschool-age children and advancing thinking about measurement properties with regard to goals (e.g., literacy/reading) across developmental (e.g., infant/toddler and preschool) and physical (e.g., preschool to early elementary school) transitions. The experience of these authors with GOM in the context of preschool and in the development of EL IGDIs specifically has changed the way we consider assessment across developmental periods. We look forward to the next decade of research and development and to further refinement of teachers' and others' capacity to assess, and thus support, the growth and development of individual children.

New Applications and Considerations

Judith J. Carta and Charles Greenwood

The growing awareness of the importance of the first few years of life as a critical time for learning is finally being translated to policies for promoting early development. In 2010, the United States is expanding programs for infants and toddlers as never before. An infusion of $1.2 billion into the Early Head Start program in 2010 alone will increase the number of infants and toddlers and their families served by this program by nearly double. Other initiatives are aiming to prevent child maltreatment and promote more positive approaches to parenting of young children. Along these lines, the U.S. Congress is considering a number of initiatives to provide funds to states for evidence-based home visitation programs for low-income families with children younger than age 3 years. The proposed New Early Learning Challenge Grants would integrate multiple federal and state funding streams and create a competitive program to push states to develop comprehensive birth-to-5 systems. These new policy directions raise a number of issues:

1. As a higher proportion of infants and toddlers are served in programs, the need for screening measures increases.

2. As the awareness for evidence-based practices for programs serving young children grows, the need for tools that programs can use to demonstrate that children are growing toward important outcomes intensifies.

3. As programs embrace the philosophy of response to intervention (RTI) and other approaches that seek to prevent failure, programs are seeking out new tools that can be used to identify children who need additional supports as early as possible and then to modify their instructional programs to more closely match children's level of need.

The authors acknowledge the contribution of Drs. Gayle Luze and Kere Hughes of Iowa State University for contributing their work on testing the feasibility of using the IGDIs as a battery of measures.

In this volume, we offer IGDIs as a new approach for screening and progress monitoring that programs for infants and toddlers can use to achieve these ends. As the focus turns toward programs that would serve more of our youngest children, the importance of ensuring that these programs are doing all they can to promote children's learning and development is underscored. Programs must be equipped with ways of determining whether children are making progress in their growth on socially validated outcomes. They must have ways of knowing when children in their charge are making sufficient progress and quickly detecting when children are not on a track to be ready for school—academically, socially, and physically. When universal screening is carried out regularly across critical areas, children who need additional evaluation can be identified and provided with greater intensity of support or intervention and more opportunities for learning.

Although considerable progress developing and using IGDIs has been reported in this book, there is still much to do in terms of research and development, practice, and broad dissemination of IGDI technology (VanDerHeyden & Snyder, 2006). In terms of *new* measures for young children, IGDIs represent just the beginning of progress monitoring measurement in early childhood with much more to come. IGDIs now exist for a small range of socially valid outcomes that can be used in programs for universal screening and for addressing the intervention needs of children who are not meeting expected rates of progress; however, many other outcomes await the development of new measures, which suggests the need for more work on new progress monitoring measures. As we look ahead, we see the need for additional work in the following areas:

1. Development of new IGDIs to address additional general outcomes

2. Research about their psychometric properties

3. Studies to improve the efficiency and usability of IGDIs

4. Research that documents the benefits of using IGDIs in intervention contexts to improve children's and families' outcomes

Need for New IGDI Development

While this book showcases initial steps at applying the general outcomes approach to the screening and progress monitoring of young children, a number of important outcome areas remain untapped. One outcome identified by most parents and professionals as critically important in the original IGDI development plan remains to be completed: an adaptive proficiency general outcome. This outcome would tap children's growing proficiency in self-help skills such as dressing, eating, toileting, and safety. While skills in this area may not necessarily predict later school readiness, they certainly are related to children's ability to function across a variety of home, school, and community environments and thus are predictive of children's later social outcomes. Thus, IGDIs in this area are a high priority for future development.

Another important outcome for which IGDIs are needed is self-regulation, that is, children's capacity to control and regulate their behavior, attention, and affect in response to external (environmental) and internal (physiological) cues (Raffaelli, Crockett, & Shen, 2005). This is an area of rapid growth during the early childhood years as infants increase their capacities for physiological self-regulation (e.g., coordinating their wake and sleep cycles) and for emotional modulation (e.g. self-soothing); as toddlers initially face challenges associated with physiological self-regulation (e.g., coordinating sleep and wake cycles) and early modulation of emotions (e.g., self-soothing); as toddlers learn to comply and control behaviors; and as preschoolers learn to delay gratification. Children with difficulties in these areas often exhibit challenging behaviors and cause much concern for parents and caregivers.

Although a number of well-established methods exist for measuring challenging behavior in individual children (Barnett et al., 2006), we are not aware of any that are available for universal screening and progress monitoring of children's proficiency in regulating their behavior using brief, easy-to-use measures such as the IGDIs.

Another important outcome of early childhood is related to numeracy and numerical literacy. Whereas some progress has occurred in developing math IGDIs for preschool-age children (VanDerHeyden et al., 2004), much less is known about infants and toddlers and the behaviors they demonstrate relative to emerging numeracy skills (Clements, Sarama, & DiBiase, 2004; Xu, Spelke, & Goddard, 2005). Work is needed to develop infant and toddler IGDIs reflecting the earliest precursors of mathematic readiness for kindergarten. Considerable conceptual work is available tracing the roots of number fluency to the earliest aspects of number sense in young children, including what are thought to be the primary building blocks of number sense (i.e., a basic understanding of the cardinality and recognition of the "intuitive numbers") (e.g., Baroody, Bajaw, & Eiland, 2009). As researchers expand the knowledge available about the early cognitive processes that are precursors to later mathematical abilities, development of IGDIs in this area should take place so that tools can monitor children's early growth and determine when children need additional support in this important area of learning.

Need for More Research About Psychometric Properties of Current IGDIs

In this volume, we have presented initial findings of the reliability and validity studies that have been completed for the IGDIs. Additional work is needed to increase sample sizes, determine benchmarks (local and national), and study the predictive validity of existing measures. Of critical importance is establishing whether the infant and toddler IGDIs for the same general outcome measurement (GOM) link to (i.e., predict) the preschooler IGDIs. This type of linkage should occur in a seamless system of progress monitoring; however, only preliminary findings exist to document the predictive relationship between IGDIs across age spans toward specific outcomes. Therefore, longitudinal data are needed to indicate how good these measures are for long-term prediction of later outcomes. It is important to know that an at-risk identification at an early point in time will accurately forecast low perform-ance months and years later. Without predictive validity, it is difficult for programs to know whether a child's performance as an infant and toddler signals his or her need for immediate early intervention and, without such intervention, what the likely preschool and later school outcomes would be. Predictive validity provides the kind of evidence necessary to assert that children need and will benefit from tier 2 and 3 interventions. However, establishing predictive validity is challenging be-cause it requires longitudinal multivariate studies of growth and development over time. More research is needed to establish the predictive validity of each IGDI. More specifically, research is needed to establish IGDI benchmarks that can be the indi-cators for deciding whether any one child is potentially at risk of not attaining de-sired outcomes in the future. Benchmarks constitute the milestones of expected performance, and they are needed for intervention decision making.

Need for Research to Improve Efficiency of iGDIs

Additional questions remain about how IGDIs can be applied in actual practice. The current IGDIs were developed individually, each on its own time line over the course of years using the methods described in Chapter 11. At that time, little thought was devoted to the issue of how multiple IGDIs might be used as a system-atic battery in programwide implementation. During the initial stages of IGDI research, it was not certain whether multiple IGDIs would be successfully devel-oped. This has since been demonstrated. At this point, an important question for programs is whether multiple IGDIs can be used for universal screening and progress monitoring within single programs? Is this feasible, what are the costs, and how can implementation of multiple IGDIs best be conducted?

Investigators at Iowa State University are seeking to advance knowledge about using the battery of IGDIs (Luze & Hughes, 2008). Their aims are to investigate the reliability and validity of the IGDIs used in this way, as well as the practicality and feasibility of using all of the indicators with infants and toddlers with and without disabilities. The questions they are answering include "What is the reliability and va-lidity of IGDIs when used together as a comprehensive set for screening, progress monitoring, and outcome assessments? Can interventionists implement all of the IGDIs with fidelity? Do interventionists use the data for decision making and plan-ning interventions over time?"

We advise programs or individual early interventionists who want to use all the infant–toddler IGDIs together to understand what is involved in adopting these tools, ensure ongoing administrative support, and approach the implementation in a systematic manner. To do this effectively, a team approach is most beneficial. A team should explore the IGDIs, understand their theoretical background and pur-poses, and organize learning and implementation procedures. In addition, inter-ventionists who learn to use the specific IGDIs that are most applicable to their practice first (e.g., the ECI for speech and language therapists, the EMI for physical therapists) appear to be more motivated to learn the remaining IGDIs.

As with any innovation in practice, there is a time commitment necessary to become proficient in using IGDIs; it is more complex than just reading about them and then trying them out once or twice. Practitioners need to meet set proficiency standards administering and scoring each IGDI, but they also need to learn how to use IGDIs in making decisions about programming and services for young children and their families. The most effective learning comes when interventionists also use other sources of support. Administrators are one source, but fellow team members or colleagues who are also learning to use the IGDIs are also valuable. Interventionists who are most successful in learning to administer and use the IGDIs are those who not only lean on their colleagues for support, but those who also push one another to higher levels of performance.

Another question related to using IGDIs more efficiently focuses on whether it might be possible to integrate the indicators so that a child could be assessed on several IGDIs at once in a single session using one set of materials. More specifically, could a battery of IGDI measures be given in a single 10-minute administration, yielding data on parent–child interaction as well as the child's communication, movement, social, and cognitive proficiency? The issue is challenging because the toys and materials used for each IGDI are largely different due to the need to best evoke the different behaviors of interest (see Chapter 11). In addition, with the Early Social Indicator, a child peer is required along with the toy set. Yet, there are obvious overlaps in toys used for individual IGDIs (e.g., the ESI and EMI), and the possibility exists that some of the individual IGDI toy sets could be combined or integrated in some creative ways to evoke the behaviors of interest.

The potential benefit of integrating IGDIs is obvious for both the assessor and the child. Shortening the need for multi-play sessions that could take up to 30–40 minutes altogether to complete the battery would result in considerable time savings. In addition, for home visitors using IGDIs, the need to carry fewer small and large, cumbersome toy collections to home visits would also be appealing. A more integrated approach combining toys and data collection across IGDIs might be possible, but work on this has yet to be undertaken.

Need for Research on Use of IGDIs for Guiding Interventions

One of the most important uses of IGDIs is identifying those children who would benefit from greater levels of intervention intensity and then using IGDIs to examine whether these changes in intervention result in higher levels of growth. More research also is needed to document whether use of IGDIs to guide interventions in this way results in important outcomes. Work is just beginning, for example, to explore the benefits of RTI decision making with infants, toddlers, and preschoolers. The Making Online Decisions (MOD) tool discussed in Chapter 9 is just one example of an RTI application of an IGDI. The MOD is currently being tested in an experimental study to determine whether the use of the ECI to guide interventions results in more positive language outcomes for children. Studies such as this have been conducted in the elementary grades to document that progress monitoring can result in a variety of benefits. These include teachers' more frequent adjustments in students' interventions, quicker identification of children who need additional or different forms of intervention, and more effective programs resulting in better student outcomes (e.g., Fuchs, Fuchs, & Hamlett, 1989; Fuchs, Fuchs, & Stecker, 1989). Findings such as these will help make progress monitoring a routine part of early childhood practice.

Conclusion

We believe IGDIs will move programs for infants and toddlers forward because they will provide practitioners, parents, program directors, and policymakers with critically important information. We hope that we have designed a new approach that will be useful to guide programs at the individual child level, the classroom level, the program level, and even the state level. We hope that the information these indicators provide will help refine programs at all levels and make them more effective in terms of improved child outcomes. Challenges remain, however, and more work is needed if we are to develop an accurate and useful system of measures with progress-monitoring features. Not the least of these challenges is the key role of caregiver and teacher training and professional development that is required for using IGDIs in an RTI approach to improving services and effectiveness. Progress has been made, but more is needed, and new developments will surely be made as we learn more about the conditions that support the systematic use of IGDIs.

References

Achenbach, T.M., & Rescorla, L.A. (2000). *Manual for the ASEBA Preschool-Age Forms & Profiles*. Burlington, VT: University of Vermont, Research Center for Children, Youth, & Families.

Acredolo, L., & Goodwyn, S. (1988). Symbolic gesturing in normal infants. *Child Development, 59*, 450–466.

Adams, M. (1990). *Beginning to read: Thinking and learning about print*. Cambridge, MA: The MIT Press.

Administration for Children and Families. (1996). *Head Start program: Final rule*. Washington, DC: Department of Health and Human Services. Retrieved May 15, 2007, from http://www.head-start.lane.or.us/administration/regulations/45CFR130x.index.html

American Educational Research Association (AERA). (1999). *The standards for educational and psychological testing*. Washington, DC: Author.

Appleyard, K., Egeland, B., van Dulmen, M.H., & Sroufe, L.A. (2005). When more is not better: The role of cumulative risk in child behavior outcomes. *Journal of Child Psychology and Psychiatry, 46*, 235–245.

Asher, S.R. (1990). Recent advances in the study of peer rejection. In S.R. Asher & J.D. Coie (Eds.), *Peer rejection in childhood* (pp. 3–14). Cambridge, England: Cambridge University Press.

Atwater, J.B., Lee, Y., Montagna, D., Reynolds, L.H., & Tapia, Y. (2009). *Classroom CIRCLE: Classroom code for interactive recording of children's learning environments (Version 2.0)*. Kansas City: Juniper Gardens Children's Project, University of Kansas.

Baggett, K.M., & Carta, J.J. (2006). Using assessments to guide social-emotional intervention for very young children: An individual growth and development indicator (IGDI) of parent–child interaction. *Young Exceptional Children Monograph Series, 8*, 67–76.

Baggett, K.M., Warlen, L., Hamilton, J.L., Roberts, J.L., & Staker, M. (2007). Screening infant mental health indicators: An early Head Start initiative. *Infants and Young Children, 20*, 300–310.

Bagnato, S.J. (2006). Of helping and measuring for early childhood intervention: Reflections on issues and school psychology's role. *School Psychology Review, 35*(4), 615–620.

Bagnato, S.J., & Neisworth, J.T. (1991). *Assessment for early intervention: Best practices for professionals*. London: Guilford.

Bagnato, S.J., Neisworth, J.T., Salvia, J.J., & Hunt, F.M. (1999). *Temperament and Atypical Behavior Scale (TABS): Early childhood indicators of developmental dysfunction*. Baltimore: Paul H. Brookes Publishing Co.

Barnett, D.W., Elliott, N., Wolsing, L., Bunger, C.E., Haski, H., McKissick, C., et al. (2006). Response to intervention for young children with extremely challenging behaviors: What it might look like. *School Psychology Review, 35*, 568–582.

Baroody, A.J., Bajwa, N.P., & Eiland, M. (2009). Why can't Johnny remember the basic facts? *Developmental Disabilities Research Reviews, 15*(1), 69–79.

Bauer, P.J., Schwade, J.A., Wewerka, S.S., & Delaney, K. (1999). Planning ahead: Goal-directed problem solving by 2-year-olds. *Developmental Psychology, 35*(5), 1321–1337.

Bavolek, S.J., & Keene, R.G. (2001). *Adult-Adolescent Parenting Inventory* (2nd ed.). Park City, UT: Family Development Resources.

Bayley, N. (1993). *Bayley Scales of Infant Development* (2nd ed.). New York: Pearson Psych-Corp.

Berkeley, S., Bender, W.N., Peaster, L.G., & Saunders, L. (2009). Implementation of response to intervention: A snapshot of progress. *Journal of Learning Disabilities, 42*, 85–95.

Bigelow, K. (2006). Communication promotion and planned activities with families experiencing multiple risks. (Doctoral dissertation, University of Kansas, 2006). *Dissertation Abstracts International, B 67/04* [Publication number: AAT 3214822].

Brady, N.C., Bredin-Oja, S.L., & Warren, S.F. (2008). Prelinguistic and early language interventions for children with Down syndrome or fragile X syndrome. In S.F. Warren & J. Reichle (Series Eds.) & J.E. Roberts, R.S. Chapman, & S.F. Warren (Vol. Eds.), *Communication and language intervention series: Speech and language development and intervention in Down syndrome and fragile X syndrome* (pp. 173–192). Baltimore: Paul H. Brookes Publishing Co.

Bricker, D., Schoen Davis, M.S., & Squires, J. (2004). Mental health screening in young children. *Infants and Young Children, 17*, 129–144.

Briggs-Gowan, M.J., & Carter, A.S. (2006). *Brief Infant Toddler Social Emotional Assessment (BITSEA)*. San Antonio, TX: Pearson PsychCorp.

Briggs-Gowan, M.J., Carter, A.S., Irwin, J.R., Wachtel, K., & Cicchetti, D.V. (2004). The Brief Infant-Toddler Social And Emotional Assessment: Screening for social-emotional problems and delays in competence. *Journal of Pediatric Psychology, 29*, 143–155.

Brooks-Gunn, J., Berlin, L., Fuligni, A.J., & Sidle, A.S. (2000). Early childhood intervention programs: What about the family? In Shonkoff, J.P. & Meisels, S.J. (Eds), *Handbook of early childhood intervention* (2nd ed., pp. 549–588). New York: Cambridge University Press.

Burchinal, M.R., Roberts, J.E., Riggins, R., Jr., Zeisel, S.A., Neebe, E., & Bryant, D. (2000). Relating quality of center-based child care to early cognitive and language development longitudinally. *Child Development, 71*, 339–357.

Burton, A.W., & Miller, D.E. (1998). *Movement skill assessment.* Champaign, IL: Human Kinetics.

Butterworth, G., & Morisette, P. (1996). Onset of pointing and the acquisition of language in infancy. *Journal of Reproductive and Infant Psychology, 14*, 219–231.

Buzhardt, J., Greenwood, C.R., Walker, D., Carta, J.J., Terry, B., Garrett, M., Haupert, S. (2009, October). *Web-based support for progress monitoring and decision making for infant and toddlers.* Poster presentation for the 2009 Division of Early Childhood conference, Albuquerque, NM.

Buzhardt, J., Greenwood, C.R., Walker, D., Carta, J.J., Terry, B., & Garrett, M. (2010). Web-based tools to support the use of infant and toddler IGDIs for early intervention decision making. *Topics in Early Childhood Special Education, 29*(4), 201–214.

Buzhardt, J., & Semb, G. (2005). Integrating online instruction in a college classroom to improve cost effectiveness. *Teaching of Psychology, 32*(1), 63–66.

Cadigan, K., & Missall, K.N. (2007). Measuring expressive language growth in young children with autism spectrum disorders. *Topics in Early Childhood Special Education, 27*, 110–118.

Caldwell, B.M., & Bradley, R.H. (1984). *Home Observation for Measurement of the Environment (HOME) Inventory.* Little Rock, AR: University of Arkansas.

Carta, J.J., Greenwood, C.R., Luze, G.J., Cline, G., & Kuntz, S. (2004). Developing a general outcome measure of growth in social skills for infants and toddlers. *Journal of Early Intervention, 26*(2), 91–114.

Carta, J.J., Greenwood, C.R., Walker, D., Kaminski, R., Good, R., McConnell, S., & McEvoy, M. (2002). Individual Growth and Development Indicators (IGDIs): Assessment that guides intervention for young children. *Young Exceptional Children Monograph Series, 4*, 15–28.

Centers for Disease Control and Prevention. (2000). *CDC growth charts.* Washington, DC: Author.

Centers for Disease Control and Prevention. (2009). *Consequences of child maltreatment.* Washington, DC: Author. Retrieved November 8, 2009, at http://www.cdc.gov/violence prevention/childmaltreatment/consequences.html

Chang, L., Schwartz, D., Dodge, K.A., & McBride-Chang, C. (2003). Harsh parenting in relation to child emotion regulation and aggression. *Journal of Family Psychology, 17*, 598–606.

Clay, M.E. (1985). *Concepts about print.* Westport, CT: Greenwood Publishing.

Clements, D.H., Sarama, J., & DiBiase, A.M. (Eds.). (2004). *Engaging young children in mathematics: Standards for early childhood mathematics education.* Mahwah, NJ: Lawrence Erlbaum Associates.

Colombo, J. (1993). *Infant cognition: Predicting later intellectual functioning.* Thousand Oaks, CA: Sage Publications.

Colombo, J. (2004). Visual attention in infancy: Process and product in early cognitive development. In M.I. Posner (Ed.), *Cognitive neuroscience of attention* (pp. 329–341). New York: Guilford Press.

Colombo, J., & Cheatham, C.L. (2006). The emergence and basis of endogenous attention in infancy and early childhood. In R. Kail (Ed.), *Advances in child development and behavior (Vol. 35).* San Diego: Elsevier.

Council for Exceptional Children. (2007). *CEC's position on response to intervention (RTI): The unique role of special education and special educators.* Arlington, VA: Author.

Cratty, B.J. (1986). *Perceptual and motor developments in infants and children* (3rd ed.). Upper Saddle River, NJ: Prentice Hall.

Cripe, J., Hanline, M.F., & Daley, S. (1997). Preparing practitioners for planning intervention for natural environments. In P. Winton, J. McCullum, & C. Catlett (Eds.), *Reforming personnel preparation in early intervention: Issues, models, and practical strategies* (pp. 309–336). Baltimore: Paul H. Brookes Publishing Co.

Crowe, L. (2002). *The language intervention toolkit.* Topeka, KS: Kansas Department of Social and Rehabilitative Services.

Cunningham, A.E., & Stanovich, K.E. (1997). Early reading acquisition and its relation to reading experience and ability 10 years later. *Developmental Psychology, 33,* 934–945.

Dale, P.S., Price, T.S., Bishop, D.V.M., & Plomin, R. (2003). Outcomes of early language delay: 1. Predicting persistent and transient language difficulties at 3 and 4 years. *Journal of Speech, Language, and Hearing Research, 46,* 544–560.

Deno, S.L. (1985). Curriculum-based measurement: The emerging alternative. *Exceptional Children, 52,* 219–232.

Deno, S.L. (1997). Whether thou goest . . . Perspectives on progress monitoring. In J.W. Lloyd, E.J. Kameenui, & D. Chard (Eds.), *Issues in educating students with disabilities* (pp. 77–99). Mahwah, NJ: Lawrence Erlbaum Associates.

Deno, S.L. (2002). Problem solving as "best practice." In A. Thomas & J. Grimes (Eds.), *Best practices in school psychology IV* (Vol. 1, pp. 37–56). Washington, DC: National Association of School Psychologists.

Deno, S.L. (2003). Developments in curriculum-based measurement. *Journal of Special Education, 37,* 184–192.

Deno, S.L., Fuchs, L.S., Marston, D., & Shin, J. (2001). Using curriculum-based measurements to establish growth standards for students with learning disabilities. *School Psychology Review, 30,* 507–525.

Deno, S.L., Mirkin, P.K., & Chiang, B. (1982). Identifying valid measures of reading. *Exceptional Children, 49,* 36–45.

Dickinson, D.K., & Neuman, S.B. (Eds.). (2006). *Handbook of early literacy research* (Vol. 2). New York: Guilford Press.

Didow, S.M., & Eckerman, C.O. (2001). Toddler peers: From nonverbal coordinated action to verbal discourse. *Social Development, 10*(2), 170–188.

Division for Early Childhood. (2007). *Promoting positive outcomes for children with disabilities: Recommendations for curriculum, assessment, and program evaluation.* Missoula, MT: Council for Exceptional Children.

Dunlap, G., Strain, P.S., Fox, L., Carta, J.J., Conroy, M., Smith, B., et al. (2007). Prevention and intervention with young children's challenging behavior: A summary of current knowledge. *Behavioral Disorders, 32,* 29–45.

Dunn, L.M., & Dunn, L.M. (1997). *Peabody Picture Vocabulary Test* (3rd ed.). Circle Pines, MN: American Guidance Service.

Early Childhood Research Institute on Measuring Growth and Development. (1998a). *Accountability systems for children between birth and age eight (Technical Report 1)* (No. 6). Minneapolis, MN: Center for Early Education and Development, University of Minnesota.

Early Childhood Research Institute on Measuring Growth and Development. (1998b). *Research and development of individual growth and development indicators for children between birth and age eight,* (4). Minneapolis, MN: Center for Early Education and Development, University of Minnesota.

Eckerman, C.O., Davis, C.C., & Didow, S.M. (1989). Toddlers' emerging ways of achieving social coordination with a peer. *Child Development, 60,* 440–453.

Eckerman, C.O., & Didow, S.M. (1996). Nonverbal imitation and toddlers' mastery of verbal means of achieving coordinated action. *Developmental Psychology, 32*(1), 141–152.

Eckerman, C.O., Whatley, J.L., & McGehee, L.J. (1979). Approaching and contacting the object another manipulates. *Developmental Psychology, 15*, 585–593.

Feil, E.G., Walker, H.M., & Severson, H.H. (1995). Young children with behavior problems: Research and development of the early screening project. *Journal of Emotional and Behavioral Disorders, 3*, 194–202.

Fenson, L., Dale, P.S., Reznick, J.S., Bates, E., Thal, D.J., & Pethick, S.J. (1994). Variability in early communicative development. *Monographs of the Society for Research in Child Development, 59*(5, Serial 242).

Fenson, L., Dale, P.S., Reznick, J.S., Thal, D., Bates, E., Hartung, et al. (1993). *The MacArthur Communicative Development Inventories: User's guide and technical manual.* San Diego: Singular Publishing Group.

Fenson, L., Marchman, V.A., Thal, D.J., Dale, P.S., Reznick, J.S., & Bates, E. (2007). *MacArthur-Bates Communicative Development Inventories (CDIs): User's guide and technical manual* (2nd ed.). Baltimore: Paul H. Brookes Publishing Co.

Fey, M.E., Catts, H.,& Larrivee, L.S. (1995). Preparing preschoolers for the academic and social challenges of school. In S.F. Warren & J. Reichle (Series Eds.) & M.E. Fey, J. Windsor, & S.F. Warren (Vol. Eds.), *Communication and language intervention series: Vol. 5. Language intervention: Preschool through the elementary years* (pp. 225–290). Baltimore: Paul H. Brookes Publishing Co.

Field, T. (1994, February). The effects of mother's physical and emotional unavailability on emotion regulation. *Monographs of the Society for Research in Child Development, 59*(2–3), 208–227.

Fisher, L., Thompson, S., Ferrari, M., Savoie, L.A., & Lukie, S. (2009). *Medical, behavior, and social problems.* Association for Research in International Adoption. Retrieved November 7, 2009, at http://www.adoption-research.org/chapter3.html

Folio, M.R., & Fewell, R. (2000). *Peabody Developmental Motor Scales* (2nd ed.). San Antonio, TX: Pearson PsychCorp.

Fuchs, D., Fuchs, L.S., & Compton, D. (2004). Identifying reading disabilities by responsiveness-to-instruction: Specifying measures and criteria. *Learning Disability Quarterly, 27*, 216–227.

Fuchs, L.S. (2004). The past, present, and future of curriculum-based measurement. *School Psychology Review, 33*, 188–192.

Fuchs, L.S., & Deno, S.L. (1991). Paradigmatic distinctions between instructionally relevant measurement models. *Exceptional Children, 57*, 488–500.

Fuchs, L.S., & Fuchs, D. (1998). Treatment validity: A unifying concept for reconceptualizing the identification of learning disabilities. *Learning Disabilities Research & Practice, 13*, 204–219.

Fuchs, L.S., & Fuchs, D. (2007). The role of assessment in the three-tier approach to reading instruction. In D. Haager, J. Klingner, & S. Vaughn (Eds.), *Evidence-based reading practices for response to intervention* (pp. 29–44). Baltimore: Paul H. Brookes Publishing Co.

Fuchs, L.S., Fuchs, D., & Hamlett, C.L. (1989). Effects of instrumental use of curriculum-based measurement to enhance instructional programs. *Remedial and Special Education, 10*(2), 43–52.

Fuchs, L.S., Fuchs, D., Hamlett, C.L., Waltz, L., & Germann, G. (1993). Formative evaluation of academic progress: How much growth can we expect? *School Psychology Review, 22*, 27–48.

Fuchs, L.S., Fuchs, D., Hintze, J., & Lembke, E. (2006, July). Progress monitoring in the context of responsiveness-to-intervention. Presentation at the Summer Institute on Student Progress Monitoring, Kansas City, MO.

Fuchs, L.S., Fuchs, D., & Stecker, P.M. (1989). Effects of curriculum-based measurement on teachers' instructional planning. *Journal of Learning Disabilities, 22*, 51–59.

Gallahue, D.L. (1989). *Understanding motor development: Infants, children, and adolescents* (2nd ed.). Carmel, IN: Benchmark Press.

Gallahue, D.L., & Ozmun, J.C. (1995). *Understanding motor development: Infants, children, adolescents, and adults* (3rd ed.). Madison, WI: Brown & Benchmark.

Garg, A., Adhikari, N., McDonald, H., Rosas-Arellano, M., Devereaux, P., Beyene, J., et al. (2005). Effects of computerized clinical decision support systems on practitioner performance and patient outcomes: A systematic review. *Journal of the American Medical Association, 293*(10), 1223–1238.

Garon, N., Bryson, S.E., & Smith, I.M. (2008). Executive function in preschoolers: A review using an integrative framework. *Psychological Bulletin, 134*(1), 31–60.

George, C., & Main, M. (1979). Social interactions of young abused children: Approach, avoidance, and aggression. *Child Development, 50,* 306–318.

Gibbs, E.D., & Teti, D.M. (1990). *Interdisciplinary assessment of infants: A guide for early intervention professionals.* Baltimore: Paul H. Brookes Publishing Co.

Gilfoyle, E.M., Grady, A.P., & Moore, J.C. (1981). *Children adapt.* Thorofare, NJ: Slack.

Goldfield, E.C. (1995). *Emergent forms: Origins and early development of human action and perception.* New York: Oxford University Press.

Goldstein, H., Kaczmarek, L.A., & English, K.M. (Vol. Eds.). (2001). *Promoting social communication: Children with developmental disabilities from birth to adolescence.* In S.F. Warren & J. Reichle (Series Eds.), *Communication and language intervention series: Vol. 10.* Baltimore: Paul H. Brookes Publishing Co.

Goldstein, H., & Morgan, L. (2002). Social interaction and models of friendship development. In S.F. Warren & M.E. Fey (Series Eds.) & H. Goldstein, L.A. Kaczmarek, & K.M. English (Vol. Eds.), *Communication and language intervention series: Vol. 10. Promoting social communication: Children with developmental disabilities from birth to adolescence* (pp. 5–26). Baltimore: Paul H. Brookes Publishing Co.

Good, R.H., Gruba, J., & Kaminski, R.A. (2002). Best practices in using dynamic indicators of basic early literacy skills (Dibels) in an outcomes-driven model. In A. Thomas & J. Grimes (Eds.), *Best practices in school psychology: Vol. 1* (4th ed., pp. 699–720). Washington, DC: National Association of School Psychologists.

Good, R., & Jefferson, G. (1998). Contemporary perspectives on curriculum-based measurement validity. In M.R. Shinn (Ed.), *Advanced applications of curriculum-based measurement* (pp. 61–88). New York: Guilford Press.

Good, R.H., & Kaminski, R.A. (2003). *DIBELS: Dynamic Indicators of Basic Early Literacy Skills* (6th ed.). Longmont, CO: Sopris West.

Good, R.H., Kaminski, R.A., Smith, S., Simmons, D.C., Kame'enui, E., & Wallin, J. (2003). Reviewing outcomes: Using DIBELS to evaluate kindergarten curricula and interventions. In S. Vaughn & K.L. Briggs (Eds.), *Reading in the classroom: Systems for the observation of teaching and learning.* Baltimore: Paul H. Brookes Publishing Co.

Good, R.H., Simmons, D.C., & Kame'enui, E.J. (2001). The importance and decision-making utility of a continuum of fluency-based indicators of foundational reading skills for third-grade high-stakes outcomes. *Scientific Studies of Reading, 5,* 257–288.

Good, R.H., Simmons, D.C., Kame'enui, E.J., Kaminski, R., & Wallin, J. (2002). *Summary of decision rules for intensive, strategic, and benchmark instructional recommendations in kindergarten through third grade (Technical Report 11).* Eugene, OR: University of Oregon.

Greenwood, C.R. (2008, June). *Developing, validating, and scaling-up continuous progress monitoring measures for intervention research and accountability in early childhood.* Paper presented at the Institute on Educational Science Project Directors' Conference, Washington, DC.

Greenwood, C.R., Anderson, R., Little, T.D., Walker, D., & Buzhardt, J. (2009, June). *Dynamic relations in early communication key skill growth trajectories of infants and toddlers.* Poster presented at the Institute on Educational Science Project Directors' Conference, Washington, DC.

Greenwood, C.R., Carta, J.J., & Walker, D. (2004). Individual Growth and Development Indicators (IGDIs): Tools for assessing intervention results for infants and toddlers. In W. Heward, T.E. Heron, N.A. Neef, S.M. Peterson, D.M. Sainato, G. Cartledge, et al. (Eds.), *Focus on behavior analysis in education: Achievements, challenges, and opportunities* (pp. 103–124). Columbus, OH: Pearson/Prentice Hall.

Greenwood, C.R., Carta, J.J., & Walker, D. (2005). Individual growth and development indicators (IGDIs): Tools for assessing intervention results for infants and toddlers. In B. Heward et al. (Eds.), *Focus on behavior analysis in education: Achievements, challenges, and opportunities* (pp. 103–124). Columbus, OH: Pearson/Prentice Hall.

Greenwood, C.R., Carta, J.J., Baggett, K., Buzhardt, J., Walker, D., & Terry, B. (2008). Best practices in integrating progress monitoring and response-to-intervention concepts into early childhood systems. In A. Thomas, J. Grimes, & J. Gruba (Eds.), *Best practices in school psychology: V* (pp. 535–548). Washington, DC: National Association of School Psychology.

Greenwood, C.R., Carta, J.J., McConnell, S.R., Goldstein, H., & Kaminksi, R.A. (2008). Center for Response to Intervention in Early Childhood. Retrieved June 5, 2008, from http://www.crtiec.org/

Greenwood, C.R., Carta, J.J., Walker, D., Hughes, K., & Weathers, M. (2006). Preliminary investigations of the application of the early communication indicator (ECI) for infants and toddlers. *Journal of Early Intervention, 28*(3),178–196.

Greenwood, C.R., Dunn, S., Ward, S.M., & Luze, G.J. (2003). The early communication indicator (ECI) for infants and toddlers: What it is, where it's been, and where it needs to go. *The Behavior Analyst Today, 3*(4), 383–388.

Greenwood, C.R., Luze, G.J., Cline, G., Kuntz, S., & Leitschuh, C. (2002). Developing a general outcome measure of growth in movement for infants and toddlers. *Topics in Early Childhood Special Education, 22*(3), 143–157.

Greenwood, C.R., McConnell, E.K., Little, T.D., & the IGDI Workgroup. (2008, June). *Dynamic relations in the early communication growth trajectories of infants and toddlers.* Poster presented at the Institute on Educational Science Project Directors' Conference, Washington, DC.

Greenwood, C.R., Walker, D., Carta, J.J., & Higgins, S. (2006). Developing a general outcome measure of growth in the cognitive abilities of children 1 to 4 years old: The early problem solving indicator (EPSI). In A. VanDerHeyden & P. Synder (Eds.), *Integrating early intervention and school psychology to accelerate growth for all children in school. Psychology Review, 35,* 535–551.

Greenwood, C.R., Walker, D., & Utley, C.A. (2001). Relationships between social-communicative skills and life achievements. In S.F. Warren & J. Reichle (Series Eds.) & H. Goldstein, L.A. Kaczmarek, & K.M. English (Vol. Eds.), *Communication and language intervention series: Vol. 10. Promoting social communication: Children with developmental disabilities from birth to adolescence* (pp. 345–370). Baltimore: Paul H. Brookes Publishing Co.

Guralnick, M.J., & Neville, B. (1997). Designing early intervention programs to promote children's social competence. In M.J. Guralnick (Ed.), *The effectiveness of early intervention.* Baltimore: Paul H. Brookes Publishing Co.

Hannan, T.E. (1987). A cross-sequential assessment of the occurrences of pointing in 3- to 12-month-old human infants. *Infant Behavior and Development, 11,* 381–410.

Harjusola-Webb, S.M. (2006). The use of naturalistic communication intervention with young children who have developmental disabilities. (Doctoral dissertation, University of Kansas, 2006). *Dissertation Abstracts International, A 67/04, 1290.* [Publication number: AAT 3216284].

Harris, S.R. (1997). The effectiveness of early intervention for children with cerebral palsy and related motor disabilities. In M.J. Guralnick (Ed.), *The effectiveness of early intervention* (pp. 327–347). Baltimore: Paul H. Brookes Publishing Co.

Harris, S.R., & McEwen, I.R. (1996). Assessing motor skills. In M. McLean, D.B. Bailey & M. Wolery (Eds.), *Assessing infants and preschoolers with special needs* (pp. 305–333). Upper Saddle River, NJ: Merrill/Prentice Hall.

Hart, B. (1991). Input frequency and children's first words. *First Language, 11,* 289–300.

Hart, B., & Risley, T.R. (1992). American parenting of language learning children: Persisting differences in family–child interaction observed in natural home environments. *Developmental Psychology, 28,* 1096–1105.

Hart, B., & Risley, T.R. (1995). *Meaningful differences in the everyday experience of young American children.* Baltimore: Paul H. Brookes Publishing Co.

Hebbeler, K., Spiker, D., Bailey, D., Scarborough, A., Mallik, S., Simeonsson, R., Singer, M., & Nelson, L. (2007, January). *Early intervention for infants and toddlers with disabilities and their families: Participants, services, and outcomes.* Final Report of the National

Early Intervention Longitudinal Study (NEILS) to the U.S. Department of Education, Office of Special Education Programs. Retrieved January 20, 2009, from http://www.sri.com/neils/pdfs/NEILS_Report_02_07_Final2.pdf

Heinicke, C.M., Fineman, N.R., Ponce, V.A., & Gutnrie, D. (2001). Relation-based intervention with at-risk mothers: Outcome in the second year of life. *Infant Mental Health Journal, 22,* 431–462.

Hofacker, N., & Papousek, M. (1998). Disorders of excessive crying, feeding, and sleeping: The Munich Interdisciplinary Research and Intervention Program. *Infant Mental Health Journal, 19,* 180–201.

Howes, C. (1988). Peer interaction in young children. *Monograph of the Society for Research in Child Development #217, 53*(1).

Howes, C., & Matheson, C.C. (1992). Sequences in the development of competent play with peers: Social and social pretend play. *Developmental Psychology. 28*(5), 961–974.

Howes, C., & Stewart, P. (1987). Child's play with adults, toys, and peers: An examination of family and child care influences. *Developmental Psychology, 23,* 423–430.

Hupp, S., & Abbeduto, L. (1991). Persistence as an indicator of mastery motivation in young children with cognitive delays *Journal of Early Intervention, 15,* 219–225.

Huttenlocher, J., Haight, W., Bryk, A., Seltzer, M., & Lyons, T. (1991). Early vocabulary growth: Relation to language input and gender. *Developmental Psychology, 27,* 236–248.

Individuals with Disabilities Education Act Amendments of 1997, PL 105-17, 20 U.S.C. §§ 1400 *et seq.*

Individuals with Disabilities Education Improvement Act of 2004, PL 108-446, 20 U.S.C. §§ 1400 *et seq.*

Irvin, L.K., Horner, R.H., Ingram, K., Todd, A.W., Sugai, G., & Boland, J.B. (2006). Using office discipline referral data for decision making about student behavior in elementary and middle schools. *Journal of Positive Behavior Interventions, 8,* 10–23.

Isaacs, J.B. (2008). Impacts of early childhood programs. Retrieved September 29, 2008, from http://www.brookings.edu/~/media/Files/rc/papers/2008/09_early_programs_isaacs/09_early_programs_isaacs.pdf.

Iverson, J.M., & Thal, D.J. (1997). Communicative transitions: There's more to the hand than meets the eye. In S.F. Warren & J. Reichle (Series Eds.) & A.M. Wetherby, S.F. Warren & J. Reichle (Vol. Eds.), *Communication and language intervention series: Vol. 7. Transitions in prelinguistic communication* (pp. 59–87). Baltimore: Paul H. Brookes Publishing Co.

Jenkins, J.R. & Jewell, M. (1993). Examining the validity of two measures for formative teaching: Reading aloud and maze. *Exceptional Children, 59,* 421–432.

Jennings, K.D., Yarrow, L.J., & Martin, P.P. (1984). Mastery motivation and cognitive development: A longitudinal study from infancy to 3 1/2 years of age. *International Journal of Behavioral Development, 7,* 441–461.

Jung, I. (2005). Cost-effectiveness of online teacher training. *Open Learning, 20*(2), 131–146.

Kagan, S.L., Rosenkoetter, S., & Cohen, N. (1997). *Considering child-based results for young children: Definitions, desirability, feasibility, and next steps.* New Haven, CT: Yale Bush Center in Child Development and Social Policy.

Kaiser, A.P., Hancock, T.B., Cai, X., Foster, E.M., & Hester, P.P. (2000). Parent reported behavioral problems and language delays in boys and girls enrolled in head start classrooms. *Behavioral Disorders, 26*(1), 26–41.

Kaiser, A.P., Hancock, T.B., & Nietfeld, J.P. (2000). The effects of parent-implemented enhanced milieu teaching on the social communication of children who have autism. *Journal of Early Education and Development [Special Issue], 4,* 423–446.

Kaminski, R., & Good, R.H. (1996). Toward a technology for assessing basic early literacy skills. *School Psychology Review, 25,* 215–227.

Kaminski, R., Cummings, K.D., Powell-Smith, K.A., & Good, R.H. (2008). Best practices in using Dynamic Indicators of Basic Early Literacy Skills for formative assessment and evaluation. In A. Thomas & J. Grimes (Eds.), *Best practices in school psychology: Vol. V* (pp. 1181–1204). Washington, DC: National Association of School Psychologists.

Kannass, K.N., & Colombo, J. (2007). The effects of continuous and intermittent distraction on attention and cognitive performance in preschoolers. *Journal of Cognition and Development, 8,* 63–77.

Kannass, K.N., Colombo, J., & Wyss, N. (in press). Now, pay attention! The effects of instruction on children's attention. *Journal of Cognitive Development.*

Kannass, K.N., & Oakes, L.M. (2008). The development of attention and its relations to language in infancy and toddlerhood. *Journal of Cognition and Development, 9*(2), 222–246.

Kennedy, C.H. (2005). *Single case designs for educational research.* Boston: Pearson.

Kirk, S. (2006). *The effects of using outcome measures and progress monitoring to guide language-promoting interventions in Early Head Start Programs.* Unpublished Doctoral Dissertation, University of Kansas, Lawrence, KS.

Kirshner, B., & Guyatt, G.H. (1985). A methodologic framework for assessing health indices. *Journal of Chronic Diseases, 38,* 27–36.

Krall, L., Kroll, A., & Christ, T.J. (2006). Computer Based Assessment System for Reading (CBAS-R) 1.0: Hierarchy and item development for fluency and decoding. University of Minnesota, Center for Reading Research.

Kuntz, S. (2001). *Caregiver Assessment of Movement Skills–Gross Motor.* Kansas City, KS: University of Kansas.

Kupersmidt, J.B., & Coie, J.D. (1990). Preadolescent peer status, aggression, and school adjustment as predictors of externalizing problems in adolescence. *Child Development, 61,* 1350–1362.

Ladd, G.W., & Price, J.M. (1986). Promoting children's cognitive and social competence: The relation between parents' perceptions of task difficulty and children's perceived and actual competence. *Child Development, 57*(2), 446–460.

Landry, S.H., Smith, K.E., & Swank, P.R. (2006). Responsive parenting: Establishing foundations for social, communication and independent problem-solving. *Developmental Psychology, 42,* 627–642.

Landry, S.H., Smith, K.E., Swank, P.R., Assel, M.A., & Vellet, N.S. (2001). Does early responsive parenting have a special importance for children's development or is consistency across early childhood necessary? *Developmental Psychology, 37*(3), 387–403.

Landry, S.H., Smith, K.E., Swank, P., & Guttenttag, C. (2008). A responsive parenting intervention: The optimal timing across early childhood for impacting maternal behaviors and child outcomes. *Developmental Psychology, 44,* 1335–1353.

Le Mare, L., & Audet, K. (2006). A longitudinal study of the physical growth and health of post institutionalized Romanian adoptees. *Paediatrics and Child Health, 11,* 85–91.

Linas, M., Carta, J.J., & Greenwood, C.R. (2009, May). *Taking a snapshot of early childhood response to intervention (RTI) across the USA.* Poster presented that the annual IES Project Directors Meeting, Washington, DC.

Long, C.E., Gurka, M.J., & Blackman, J.A. (2008). Family stress and children's language and behavior problems. *Topics in Early Childhood Special Education, 28,* 148–157.

Lonigan, C.J., Wagner, R.K., Torgesen, J.K., & Rashotte, C.A. (2002). *Preschool Comprehensive Test of Phonological & Print Processing.* Austin, TX: PRO-ED.

Luze, G.J. (2001). *Pilot investigations towards developing a social general outcome measure for infants and toddlers.* Kansas City: Early Childhood Research Institute on Measuring Growth and Development, Juniper Gardens Children's Project, University of Kansas.

Luze, G.J., Greenwood, C.R., Carta, J.J., Cline, G., & Kuntz, S. (2002). *Developing a general outcome measure of growth in social skills for infants and toddlers.* Kansas City: Early Childhood Research Institute for Measuring Growth and Development, Juniper Gardens Children's Project, University of Kansas.

Luze, G.J., & Hughes, K. (2008). Using individual growth and development indicators to assess child and program outcomes. *Young Exceptional Children, 12*(1), 31–41.

Luze, G.J., Linebarger, D.L., Greenwood, C.R., Carta, J.J., Walker, D., Leitschuh, C., & Atwater, J.B. (2001). Developing a general outcome measure of growth in expressive communicatoin of infants and toddlers. *School Psychology Review, 30,* 383–406.

Lyon, G.R. (1996). The need for conceptual and theoretical clarity in the study of attention, memory, and executive function. In. In G.R. Lyon & N.A. Krasnegor (Eds.), *Attention, memory, and executive function.* Baltimore: Paul H. Brookes Publishing Co.

McConnell, S.R. (2000). Assessment in early intervention and early childhood special education: Building on the past to project into the future. *Topics in Early Childhood Special Education, 20,* 43–48.

McConnell, S.R. (2008, October). *Foundations in measurement for response to intervention in early childhood: What we'll do and what we hope to learn.* Paper presented at the Division of Early Childhood, Council for Exceptional Children, Minneapolis, MN.

McConnell, S.R., McEvoy, M.A., & Priest, J.S. (2002). Growing measures for monitoring progress in early childhood education: A research and development process for Individual Growth and Development Indicators. *Assessment for Effective Intervention, 27*(4), 3–14.

McConnell, S.R., & Missall, K.N. (2008). Best practices in monitoring progress for preschool children. In A. Thomas & J. Grimes (Eds.), *Best practices in school psychology* (5th ed., pp. 561–573). Washington, DC: National Association of School Psychologists.

McConnell, S.R., Priest, J.S., Davis, S.D., & McEvoy, M.A. (2002). Best practices in measuring growth and development for preschool children. In A. Thomas & J. Grimes (Eds.), *Best practices in school psychology: IV* (Vol. 2, pp. 1231–1246). Washington, DC: National Association of School Psychologists.

McCormick, L. (1990). Sequence of language and communication development. In L. McCormick & R. Schiefelbusch (Eds.), *Early language intervention: An introduction* (2nd ed., pp. 72–105). Columbus, OH: Merrill.

McEvoy, M.A., Odom, S.L., & McConnell, S.R. (1992). Peer social competence intervention for young children with disabilities. In S.L. Odom, S.R. McConnell, & M.A. McEvoy (Eds.), *Social competence of young children with disabilities: Issues and strategies for intervention* (pp. 37–64). Baltimore: Paul H. Brookes Publishing Co.

McLean, L. (1990). Communication development in the first two years of life: A transactional process. *Zero to Three,* 13–19.

Meisels, S.J. (1996). Charting the continuum of assessment and intervention. In S.J. Meisels & E. Fenichel (Eds.), *New visions for the development and assessment of infants and young children* (pp. 27–52). Washington, DC: Zero to Three.

Missall, K.N. (2002). Reconceptualizing school adjustment: A search for intervening variables. *Dissertation Abstracts International, 63*(5A), 1712.

Missall, K.N., Carta, J.J., McConnell, S., Walker, D., & Greenwood, C.R. (2008). Using individual growth and development indicators to measure early language and literacy. *Infants and Young Children, 21,* 241–253.

Missall, K.N., McConnell, S.R., & Cadigan, K. (2006). Early literacy development: Skill growth and relations between classroom variables for preschool children. *Journal of Early Intervention, 29,* 1–21.

Missall, K., Reschly, A., Betts, J., McConnell, S., Heistad, D., Pickart, M., Sheran, C., & Marston, D. (2007). Examination of the predictive validity of preschool early literacy skills. *School Psychology Review, 26*(3), 433–452.

Mize, J., & Ladd, G.W. (1990). Toward the development of successful social skills training for preschool children. In S.R. Asher & J.D. Coie (Eds.), *Peer rejection in childhood* (pp. 338–361). Cambridge, England: Cambridge University Press.

Mowder, B.A. (1997). Typical infant development. In A.H. Widerstrom, B.A. Mowder, & S.R. Sandall (Eds.), *Infant development and risk: An introduction.* Baltimore: Paul H. Brookes Publishing Co.

Mueller, E. (1972). The maintenance of verbal exchanges between young children. *Child Development, 43,* 930–938.

Mueller, E., & Silverman, N. (1989). Peer relations in maltreated children. In D. Cicchetti & V. Carlson (Eds.), *Child maltreatment: Theory and research on the causes and consequences of child abuse and neglect* (pp. 529–578). New York: Cambridge University Press.

Murray, A. (2002). *Implementing a language intervention in a childcare setting using prelinguistic language-teaching techniques.* Unpublished Master's Thesis, University of Kansas, Lawrence.

National Center for Education Statistics. (2009). *The condition of education.* Washington, DC: U.S. Department of Education, Institute of Education Sciences.

National Center on Student Progress Monitoring (NCSPM). (2006). *Review of progress monitoring tools: Standards.* National Center for Progress Monitoring. Retrieved October 16, 2006, at http://www.studentprogress.org/

National Early Childhood Accountability Task Force. (2007). *Taking stock: Assessing and improving early childhood learning and program quality.* Philadelphia: Pew Charitable Trusts.

National Research Council. (2001). Eager to learn: Educating our preschoolers. Washington, DC: Commission on Behavioral and Social Sciences and Education, National Academies Press.

National Research Council. (2008). *Early childhood assessment: Why, what, and how.* Washington, DC: Division of Behavioral and Social Sciences and Education, National Academies Press.

National Research Council and Institute of Medicine. (2000). *From neurons to neighborhoods: The science of early childhood development.* Washington, DC: Board on Children, Youth, and Families, Commission on Behavioral and Social Sciences and Education, National Academies Press.

Neisworth, J.T. (2000). Assessment. In S. Sandall, M.E. McLean, & B.J. Smith (Eds.), *DEC recommended practices in early intervention/early childhood special education* (pp. 11–16). Longmont, CO: Sopris West.

Neisworth, J.T., & Bagnato, S. (2001). Recommended practices in assessment. In S. Sandall, M.E. McLean, & B.J. Smith (Eds.), *DEC recommended practices in early intervention/ early childhood special education* (pp. 17–28). Longmont, CO: Sopris West.

Newton, R., & Doonga, N. (2007). Corporate e-learning: Justification for implementation and evaluation of benefits. A study examining the views of training managers and training providers. *Education for Information, 25*(2), 111–130.

NICHD Early Child Care Research Network. (2000). Characteristics and quality of child care for toddlers and preschoolers. *Applied Developmental Science, 4,* 116–135.

No Child Left Behind Act of 2001, PL 107-110, 115 Stat. 1425, 20 U.S.C. §§ 6301 *et seq.*

Noell, G.H., Witt, J.C., Gilbertson, D.N., Ranier, D.D., & Freeland, J.T. (1997). Increasing teacher intervention implementation in general education settings through consultation and performance feedback. *School Psychology Quarterly, 12,* 77–88.

O'Connor, R.E., Notari-Syverson, A., & Vadasy, P.F. (1996). Ladders to literacy: The effects of teacher-led phonological activities for kindergarten children with and without disabilities. *Exceptional Children, 63*(1), 117–130.

Odom, S., McConnell, S., & Brown, W. (Eds.). (2008). *Social competence of young children: Risk, disability, and intervention.* Baltimore: Paul H. Brookes Publishing Co.

Office of Special Education Programs. (2007). Part C State Performance Plan (SPP) and Annual Performance Report (APR). Retrieved online December 7, 2008, from http://www.rrfc network.org/content/view/490/47/

Parten, M.B. (1932, October). Social participation among pre-school children. *The Journal of Abnormal and Social Psychology, 27*(3), 243–269.

Payne, V.G., & Isaacs, L.D. (1991). *Human motor development: A lifespan approach* (2nd ed.). Mountain View, CA: Mayfield.

Phaneuf, R.L., & SilbergIitt, B. (2003). Tracking preschoolers' language and preliteracy development using a general outcome measurement system. *Topics in Early Childhood Special Education, 23,* 114–123.

Priest, J.S., McConnell, S.R., McEvoy, M.A., & Shin, J. (2000, December). *Early Childhood Research Institute on Measuring Growth and Development: Progress in five domains.* Paper presented at the annual conference of the Division for Early Childhood, Council for Exceptional Children, Albuquerque, NM.

Priest, J.S., McConnell, S.R., Walker, D., Carta, J.J., Kaminski, R., McEvoy, M.A., et al. (2001). General growth outcomes for children: Developing a foundation for continuous progress measurement. *Journal of Early Intervention, 24*(3), 163–180.

Priest, J.S., McConnell, S.R., Walker, D., Carta, J.J., Kaminski, R.A., McEvoy, M.A., Good, R.H., Greenwood, C.R., & Shinn, M.R. (1998). *General growth outcomes for children between birth and age eight: Where do we want young children to go today and tomorrow?* Technical Reports of the Early Childhood Research Institute of Measuring Growth and Development, University of Minnesota, Minneapolis.

Priest, J.S., Silberglitt, B., Hall, S., & Estrem, T.L. (2000). *Progress on preschool IGDIs for early literacy.* Paper presented at the meeting of the Heartland Area Education Association, Des Moines, IA.

Radloff, L.S. (1977). The Center for Epidemiologic Studies Depression (CES-D) Scale: A self-report depression scale for research in the general population. *Applied Psychological Measurement, 1,* 385–401.

Raffaelli, M., Crockett, L.J., & Shen, Y. (2005). Developmental stability and change in self-regulation form childhood to adolescence. *The Journal of Genetic Psychology, 166,* 54–75.

Ramey, C.T., Breitmayer, B.J., & Goldman, B.D. (1984). Learning and cognition during infancy. In M.J. Hanson (Ed.), *Atypical infant development* (pp. 237–279). Baltimore: University Park Press.

Raver, C.C. (2003). *Young children's emotional development and school readiness.* Champaign, IL: ERIC Clearinghouse on Elementary and Early Childhood Education.

Regional Resource Center Program. (2008). SPP/APR information. Washington, DC: Author. Retrieved June 12, 2009, from http://www.rrfcnetwork.org/content/view/490/47/

Reschly, A., & Missall, K.N. (2005, August). *Examining literacy development from preschool to first grade.* Poster presentation at the annual meeting of the American Psychological Association, Washington, DC.

Reschly, D.J., & Ysseldyke, J.E. (2002). Paradigm shift: The past is not the future. In A. Thomas & J. Grimes (Eds.), *Best practices in school psychology: IV* (Vol. 1, pp. 3–20). Bethesda, MD: National Association of School Psychologists.

Rimm-Kaufman, S.E., Pianta, R.C., & Cox, M.J. (2000). Teachers' judgments of problems in the transition to kindergarten. *Early Childhood Research Quarterly, 15,* 147–166.

Rosenberg, S.A., & Smith, E.G. (2008). Rates of Part C eligibility for young children investigated by child welfare. *Topics in Early Childhood Special Education, 28*(2), 68–74.

Roseth, C., & Missall, K. (2008, February). *Preschoolers with disabilities: What do we learn from Early Literacy Individual Growth and Development Indicators?* Poster presentation at the biennial Conference on Research Innovations in Early Intervention, San Diego.

Rubin, K.H., Bukowski, W., & Parker, J.G. (1998). Peer interactions, relationships, and groups. In W. Damon (Series Ed.) & R.M. Lerner (Vol. Ed.), *Handbook of child psychology: Vol. 1. Theoretical models of human development* (5th ed, pp. 619–700). New York: Wiley.

Ruff, H.A., & Capozzoli, M. (2003). Development of attention and distractibility in the first 4 years of life. *Developmental Psychology, 39,* 877–890.

Sandall, S.R., Hemmeter, M., Smith, B., & McLean, M. (2005). *DEC recommended practices: A comprehensive guide for practical application in early intervention/early childhood special education.* Longmont, CO: Sopris West.

Schultz, T., Kagan, S.L., & Shore, R. (2007). Taking stock: Assessing and improving early childhood learning and program quality. Washington, DC: The Report of the National Early Childhood Accountability Task Force, PEW Charitable Trusts.

Schwartz, I., Carta, J.J., & Grant, S. (1996). Examining the use of recommended language-intervention practices in early childhood special education classrooms. *Topics Early Childhood Special Education, 16,* 251–272.

Shinn, M.R. (1989). *Curriculum-based measurement: Assessing special children.* New York: Guilford Press.

Shonkoff, J.P., & Phillips, D.A. (2000). *From neurons to neighborhoods: The science of early childhood development.* Washington, DC: National Academies Press.

Siegler, R.S., & Alibali, M.W. (2004). *Children's thinking* (4th ed.). Upper Saddle River, NJ: Prentice Hall.

Small, C.J. (2004). *A collaborative intervention to increase the communication use of toddlers with and without disabilities in inclusive child care environments.* Unpublished master's thesis, University of Kansas, Lawrence, KS.

Smith, K.U., & Smith, W.H. (1962). *Perception and motion.* Philadelphia: W.B. Saunders.

Snow, C.E. (1991). The theoretical basis for relationships between language and literacy development. *Journal of Research in Childhood Education, 6*(1), 5–10.

Snow, C.E., Burns, M.S., & Griffin, P. (Eds.). (1998). *Preventing reading difficulties in young children.* Washington, DC: National Academies Press.

Sparrow, S., Balla, D., & Cicchetti, D. (1998). *Vineland Social-Emotional Early Childhood Scales.* Circle Pines, MN: American Guidance Service.

Squires, J., & Bricker, D. (2007). *An activity-based approach to developing young children's social emotional competence.* Baltimore: Paul H. Brookes Publishing Co.

Stecker, P.M., & Fuchs, L.S. (2000). Effecting superior achievement using curriculum-based measurement: The importance of individual progress monitoring. *Learning Disability Research and Practice, 15,* 128–134.

Sterling-Turner, H.E., Watson, T.S., Wildmon, M., Watkins, C., & Little, E. (2001). Investigating the relationship between training type and treatment integrity. *School Psychology Quarterly, 16,* 78–89.

Stoel-Gammon, C. (1998). Role of babbling and phonology in early linguistic development. In S.F. Warren & J. Reichle (Series Eds.) & A.M. Wetherby, S.F. Warren, & J. Reichle (Vol. Eds.), *Communication and language intervention series: Vol. 7. Transitions in prelinguistic communication* (pp. 87–111). Baltimore: Paul H. Brookes Publishing Co.

Strother, J. (2002). An assessment of the effectiveness of e-learning in corporate training programs. *International Review of Research in Open and Distance Learning, 3*(1), 1–17.

Sugai, G., Lewis-Palmer, T., & Hagan, S. (1998). Using functional assessments to develop behavior support plans. *Preventing School Failure, 43,* 6–13.

Tamis-LeMonda, C.S., Bornstein, M.H., & Baumwell, L. (2001). Maternal responsiveness and children's achievement of language milestones. *Child Development, 72,* 748–767.

Thelen, E., & Smith, L.B. (1994). *A dynamic systems approach to the development of cognition and action.* Cambridge, MA: The MIT Press.

Tilly, W.D., III. (2002). Best practices in school psychology as a problem-solving enterprise. In A. Thomas & J. Grimes (Eds.), *Best practices in school psychology* (4th ed., pp. 21–36). Bethesda, MD: National Association of School Psychologists.

Torgesen, J.K., & Bryant, B.R. (1994). *Test of Phonological Awareness.* Austin, TX: Pro-Ed.

Tronick, E.Z., Cohn, J., & Shea, E. (1986). The transfer of affect between mothers and infants. In T.B. Brazelton & M.W. Yogman (Eds.), *Affective development in infancy.* Norwood, NJ: Ablex.

Vandell, D.L., Wilson, K.S., & Buchanan, N.R. (1980). Peer interaction in the first year of life: An examination of its structure, content, and sensitivity to toys. *Child Development, 51,* 481–488.

van den Boom, D.C. (1994). The influence of temperament and mothering on attachment and exploration: An experimental manipulation of sensitive responsiveness among lower-class mothers with irritable infants. *Child Development, 65*(5), 1457–1477.

van den Boom, D.C. (1995). Do first-year intervention effects endure? Follow-up during toddlerhood of a sample of Dutch irritable infants. *Child Development, 66,* 1798–1816.

VanDerHeyden, A.M., Broussard, C., Fabre, M., Stanley, J., Legendre, J., & Creppell, R. (2004). Development and validation of curriculum-based measures of math performance for preschool children. *Journal of Early Intervention, 27,* 27–41.

VanDerHeyden, A.M., & Snyder, P. (2006). Integrating frameworks from early childhood intervention and school psychology to accelerate growth for all young children. *School Psychology Review, 35*(4), 519–534.

VanDerHeyden, A.M., Snyder, P.A., Broussard, C., & Ramsdell, K. (2008). Measuring response to early literacy intervention with preschoolers at risk. *Topics in Early Childhood Special Education, 27,* 232–249.

Wackerle, A., & McConnell, S.R. (2007, March). *General outcome measures of early literacy development: Evidence of validity and reliability across ages.* Paper presented at the National Association of School Psychologists, New York.

Walker, D., Bigelow, K., & Harjusola-Webb, S. (2008). Increasing communication and language-learning opportunities for infants and toddlers. *Young Exceptional Children Monograph Series 10,* 105–121.

Walker, D., Bigelow, K., Harjusola-Webb, S., Small, C., & Kirk, S., (2004). *Strategies for promoting communication and language of infants and toddlers.* Kansas City, MO: Juniper Gardens Children's Project.

Walker, D., Carta, J.J., Greenwood, C.R., & Buzhardt, J. (2008). The use of individual growth and developmental indicators for progress monitoring and intervention decision making in early education. *Exceptionality, 16*(1), 33–47.

Walker, D., Greenwood, C.R., & Buzhardt, J. (2009). *The effects of a web-based scalability model for the IGDI measurement systems under high versus low traditional professional development.* Technical Report, Juniper Gardens Children's Project, University of Kansas, Kansas City, KS.

Walker, D., Greenwood, C.R., Buzhardt, J., Carta, J.J., Baggett, K., & Higgins, S. (2008, July). Developing and testing a model for the use of progress monitoring measures for infants land toddlers. Poster presentation for the 2008 OSEP Project Directors Meeting, Washington, DC.

Walker, D., Greenwood, C.R., Hart, B., & Carta, J.J. (1994). Improving the prediction of early school academic outcomes using socioeconomic status and early language production. *Child Development, 65,* 606–621.

Warren, S.F., & Walker, D. (2005). Fostering early communication and language development. In D.M. Teti (Ed.), *Handbook of research methods in developmental science* (pp. 249–270). Malden, MA: Blackwell.

Warren, S.F., Yoder, P.J., & Leew, S.V. (2001). Promoting social-communicative development in infants and toddlers. In S.F. Warren & J. Reichle (Series Eds.) & H. Goldstein, L.A. Kaczmarek, & K.M. English (Vol. Eds.), *Communication and language intervention series: Vol. 10. Promoting social communication: Children with developmental disabilities from birth to adolescence* (pp. 121–149). Baltimore: Paul H. Brookes Publishing Co.

Wetherby, A.M., & Prizant, B.M. (1992). Profiling young children's communicative competence. In S.F. Warren & J. Reichle (Series & Vol. Eds.), *Communication and language intervention series: Vol. 1. Causes and effects in communication and language intervention* (pp. 217–253). Baltimore: Paul H. Brookes Publishing Co.

Whitehurst, G.J., & Lonigan, C.J. (1998). Child development and emergent literacy. *Child Development, 69,* 848–872.

Whitehurst, G.J., & Lonigan, C.J. (2001). Emergent literacy: Development from prereaders to readers. In S.B. Neuman & D. Dickinson (Eds.), *Handbook of early literacy research* (pp. 11–29). New York: Guilford Press.

Whitehurst, G.J., Zevenbergen, A.A., Crone, D.A., Schultz, M.D., Velting, O.N., & Fischel, J.E. (1999). Outcomes of an emergent literacy intervention from Head Start through second grade. *Journal of Educational Psychology, 91,* 261–272.

Wiggins, C., Fenichel, E., & Mann, T. (2007, April). Developmental problems of maltreated children and early intervention options. Retrieved November 7, 2009, at http://aspe.hhs .gov/hsp/07/Children-CPS/litrev/part1.htm#A-Health

Willatts, P. (1999). Development of means-end behavior in young infants: Pulling a support to retrieve a distant object. *Developmental Psychology, 35,* 651–667.

Wolery, M. (1989). Using assessment information to plan instructional programs. In D.B. Bailey & M. Wolery (Eds.), *Assessing infants and preschoolers with handicaps* (pp. 478–495). Englewood Cliffs, NJ: Merrill/Prentice Hall.

Xu, F., Spelke, E.S., & Goddard, S. (2005). Number sense in human infants. *Developmental Science, 8*(1), 88–101.

Yoder, P., & Warren, S. (2002). Effects of prelinguistic milieu teaching and parent responsivity education on dyads involving children with intellectual disabilities. *Journal of Speech, Language and Hearing Research, 45,* 1158–1175.

Zanolli, K., Paden, P., & Cox, K (1997). Teaching prosocial behavior to typically developing toddlers. *Journal of Behavioral Education, 7,* 373–391.

Zelazo, P.D., Carter, A., & Reznick, J.S. (1997). Early development of executive function: A problem-solving framework. *Review of General Psychology, 1*(2), 198–226.

Zilkowski, R.A., & Goldstein, H. (2008). Effects of an imbedded phonological awareness intervention during repeated book reading on preschool children with language delays. *Journal of Early Intervention, 31,* 67–90.

Zimmerman, I.L., Steiner, V.G., & Pond, R.E. (1992). *Preschool Language Scales* (3rd ed.). San Antonio, TX: Pearson PsychCorp.

Appendix
Web Site Resources and Support

Table of Contents

Publicly Accessible Web Site

The Home Page for the IGDI Web Site

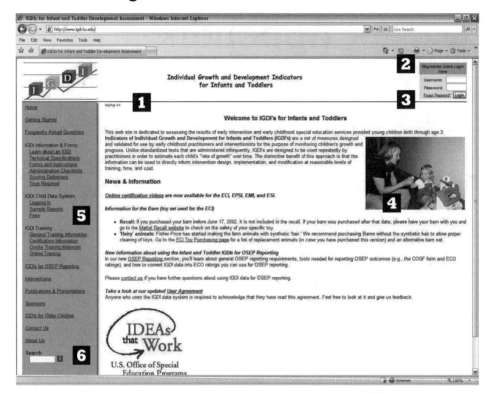

1. Alternative "crumb trail" navigation to improve user navigation and orientation

2. User login fields at top of all web pages

3. Automatic and secure password recovery

4. "Alternate" text descriptions for all images to improve accessibility

5. Main menu design and label titles informed by user testing

6. Site-specific search engine powered by Google technology

Assessment Descriptions, Forms, and Instructions

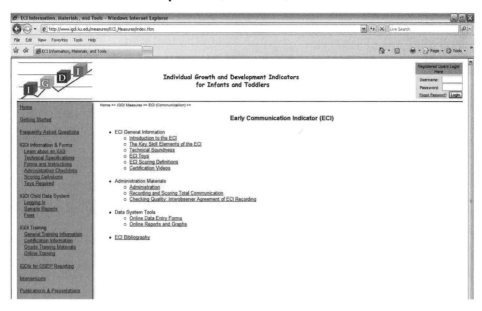

Comprehensive descriptions of each IGDI measure are provided, including technical adequacy, administration guidelines, observation forms, sample assessment videos, sample reports and graphs, toys required, and scoring definitions.

Access is provided to all forms necessary to conduct IGDI assessments, reliability checks, and administration fidelity assessments.

Certification Instructions and Resources

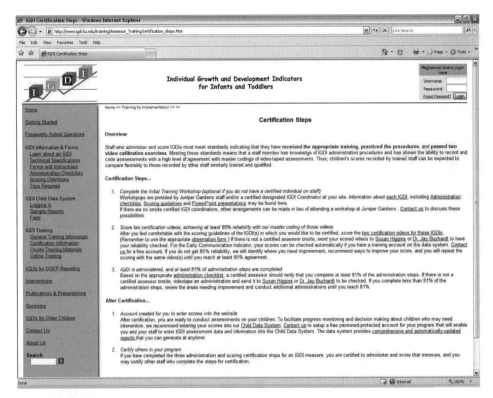

Complete instructions for becoming a certified assessor are available. Full certification can be achieved using resources available on the web site.

Password-Protected Online Data System

User Login Welcome Screen

 Individual Growth and Development Indicators for Infants and Toddlers

Logout
Print this page

Test, Director, you are currently logged in as a Program Coordinator.

Child Information & Data
Child information
Communication (EC)
Problem Solving (EPSI)
Parent/Child Interaction (IPCI)
Reports

My Program(s)
Edit program
Program users

My Information
Contact information
Change password
Change username

Welcome page
Logout

Welcome Director Test to the Official IGDI website for Infants and Toddlers.

You are be able to access all the necessary functionality of the site for a Program Coordinator. As a Program Coordinator you are able to access those menus needed to add, modify and view results for the children and staff in your program. You may also view results and print reports as needed to manage your Project and Programs.

In order to maintain a more secure system for your data, we have removed some of the functionality from your browser (e.g., your back, forward and refresh buttons) while you are logged into the IGDI Data System. Please use the links to the left and/or the Quicklinks above to navigate the system.

⊟ Children Who Are Off Target in Communication Development and Who Warrant Special Attention

Child Name	Proficiency Status
Valient, Prince	Slightly Below Benchmark
Webb, Sasha	Slightly Below Benchmark
Cute, Jacob (Social IFSP)	Below Benchmark
Cute, Kevin	Below Benchmark
House, Danny	Below Benchmark
Lewis, Bill	Below Benchmark
Smith, John T.	Below Benchmark

The following children are 6 months of age and need ECI Assessment.

The following children have not had ECI data entered in the last 3 months.

- Lynn, Buzhardt

Immediately upon logging in, a program director sees the children whose most recent assessment was below or slightly below benchmark. Also available are a list of children who are at least 6 months old and have not been assessed, as well as those who are in need of a quarterly assessment.

Options Available at Login (Option availability depends on user access level)

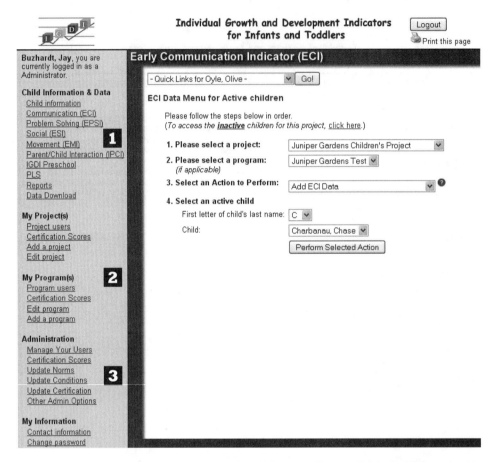

1. This set of links provides options for adding and/or modifying children in the system, adding and/or modifying data, and viewing reports.

2. Depending on the user's access level, he or she can add and/or modify projects, programs, or users.

3. Administrators (e.g., research staff) have full access to all programs, projects, and users in the system. They can also update norms, edit intervention and/or condition lists, and edit user levels.

Online Data Entry Form

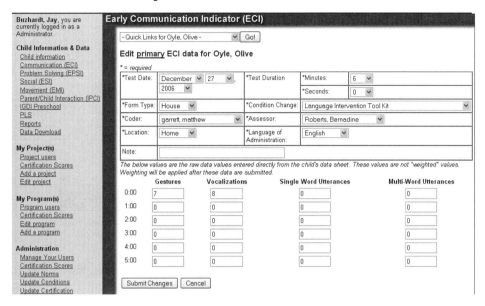

User-tested online data entry forms mirror the pen-and-paper data entry forms to facilitate ease of use. Data can be modified later if errors are made. Immediately after submitting data, those data are available in the appropriate reports (see the following section).

Dynamically Generated Online Reports: The Individual Child Report

Reports can be rather lengthy; therefore, we only show highlights of each type of report. Examples of full reports are available on the IGDI web site.

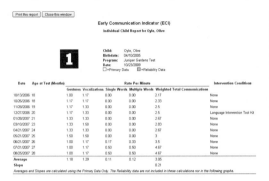

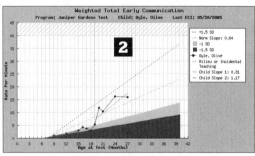

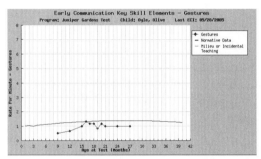

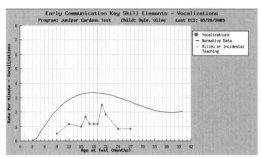

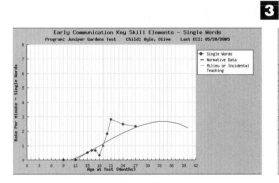

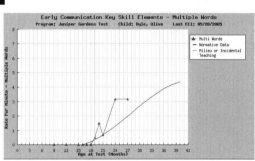

1. Tabular summary of child's entire assessment history

2. Total communication data plotted against norms with –1 and –1.5 *SD* in shaded areas. Also provides user-defined intervention lines and calculated slope.

3. Key skill elements plotted against curvilinear norms with user-defined intervention lines

The Program Report

This shows an example of a program nested within a state's Early Head Start project. The project report (not shown here) provides the same type of information as the program report, except that it reflects data across *all programs* within the project. For example, the Missouri Early Head Start project report contains data from all 15 programs in Missouri.

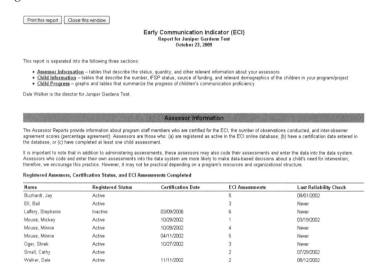

Assessor Information provides critical information for administrators to manage and maintain certification of their assessors.

Child Information provides aggregate child demographics and information about child disabilities, funding status, and so forth.

Child Progress

These reports provide information on the children's progress developing communication proficiency, and thus, the program's effectiveness.

How Many Registered Children Have ECI Data?

In Juniper Gardens Test, 45 active children have been registered. A total of 155 ECI observations have been conducted with these children. 127 of these were monthly monitoring observations (i.e., they occurred 25-40 days following the last observation) across 23 children.

How Many Primary ECI Observations Do Individual Children Have at This Point?

Cumulative Number of ECI Observations	Percentage of Children with that Number of Observations
0	17.8
1	17.8
2	17.8
3	8.9
4	6.7
5	2.2
6	11.1
7	2.2
8	6.7
>8	8.9
	100.0

Type and Location of Observations

Form Type	Number of Observations	Percentage of Total
Barn	102	65.8
Home	75	48.4
Center	25	16.1
Other	2	1.3
House	53	34.2
Home	39	25.2
Center	14	9
Other	0	0
Total Observations	155	100.0

Languages of Administration

Language of Administration	Number of Observations	Percentage of Total
English	153	98.7
Spanish	0	0
Creole	0	0
Mandarin	2	1.3
Cantonese	0	0
Japanese	0	0
Vietnamese	0	0
Other	0	0
Total Observations	155	100.0

Communication Distribution for Children in the Program

This frequency histogram shows the number of children at various levels of total communication fluency across the range of 0 to 43 (the maximum level), based on their most recent assessments. This distribution provides a point in time look at the communication status of all children in the program. Based on the total communication fluency of a 36 month old as a desired outcome for all children to achieve, we define three groups of communicators based on the total communication score: Fluent, Emerging, and Novice.

Fluent communicators are children with total communcation scores of 12 per minute and higher (They have all key skills in evidence).
Emerging communicators are children with total communication scores between 6 and 12 per minute (They are aquiring words and multiple words).
Novice communicators are children in transition from prelinguistic to spoken language between 0 and 6 per minute. (They are primarily prelinguistic communicators).

Clearly, children's age and experience strongly affects the numbers of children at these levels in a project, as does the conditions in their lives that promote communication. This chart enables program staff the ability to know where on the path to communication proficiency their children are at this point in time.

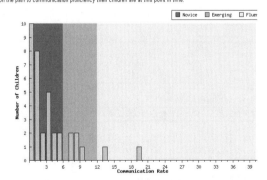

Child Progress provides aggregated data regarding child performance on the IGDIs, including how they are being administered and interventions used.

Children Who Are on Target, Slightly Below (> = -1.0 SD), or Below Benchmark (> = -1.5 SD) in Total Communication Development Based on Their Latest ECI Measurement

The first table below shows the number and percentage of children in each age group whose most recent ECI total communication rate is on target, slightly below (-1.0 SD), or below benchmark (-1.5 SD) as indicated by normative benchmarks. Benchmarks are based on the performance of children in previous research.

*Age Group	Proficiency Status			
	On Target	Slightly Below Benchmark	Below Benchmark	Total
1-11 Months	2 100%	0%	0%	2 100.0%
12-23 Months	1 8.3%	3 25%	8 66.7%	12 100.0%
24-35 Months	5 27.8%	2 11.1%	11 61.1%	18 100.0%
36-47 Months	2 50%	1 25%	1 25%	4 100.0%
Overall	11 29.7%	6 16.2%	20 54.1%	37 100%

*Age of children at their last observation

Proficiency Status shows percentage of children on target, slightly below benchmark, and below benchmark. Recall that "below benchmark" is 1 *SD* below benchmark, and "slightly below" is 1.5 *SD* below benchmark.

Children Who Are Off Target in Communication Development and Who Warrant Special Attention

Child Name	Proficiency Status	Currently on Monthly Monitoring?*	Total Number of Monthly Monitoring Assessments**
Valient, Prince	Slightly Below Benchmark	Yes	5
Webb, Sasha	Slightly Below Benchmark	No	0
Springsteen, Bruce	Slightly Below Benchmark	Yes	5
Hill, Abbey	Slightly Below Benchmark	No	4
Charbanau, Chase	Slightly Below Benchmark	Yes	3
Trujillo, Daniel	Slightly Below Benchmark	No	0
Abani, Chance	Slightly Below Benchmark	Yes	2
House, Danny	Below Benchmark	No	0

Children Below Benchmark lists specific children whose last assessment was slightly below benchmark or below benchmark, as well as whether or not they are on monthly progress monitoring (i.e., receiving assessments every 45 days or more).

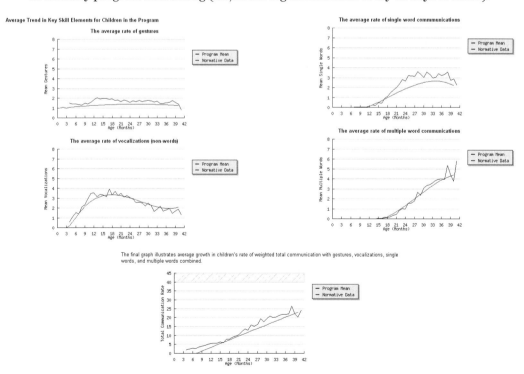

Child Progress shows graphs of children's aggregate performance for each key skill element and total measure (in this case, Total Communication for the ECI).

Child Roster Reports

| Print this report | Close this window |

Child Roster
Report for Juniper Gardens Test
October 23, 2009

Active Children

Name	Current Age	Gender	IFSP	Language	Funding
Abani, Chance	12 months	Male	Yes - Communication	English	Federal
Better, Max	47 months	Male	No	English	State
Buzhardt, Morgan	50 months	Female	No	English	None
Charbanau, Chase	44 months	Male	No	English	Federal
Child, Test	45 months	Male	No	English	State
Cute, Dana	98 months	Female	Yes - Motor	English	State
Cute, Jacob	109 months	Male	Yes - Social	English	State
Cute, Kevin	99 months	Male	No	English	State
Vallent, Prince	116 months	Male	No	English	State
Webb, Sasha	87 months	Female	Yes	Other	State
Williams, Roy	116 months	Male	No	English	State
Total Children: 46					

Inactive Children

Name	Current Age	Gender	IFSP	Language	Funding
1083, 1083	23 months	Male	No	English	Other
1091, 1091	26 months	Male	No	English	Other
ASD_Sample, Brandon	112 months	Male	Yes - Communication	English	State
ATEST, TEST	117 months	Male	No	Mandarin	Federal
Buzhardt, Jay	436 months	Male	No	Spanish	State
Buzhardt, Morgan	50 months	Female	No	English	Federal

Child roster reports provide a quick look at each child in a program or project. Separate tables are provided for active and inactive children. These data are aggregated in the program and/or project reports.

Customizing Reports

Reports

| Add a child ▾ | Go! |

Report Menu

Please follow the steps below in order to view a report. (*Note: the report will open in a new window and may take several minutes to load*)

1. Please select a project: | Juniper Gardens Children's Project ▾

2. Please select a program: | Juniper Gardens Test ▾
(if applicable)

3. Please select a report: | ECI - Full Program Report ▾

| Open Report | Customize this report | **1**

Report Menu

Please follow the steps below in order to view a report. (*Note: the report will open in a new window and may take several minutes to load*)

1. Please select a project: | Juniper Gardens Children's Project ▾

2. Please select a program: | Juniper Gardens Test ▾
(if applicable)

3. Please select a report: | ECI - Full Program Report ▾

4. Filters: Select the criteria below for which you would like to create a report. For example, if you want a report of all one year old girls with an IFSP, you would select "1 Year Olds", "Female", and "Children with an IFSP" and click "Open Report".

Age Group:
(at the time of the last observation)
☐ Under 1 year
☑ 1 year olds
☑ 2 year olds
☐ 3 year olds

Gender: ☐ Male   ☐ Female

IFSP:
☐ Children without an IFSP
☑ Children with an IFSP

Area of Disability:
☐ Communication
☐ Social
☐ Motor   **2**
☐ Cognitive
☐ None

Language:
☐ English
☐ Spanish
☐ Creole
☐ Mandarin
☐ Cantonese
☐ Japanese
☐ Vietnamese
☐ Sudanese
☐ Arabic
☐ Other

| Open Report | Cancel customized report |

---

1. Before opening a report, you can choose to limit the parameters of the report by customizing it first.

2. Select how you want to limit the report. The more options you choose, the more constrained the data will be that are included in the report.

For more individualized reporting, use the "Data Download" function to export the data into a local spreadsheet or database (described next).

Data Download

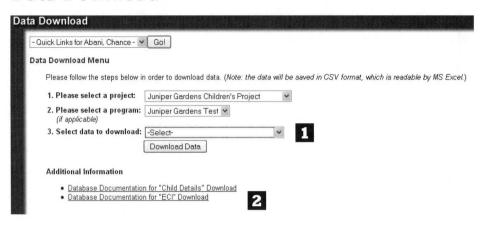

1. Select data to download (e.g., child roster, ECI data, IPCI data). Data are downloaded in a universal format that is recognized by most common spreadsheet and statistical software.

2. Documentation available for download that describes each field or column of the data.

Index

Page numbers followed by *f* indicate figures; those followed by *t* indicate tables.